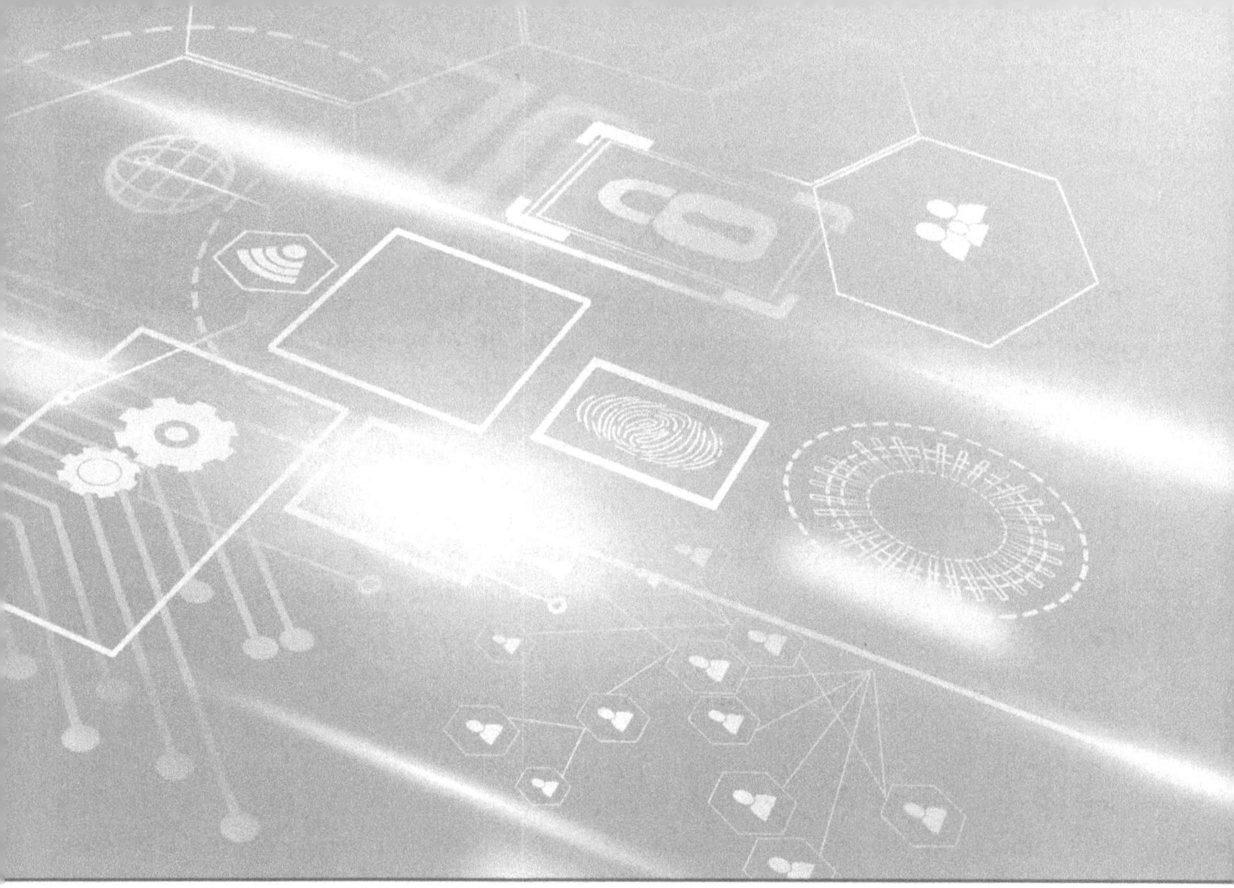

Showing the Value of the Legal Department

More Than Just a Cost Center

Sterling L. Miller

AMERICAN BAR ASSOCIATION
Business Law Section

Cover design by Catherine Zaccarine.

Printed in the United States of America.

25 24 23 5 4 3

ISBN: 978-1- 63905-045-1

Discounts are available for books ordered in bulk. Special consideration is given to state bars, CLE programs, and other bar-related organizations. Inquire at Book Publishing, ABA Publishing, American Bar Association, 321 N. Clark Street, Chicago, Illinois 60654-7598.

www.shopABA.org

Table of Contents

Introduction–How We Got Here

I have been a lawyer for over thirty years. When I came out of law school, fax machines were the "cool" technology. So, I have seen a lot of changes. One change in particular has been the evolution of the role of in-house lawyers. When I was in law school, going in-house was considered a step down, a low-value backwater of the legal profession. Today, there are dozens of applicants for any in-house position, and it is a coveted role and a desired career move by most lawyers, including big law partners. That is incredible. The evolution of the in-house lawyer is part of this book.

Many of you probably know a lot about me because of my blog, "Ten Things You Need to Know as In-House Counsel," which I started in 2014 and, somehow, am still writing here in late 2021. I graduated from the Washington University in St. Louis School of Law and spent the first six years of my legal career as a litigation associate at a large law firm in St. Louis. I then went in-house at American Airlines in the mid-1990s. I left American when it spun-out its Sabre technology division and over time became general counsel for Travelocity.com, Sabre Corporation, and Marketo, Inc. In between some of those stops I went back to law firm life with the boutique law firm Hilgers Graben PLLC where I am currently the CEO and Senior Counsel, based in Dallas, Texas. It has been a fantastic journey and I have enjoyed every minute of it. I am fortunate in that I love being a lawyer.

And I love to write. Which explains the blog and the books. A completely unexpected benefit of writing about in-house legal issues is that I am contacted daily by in-house lawyers from all over the world. For someone who grew up in small town York, Nebraska, it boggles my mind to have conversations with lawyers in Brazil, London, Australia, India, Canada, France, Mexico, and many other countries (and from all around the United States). Most reach out because of something they read in the blog and it resonated with them, or they have a question and just want to talk to someone who has sat in the chair. One thing I can tell you is that, for the most part, the issues in-house lawyers face in the United States, are the same issues in-house lawyers around the world are dealing with.

Starting about three years ago, I began to get a lot of questions about the topic of this book, i.e., "How do I show the value of the legal department?" For some, it was an internal exercise, just something they wanted to do on their own. For most, however, the question arose because of demands by the business to explain (or justify) the cost of the legal department and why it was worth the investment or worthy of additional resources. Regardless of the "why," it was clear to me that most in-house lawyers struggled with the question.

Fortunately, I had a lot of experience with it. Initially, trying to figure out the value generated by my legal team was just to satisfy my own curiosity, i.e., is it possible to develop ways to show the value of the different things the legal department does? While metrics and numbers were nice, my focus was on finding ways to show value that did not rely solely on numbers but, rather, on finding other ways to highlight the work, the results, and the value of problems avoided or solved before they became bigger, more expensive problems. Over the years, I developed several ways to do this and at review time I always brought the CEO a binder of "value" generated by the department. I summed it up as "enhancing value creation" and "minimizing value destruction." It was a mix of numbers, charts, and good old fashion marketing 101. The last point is something many in-house lawyers overlook. But, as I often told my teams, "The business sees us as a cost center. Always be marketing. That is how we change the perception." And it worked! While I did not always get everything I asked for or thought I needed, I faired better than most others. And the departments I ran were always well-respected by the business, sought-after partners, and had great client survey scores and employee engagement scores. We were winning hearts and minds externally and internally.

I was happy to share with others what I had learned over many years of simply figuring it out, i.e., there is no course at law school on how to show value. But, there should be. Over the past few years, several things crystalized for me when it came to showing the value of the legal department. First, everything the legal department does generates value in some way and is a potential achievement you can tout. You are only limited by your imagination. Second, how you tell the story is up to you. Lawyers are, by nature, tremendous story tellers. Turn that skill into an advantage. Third, do not wait to be asked by the business about value-generation, be proactive in marketing the legal department to the business. Always be marketing. This way you control the narrative about, and the perception of, the legal team and its value. It does not mean you can cover up crummy work or bad attitudes, but it does mean that you can take advantage of the fact that most businesspersons do not know much about the law or lawyers other than they do not like paying legal bills and they think we kill deals. Marketing is about making them happy to pay those bills and believing they have the best legal team in the country, one that gets things done, showing them that the return on their investment is real, measurable, and makes sense, i.e., the narrative you are telling them rings true. The hard part is figuring out how to bring all of the different pieces together to tell the best story. That is where I hope this book fits into the puzzle.

After I found myself helping many in-house lawyers think about the value question, I came up with a "Ten Things" blog in 2020 that captured several of my ideas. It quickly became one of the most read pieces I had written and generated even more inquiries from in-house lawyers all over the globe. It also made me realize that I had a lot more to say on the topic than I could squeeze into a 3,000 word blog post. So, when the American Bar Association approached me about writing a third book for them, I knew I wanted to write on the topic of how to show the value of the legal department.

What follows are my thoughts and ideas on how best to go about doing so. I certainly have no monopoly on how best to accomplish this task but I can say that what I have included in this book worked at three different companies. It does not happen overnight, but if you adopt (or adapt) the concepts, ideas, checklists, and actions I set out, you will no longer need to cower when someone from the business asks you to come up with ways to show the value of the department. You will be armed and ready, the master of value creation and the guardian against value destruction. In-house legal departments have a great story to tell. Go tell it. You are so much more than a cost center.

Sterling Miller

Acknowledgments

I have been fortunate throughout my career as an in-house lawyer to have had the benefit of many mentors. The willingness of people to spend time with me, to show me the ropes, and–more importantly–take the time to give feedback, explanations, and more, has always amazed me. It is certainly something I have tried to give back to the generation coming up behind me. I want to single out Dave Schwarte, the late Andy Steinberg, Laura Einspanier, Jeff Everett, Jim Brashear, Keenan Conder, Jonathan Perkel, Gabriel Walker, Bruce Charendoff, Sonia Ferguson, and Iain Lindsay for being great mentors, teachers, and friends as I came up the in-house ranks.

While too many to name, my legal department colleagues and teams at American Airlines, Sabre Corporation, Travelocity.com, and Marketo made work fun and made me look good–even when I did not deserve to. Thank you!

On the business side, thanks to Mark Miller, Sam Gilliland, Michelle Peluso, Gary Kusin, Steve Lucas, Greg Webb, Hugh Jones, Greg Wolf, and Chris Wilding for your patience, trust, and guidance on what it takes to be a successful businessperson in addition to a good lawyer.

To the many outside counsel I have worked with over the years, who have saved my butt more times than I can count, with particular thanks to Steve Stodghill, Tom Melshiemer, Brian Stagner, Chris Lind, and Karma Giulianelli.

Thank you to the team at the ABA's publishing arm for seeing value in a book like this (pun intended) and for their help and guidance and, most importantly, edits! In particular, Rick Paszkiet, Rebecca Hicks, and Caitlin McCauley.

To the readers of the "Ten Things You Need to Know as In-House Counsel" blog. Thanks for reading, spreading the word, and buying the books! And thanks to many in-house lawyers who have shared their own ideas with me, either taking my ideas and making them better or going in directions I had not considered. I am looking at you Jennifer Picenoni, General Counsel at Lindt & Sprngli; Karen Ell, General Counsel at KIVA; and Son-U "Michael" Paik, General Counsel at SeAH.

To my mom and dad, Carole and Tom Miller, who bought me my first typewriter so long ago and encouraged me to write . . . a lot!

Thank you to our fabulous daughters, Maren and Zoey, who make me laugh, keep me honest, and are already smarter than me and they are still in school; Maren at San Diego State University and Zoey at the University of Texas Law School.

Finally, to my amazing, incredible, beautiful wife, Inger, who came up with the title of the book, always tells me the truth, and is Denmark's best export since Carlsberg beer! Thank you for your understanding, patience, and support. Love you!

Showing the Value of the Legal Department–An Overview

Over the past five to ten years, there is one question being asked that stumps most in-house lawyers: How do I show the value of the legal department? While many ask themselves this question, the business is asking the question more and more—the folks paying the bills. The latter situation is when the answer is critical. Yet, having sat in the general counsel chair three times, there is little more elusive than the answer to this particular question. Is Sasquatch real? What is the meaning of life? Is the designated hitter a good thing? These riddles are child's play next to the Mount Everest of enigmas presented by the challenge of how to show the value of the legal function.[1] Not surprisingly, there is no one way to show value. Rather, for most departments, it is a series of different deliberate steps taken over time. In other words, value is something you earn, like a merit badge in Girl Scouts.

The place where most in-house lawyers start when it comes to trying to show their value to the business is with numbers, i.e., raw math. Doing so is a mistake, especially if numbers are all you bring to the conversation. Why? Because the biggest hurdle in proving the value of the legal department is the simple fact that value is subjective. Highly subjective. Like most things, the value of something lies in the eye of the buyer and it is no different when it comes to legal services, whether in-house counsel or an outside law firm provides it. Consequently, the first thing you must realize is *perception* is going to matter—a lot. While first impressions matter, anything based on perception is going to take time to develop. You cannot simply point to a chart or graph and scream, "See, look at all the value we're providing here in the legal department!"[2] There is a place for charts and numbers in the value equation (and we will get to that later), but relying

1 Notice, I am not going down the path of "proving" the value of the legal department. That is a fool's errand and proof that words matter. If you can *prove* it, you should be writing your own book! Otherwise, we will stick with "showing" as our verb of choice. Alternatively, the mere fact that the business is willing to pay for an in-house legal department is proof of value, i.e., the business does in fact value legal services. Showing the business what they are getting for their money is a more challenging question—and the one we will tackle here.

2 Actually, you could do this, but it may shorten your career . . . by a lot.

solely on metrics to prove value in this instance is foolhardy, like showing up for a knife fight with a piece of lead pipe. Trying to show *qualitative* value with a *quantitative* analysis will leave you far short of shore—so far away you will likely drown in an ocean of numbers. Instead, you need to get comfortable with the fact that the task requires a multi-prong, multi-year plan that is part marketing, part charm, part snake oil, and part numbers. Your quarry is elusive and, potentially, fleeting, i.e., value can often come down to this: "What have you done for me lately, legal department?" In other words, you can be a hero today but, like Sisyphus, you will be back pushing the value boulder up the hill again and again starting tomorrow.

This all sounds hard, right? While it is not easy, do not throw in the towel. There are many things you can do to make the value boulder lighter and the hill less steep and this book will explore many of them. I will go into a lot more detail in different chapters, but here are some of the key things to keep in mind while reading this book and starting to think about how to show value.

To start, given that value is subjective, your top priority becomes *marketing* the legal department to the business, i.e., developing a concentrated, long-term effort to build the brand of the legal team with the business. To do this, you need to understand *why* being able to show value matters along with the daily challenge of trying to prove the unprovable. Here are three things you need to get started:

- A willingness to always be marketing, that is, be ready to promote the value of the legal department day in and day out, at every opportunity, until it becomes second nature and a critical part of what you—and the legal team—do every day. You need to advertise the value of the department, just like the company advertises its products and services. Congratulations, you are now a marketer!
- A laser-like focus on the soft skills and understanding the internal politics present at your company.[3] *How* you say it is as important as *what* you are saying. Meaning, a little bit of charm, a little bit of deference, and a little bit of P.T. Barnum showmanship can go a long way in how the legal department is *perceived*—good or bad—by the business. Showmanship counts.
- Recognize that no one in the business has any idea how (technically) good of a lawyer anyone in the legal department is. Very few will recognize your mastery of the nuance of corporate law, litigation, or any other legal skills. As far as the business knows, you and your team are the greatest team of legal minds in the country and you should all be sitting on the Supreme Court. While excellent legal skills are table stakes as an in-house lawyer, understand the need to spend time on the attributes the business does know

3 If you need help with soft-skills, read Dale Carnegie's *How to Win Friends and Influence People*. First published in 1936, it is still relevant with dead-on advice on interacting with people in ways that drive your success. It is a classic for a reason.

how to evaluate, things like responsiveness, helpfulness, hard work, likeability, communication skills, and a service-first attitude. Mastering these attributes will lead to many more satisfied customers than dissatisfied ones. And high customer satisfaction goes hand-in-hand with high perceived value.

The three points above fold nicely into what I call the Four Ps of being a successful in-house lawyer. Generally, in-house lawyers must be: 1) practical, 2) proactive, 3) polished, and 4) a performer (i.e., showman). If you exhibit these four attributes, along with the other three mentioned above, you will be well on your way to being valued legal counsel.

Alas, while important, these attributes are fairly useless to an in-house lawyer, unless you spend time learning the business you support and what really matters to the people running the business. Simply put, it is difficult to show value if the members of the legal department do not truly understand how the business operates, how it makes money, or are spending inordinate amounts of time on projects the business does not care about. The legal team must become masters of the company's products and services, its business model, its goals, its top customers, competitors, and vendors. And you need a basic understanding of finance and the company's financial results. There is little more valuable than a legal team that is engaged and vested in the success of the business and that provides advice and counsel tied to the fact that the team truly understands the business and the aspirations, issues, threats, and opportunities it faces.

Lawyers have unique skills that cut across many problems the business faces. These skills include the ability to operate at a high level with less than perfect information, how to analyze problems from multiple viewpoints, how to write a coherent sentence, how to distill complex issues and make them simple to understand, and how to deal with pressure, ambiguity, and tight deadlines. Many in-house lawyers take these skills for granted and assume everyone at the company has the same level of talent. They do not. More and more, businesses are realizing their legal team has a deep bench of valuable assets that can be deployed for more than just grinding out legal work. This has led to the call for in-house lawyers to become strategic business partners of the business (though, usually, no one explains to you what strategic means or entails). Here is a quick and recent example: the COVID-19 global pandemic that began in 2020 presented challenges that cut across just about every aspect of a business. Many in-house lawyers stepped up during this time because guess who shines bright during a crisis? Yep, the legal team. We are trained to run to the fire, not away from it. Lawyers are uniquely skilled in dealing with the uncertainty and challenges of a crisis, from drafting communications and policies, to digging into the details of government orders and programs, to herding big projects and keeping a dispersed team focused on the objective. These are the moments your business colleagues say,"Thank goodness legal is involved!" Instant value add! This is all in lock-step with the continued evolution of in-house lawyers from managing discreet legal projects and outside counsel to taking on multiple non-legal functions within the company (expanding their "purview pie" and mandate along the way) and weighing in on issues and problems not because they have spotted legal issues, but because they have a viewpoint worth listening to.

Another straightforward way to show value is to simply get [expletive] done. Consistently and with urgency. As tough as it sounds, no one hired in-house lawyers to tell them, "No, you can't do that." They hired you and your team to exhaust all your creativity to find ways to get things done. A legal team really only has two goals: enhance value creation and minimize value destruction. When it comes to value creation, figuring out how to get to yes, and convincing the business that you are the "Department of Yes" will push you and your team farther along to the good side of the value continuum. Everyone on the team needs to buy into this concept. Likewise, being a teacher and helping the business do things for themselves (self service) provides incredible value because not only is legal getting out of the way, it is providing the knowledge and tools the business needs to move at its own pace, however slow or fast that may be. When it comes to limiting value destruction, it means being a watchdog when it comes to risk and process, to partner consistently and willingly with other parts of the business, and thinking strategically about whatever comes across your desk and how it might impact the company and its plans.

As I hinted at above, there will be some math (sorry). Business people love numbers. Smart in-house lawyers know how to speak this language in almost everything they do. It can be as simple as using a decision tree to walk the C-Suite through litigation options, or as tricky as consistently hitting your monthly spending forecasts and accruals with accuracy month after month. If you can distill a legal issue or advice down to numbers (and graphs and charts), you are ahead of the curve with the business. In later pages, I will discuss basic finance concepts, data analytics, building a budget, how to present legal issues to business people (e.g., using 2x2 matrices), and I will tackle the dreaded multi-headed monster known as KPIs (key performance indicators). Why? Because there are, in fact, ways to measure and mathematically show the value the legal team generates. And the math does not all need to be internal. You can develop benchmarks to measure key aspects of the legal department vs. a set of similar departments. Of course, the problem with benchmarks is that finding a set of similar departments is hard. Finding benchmarking data about other legal departments with similar characteristics to your department, that support something similar to your company's business (and complexity), and deal with the same types of legal work expected from you and your team is painfully hard. It is even worse when the business does it for you and then uses those mismatched benchmarks to call out the legal department. As you will see, benchmarks are interesting because usually you can find one to support whatever argument you want to make about the legal department, good or bad. So, being proactive and keeping a few good benchmarks in your back pocket is an excellent idea for when the value discussion happens.

Besides numbers, graphs, and colorful dashboards, sometimes you have to lay it all out for the business and *tell them* what value the legal team delivers. In its simplest form, this is a written report to the executives of the company noting the significant achievements of the legal team (enhancing value creation). It can even include a discussion about problems *avoided* because the legal team was on the ball (limiting value destruction). This effort includes making sure the right people in the business know when something good happens that the legal team did on its own or as part of the team. Do not be afraid to toot the horn for yourself and the department—always be marketing! In other words, if you sit around and wait for the business to recognize on its own how awesome the legal department is, you may be waiting awhile.

One of the most important pieces of the puzzle that shows the value of the legal department is your internal clients' satisfaction levels with the legal function. There are two parts to this equation. The first, which we just discussed, is to focus on letting clients know what legal is doing to drive value to the business. The second is to make it easy for your clients to love you and the department and to continually measure client satisfaction levels to ensure that the legal department is focused on what matters to the business. Some keys here are to talk with your clients and find out what the legal team can do that is important to them and to utilize surveys to get valuable insights into how the business sees the legal team and the value it provides. This book will discuss how to do all of this.

Lastly, as you begin to build the value perception in the minds of the business, you need to start thinking about how to take all of the things you are doing to show value and turn them into more resources for the legal department. We will explore the ways to capitalize on the value perception to get more money, more people, more whatever from the business because you have both shown why it is needed and established your credibility and value with the business.

Sadly, you can do everything right and be the most dialed-in in-house lawyer of all time, finding solutions to tricky business and legal issues, and turning projects faster than anyone has a right to expect. For some people, it still will not matter. They just do not value the legal department. It may be because of a prior bad experience or a deep-rooted belief that lawyers are nothing more than a necessary evil. Regardless of what you do, how you do it, or how fast you get it done, there is just no pleasing some people. When this happens, you need to recognize it for what it is and keep moving forward. It does not mean you give up or give less of an effort, but realize not everyone is going to be a fan of you or your team. Still, showing value requires you and your team be constantly moving toward your goals and objectives. Like a shark, you need to get busy swimming or get busy dying. Sitting on your butt is not an option unless your plan is to sink to the bottom of the corporate ocean.

Okay, enough with the overview. Let's get swimming! I am excited to get started and the chapters that follow will walk you through the detail of what I laid out above. Just keep in mind that there is no magic bullet when it comes to showing the value of the legal department. It is the accumulation of a lot of different steps taken persistently over time. And it is all intertwined and tied together. Everyone on the legal team needs to understand why proving value is so important and buy into the effort as it only takes one or two "bad experiences" to undo months and months of effort. However, you are on the right path. You have laid out your hard-earned doubloons for this book, you are willing to engage and learn, and you are smart. All good things. Ready? Dive in!

The Evolution of the In-House Lawyer

The Dark Ages

Over the past few decades, we have witnessed the incredible evolution of the in-house legal profession in the United States. As recently as the late 1980s, taking a job as in-house legal was something many in law school saw as a last resort, a sleepy backwater for the practice of law. At that time, the role of many in-house lawyers consisted primarily of managing outside counsel, that is, outside counsel did the work, and in-house counsel paid the bills. To add to the "glamour," the general counsel sometimes had little say over who the company engaged for legal counsel. Often, the CEO or CFO selected outside counsel based on friendship, school ties, or other affiliation. In-house counsel's input was limited—if asked for at all. Outside counsel did the work, in-house counsel paid the bills. And no one really cared about the cost of legal bills, they were a necessary evil that had to be paid. Some law firms even submitted invoices that set out a flat amount owed each month for services rendered. No detail, no explanation, no accountability. Moreover, for those lawyers stuck in house, their purview was strictly limited to legal issues. Likewise, no one worried much about the value the in-house lawyers provided. No one wanted to hear from them, except as needed to answer *specific* legal questions. There was no need to weigh in on business terms or business issues. All-in-all, not exactly the happening spot for the best and the brightest legal minds of the land. It also led to an unfair stigma that the legal team was reactive and not proactive, as if they were waiting around in the basement for someone to call them with an issue.

Unshackled

Starting back in the 1990s, however, there was a discernible shift in the role of in-house counsel. Cost pressures and other factors forced companies to start expanding their in-house legal teams (which were usually—and still are—significantly less expensive to pay for than outside counsel), upgrading the caliber of legal talent, and bringing more legal work in-house—and out of the hands of outside counsel. Over time, in-house lawyers became a vital part of the business by marrying their deep knowledge of the company, its business, and risk profile, with top-flight legal skills. Their skills were gradually, but surely, coming on par with those of outside counsel, certainly as to more routine matters like contract preparation, dispute resolution, employment law, and the like. Outside counsel was still important, but more so for specialized legal issues or tasks that in-house legal departments lacked the ability (or funding) to hire (e.g., ERISA or M&A specialists) or provide the infrastructure to properly support, like true litigation. Legal department members became more integrated into the business, often embedded within different work groups to further enhance the value and ability of those lawyers to serve the particular needs of that part of the business. Businesses even started asking their in-house counsel for their thoughts about issues other than purely legal matters—and found the lawyers had a lot to add! General counsel took control of hiring outside counsel and outside counsel needed to show their value and justify their cost, including submitting detailed invoices for services provided. On the downside, businesses started demanding accountability from the legal department and the days of "legal is different" started coming to a close, primarily when it came to head count, budgets, and predictability of legal spend. Simply put, the days of blank checks for the legal team were over, and those who did not adapt were victims of the laws of "business Darwinism" —a new form of natural selection.

Newly Discovered Resource

Enter the 2000s, not only did they survive the Y2K computer scare, but in-house legal departments evolved even further. In-house lawyers, in particular general counsel, are now key members of the senior management of the company. To start, their teams are no longer located in one building, in one city. The teams are scattered around the globe, wherever the company does business. General counsel have become (and are expected to be) strategic advisors and not just lawyers. They must be able to look at a myriad of issues facing the company and help it solve problems or take opportunities by bringing their legal skills *and* business acumen and savvy to the table. General counsel (and team) are a newly discovered resource more and more businesses begin taking advantage of. Once senior management figured it out, the gold rush was on so to speak. The same expectations around the marriage of legal skills and business acumen fall on the *entire* legal team, who must all bring the same problem-solving mentality to the office every day. Doing good legal work is the ante in this new game. Hiding behind a mantra of "it's not legal work, so don't ask me" does not cut it anymore. The legal team is expected to pitch in wherever, whenever, and however they can, regardless of whether the issue is legal, business, or —more frequently—some combination thereof. Ironically, in-house legal departments now look for outside firms that can handle mundane bulk matters at a low price point, freeing up in-house lawyers to focus on the company's more challenging and valuable legal work—a 180-degree change from the Jurassic-period of in-house practice. Outside law firms find themselves competing to win the business of in-house legal departments, including by responding to elaborate RFP processes.

Lawyers as Leaders

And the evolution goes on, a stunning climb from out of the primordial ooze that was the practice of law in-house just a generation or two ago. Here in the 2020s,[4] we are now witnessing the next big step for in-house counsel as businesses are tuning to the fact that lawyers bring a wide range of valuable skills to the office every day. They are usually highly articulate, excellent writers, solve problems with sparse information and little time, and stay calm in the middle of a crisis. They also enable business strategy, see things as they are and not how we wish they would be, manage unwieldy projects with gusto and ease, and analyze problems by looking at issues from multiple angles and viewpoints—to name a few of the skills that many in the legal department simply take for granted. They do so, even though most employees outside the department lack these skills, or at least lack them in terms of a complete package. This has led companies to elevate in-house lawyers into new roles, such as chief administrative officer or chief legal officer whereby the CAO or CLO manages not just the legal function, but might also be chief of staff for the CEO. The CAO or CLO also might manage such diverse groups as corporate communications, crisis management, social responsibility initiatives, real estate and facilities, human resources, government affairs, compliance, risk management, corporate strategy, record management, among many other non-legal functions. General counsel are even being promoted to CEO, as boards of directors recognize the skills and intelligence someone with a legal background can bring to the job, especially when that person has merged legal skills successfully with business skills. Outside counsel does the work, in-house counsel runs the show!

Of course, the history mentioned is a very broad generalization of how the practice of law in-house has changed. If you surveyed all of the in-house legal teams in existence today (and there are thousands) you will find them at various stages along this evolutionary continuum. Regardless of any one situation or point in time, no one can deny that the role and responsibilities of in-house lawyers have—and continue—to evolve to the benefit of the company and the legal team.

No matter how evolved the legal function is, the operators of the business still (rightly) demand to know the value the legal function provides, as they do with

---

4 If you are reading this book in the 2030s or beyond, email me and tell me what the heck is going on now! That is sterling.miller@sbcglobal.net.

any other part of the organization. However, it is easier to show the value of the legal department the more evolved it is. The mere fact a company has a legal department means it sees some level of inherent value in the group, but whether that team (or person) is truly integrated into the business, receives adequate resources to do the job, or is listened to when they weigh in on legal and other issues, is all a function of how well the legal department can show its value to the business. As a result, it is important everyone in an in-house legal department understands the importance of being able to show value and, more importantly, the myriad of ways to accomplish this task. Interested? Great. Read on!

Winning Hearts and Minds

As noted previously, a common mistake many in-house lawyers make when first tasked with showing the value of the legal department is to go straight to the math, i.e., using only numbers to demonstrate quantitatively the value the legal team provides. There will be math involved, just later in this book. But, as you can probably guess by the title of this section, in my experience it is far more important to win the hearts and minds of business as a key component of the process of showing value vs. a chart or graph full of numbers. Because value is in large part perception, in-house lawyers must recognize this and work hard to ensure (or change) the business's perception of the legal department to one of a team of value generators and value protectors. Fortunately, there are many ways you can do this, from basic marketing to changing the way legal issues are presented to the business. In the following pages, I will set out in detail these strategies to show value starting with the most important—marketing the legal department to the business!

Market the Legal Department

Being a cost center is tough. Unfortunately, at the end of the day, that is how the legal department typically is viewed– as a cost center the business must manage. And if the business sees the department as *just* a cost center, then the legal department will line up with the rest of the cost centers when the budget axe comes falling or the layoff guillotine gets cranked up. This means it is in the interest of all in-house lawyers (not just the general counsel) to focus on how to continually and systematically market the department to the business. This is important because while it is a cost center, the department is an *extremely valuable* cost center and one the business should understand and believe delivers high value to the company. If the business does not see this, the blame lies almost exclusively on the department.

Sadly, the only experience most in-house lawyers have with the marketing of legal services are the pitch materials from law firms. These types of materials do not work when trying to show the importance of the legal department and the value it adds.. Instead, think like the marketing team that touts your company's products and services to the world. And while you may not have thought marketing skills were necessary to be a successful lawyer, especially an in-house lawyer, they most definitely are. Here, we will discuss some basic and straightforward ways you can market the legal department to the business to help them understand what the department does and the value it brings to the company, along with developing friends and allies throughout the entire company—never a bad thing for a cost center to have in its back pocket.

All legal departments need to have a great intranet website to interact with their internal clients. For many employees, the legal department website is their first (and perhaps only) interaction with the legal team. If the website is bad, then the experience is bad, just like with any company's website. A great legal department website is simple, clean, and practical. It is also the beginning of self-service for the business—something that will be discussed in more detail later in the book. For now, self-service is important because it allows the business to quickly get the answers it needs, without the detailed involvement of any in-house lawyers. In doing so, it is critical the website stick to covering the following basic services:

- Frequently Asked Questions (FAQs). Determine the questions most frequently asked from clients, and build a set of FAQs around those. Plan on reviewing the FAQs every month and update, add, or subtract as necessary. For example, "What do we do if we get a subpoena?" is a common question. The more information like this you can put into the self-service category, the less work for lawyers in the department, and more likely, you'll have a happy internal client who found the answer(s) needed, without waiting.
- Contract templates. If you have form contracts the business must or should use, put those on the website and make them available to the business. Include instructions noting that if the client must alter a form contract, doing so requires the input and approval of the legal department. If you have a form that is requested frequently, such as a non-disclosure agreement, put a big button on your website noting "Need an NDA? Click here." If something this simple saves attorneys from having to find the same form and e-mail it to the client, you'll save time and money, and your clients will appreciate the ability to help themselves in real time.
- Who does what? In most businesses, every employee (regardless of rank) thinks every lawyer in the department is an expert on every legal topic. For example, litigation lawyers must know about contract drafting and contract lawyers must know about litigation. While that may be true to some extent, make sure clients are reaching out to the right lawyers in the first instance. The solution is to create a simple chart that sets out who does what, along with direct contact information (including mobile phone numbers). Clients will appreciate getting to the right person on the first try.

- Request for legal services form. Another helpful item on your website is a form clients can complete to set out what they need help with from the department. Typically, this is an online form that requires the client to give details about the request and attach the relevant documents. This allows the lawyer assigned to the project to get up to speed much quicker, and it invests the employee in the process because it requires them to think through the request and attach relevant information and documents.
- Articles of interest. To the extent you prepare articles (e.g., a blog) for the business about important legal topics, the website is the place to store them (even link the postings back to your FAQs).
- Basic corporate information. Consider a section that includes basic information about the company, for example, locations of the different offices, key phone numbers, a location for company policies, and other items an employee would find useful.

Additionally, the legal department must communicate frequently with the employees of the company. Ultimately, the goal is for the department to be approachable and a resource where employees know they can go for help. Ideally, you can communicate with the entire employee base in some manner on, at least, a monthly basis. It might be a series of short articles emailed to the employee base monthly, or it can be a video blog where one of the lawyers discusses a key topic. You can also host lunch-and-learns, where employees are invited to sit down with lawyers from the legal department and get updates on key legal issues facing the company (within reason) along with a chance to ask questions or raise concerns directly with the legal team. The lunch-and-learn can be offered virtually so remote employees can join. Alternatively, consider having a couple of lawyers available in person at a table in a popular spot in the office (e.g., near the cafeteria), where employees can just stop by and say hello or ask any questions. The bottom line is frequent communication allows the employee base and management to see the legal department in a positive light, visible and actively involved in day-to-day interactions with their business colleagues. Consider hosting a series of boot camps for different business units; spending time getting to know your clients (and vice versa), understand key business and legal issues a part of the business faces, hear concerns, and handle questions, all with a focus on trying to cooperatively solve some issue the business has raised with the department over the past year, e.g., asking for shorter contracts. The idea here is to spend the better part of a day with the business unit with each side getting to know the other better, discuss how each can help the other get more done, clear up misperceptions and nagging issues, discuss the challenges both sides face, and —most importantly—solve a specific complaint or concern. Such a meeting shows the business that the legal team is open-minded and willing to change things up to provide better service. The business will appreciate this, especially if the result is what they perceive to be a better process to handle their legal needs.

Generally, the accomplishments of the legal team go unnoticed by most of the business. Is it because they do not care? No. At least I hope not. Typically, it is because they just do not know about them. If you are waiting for someone in the employee ranks or C-Suite to know when the legal team has pulled off something particularly good for the business, you may wait a long time. The solution is simple: tell them. Consider a monthly (or weekly) report where you capture the important matters the department handled at that time. Include the basics, such as a short description of the matter, what is at stake, and how the legal team is solving (or solved) the problem. This list is then circulated to the executive team and other management members throughout the company. In other words, a comprehensive summary of what was going on in the legal department that month with an emphasis on the value it is delivering to the company. The list can track to the legal department's goals for the year which, in turn, should line up with the company's strategic goals for that year—another clear indicator of value delivered by the legal team. The point being, the legal department is rowing hard in the same direction as the business and is part of the business team.

A common complaint or misperception within a business is that the legal department does not care about the business, i.e., they only spend time on legal stuff. What the business is really saying here is that it wants the department to become more engaged in learning and understanding the business because that is when the department can add the most value to the company, i.e., when legal (or other) advice is given based on a deep understanding of the goals, risks, competitive landscape, and nuances of the business. The most visible and straightforward way to engage with the business in this manner is to find ways to be part of the various staff meetings, annual meetings, and other periodic meetings of the different parts of the business. This includes strategic and recurring business meetings held by business units. By participating in these types of meetings, in-house lawyers learn more about the business and the issues faced by that operating unit, including hearing firsthand about some idea or strategy the business wants to undertake and any potential legal (or other issues you foresee)—allowing you to advise on and solve problems in real-time versus on the eve of a new product launch that must be delayed to work out the legal concerns.[5] Embedding the legal team into the business in this manner is the best way to show the department (a) is fully engaged in the business; (b) is interested in learning about what the business needs to be successful; (c) is looking to solve issues early and with a practical mindset; and (d) that the legal team is approachable and accessible to the business.

5 Rest assured, even though the legal department had no notice of the project until launch, the fact that it has to be delayed or stopped completely will fall at the feet of the lawyers and not the business people who failed to include the department in the process.

Virtually every business needs volunteers for various projects. It might be for charitable causes in the community or a special strategic project within the company. In many companies, the members of the legal department rarely participate in these projects. The usual reason given is "We're too busy!" This is a mistake. While the legal team definitely is busy, it is hard to argue that the legal team is any busier than other parts of the business. Part of the process of establishing a positive impression of the legal department is to get involved in projects outside the day-to-day legal work. Here are some quick examples:

- mentor for individuals or clubs within the business organization;
- special projects within the company, e.g., a cross-functional team put together to help spot future business or strategic opportunities for the company;
- annual charity program (or a particular charitable event);
- training sessions for employees not tied to legal issues, e.g., public speaking and presentations, better writing, and how to spot dangerous emails.

When members of the legal team take on the role of ambassadors and teammates to the business, they foster goodwill and good feelings about the legal department overall.

One of the easiest ways to market the legal department is to increase responsiveness. "We need legal to get things done faster," is a common complaint by the business. This does not necessarily mean turning projects around faster (though that always helps). Rather, it is more basic than that, as in "just keep me updated about what the hell is going on with my project." Simple solutions include setting a department rule that all phone calls and emails must be returned within 24 hours or less. Requiring your attorneys to provide updates to clients at least weekly, even if the update is there is nothing new going on, or your project can't be worked on right now, but know it is important and it is on the list. When attorneys are out of the office, ensure they have an out-of-the-office message turned on in e-mail and voice mail. Include an emergency phone number in the "OOO" internal message. And, of course, no matter when you respond, always be courteous and professional. This is not always easy, but you are a *service* organization, so put ego and pride to the side and focus on the fact this is someone who needs help, and consider what you can do to help them.

Believe it or not, it is always a big deal when someone from headquarters visits one of the company's remote locations. It may seem like a non-event, but for the employees on the ground there, it is a chance to show off their office, to tell you what is going on in their region of the country or the world, and to hear from you about some of the key issues and opportunities facing the company and the legal department. Make a point to visit the different office locations whenever possible and, when you schedule these trips, work with the local manager to set up a lunch-and-learn or coffee break, a tour of the offices, or drinks with some of the local employees. It only takes an hour or so, but you will learn a lot, meet some really interesting people, and leave a positive impression with those employees and that office. You will almost assuredly find that the legal team has a much easier time working with that office after such a visit.

To sum up, when it comes to marketing the legal department, there is nothing difficult or radical involved to be successful. It takes time and a willingness to recognize that the value of the legal department is not the value assigned by the legal team. It is the value the business and other staff groups assign to the department. You must be aware of this fact constantly and look for ways to continually and deliberately market the department and what it does for the company. If you do not, no one else will.

Make it Easy for Your In-House Clients to Love You

One of the great benefits of being an in-house lawyer is you do not have to spend time chasing clients and developing business. All the work you will ever need is typically right in front of you—24/7. One of the downsides of being an in-house lawyer is that you only have one client—the company—and you need to keep them happy. While the company is your official client, the reality is you likely have many in-house bosses. Almost every employee of the company might need to come to you for help. The challenge is in keeping them happy—because happy clients think the legal department is valuable; unhappy clients think the opposite. If they love you, all is right. If not, then you have some work to do. In-house clients present many challenges beyond simply expecting you to do good legal work—they expect you to do more than provide legal advice, that is, they want you to be part of the business as well. Learning how to manage all of these expectations and demands is a key part of being a successful in-house lawyer. And the more successful you are at it, the more value you provide in the minds of your business colleagues.

There are many things you can do (and not do) to keep them happy. While a lot of it is fairly basic, even the basic stuff is not always apparent unless you sit down and think about it. Below we discuss some things you can do to get your in-house clients to love you and the legal department. If you are successful, it is one more step in winning the hearts and minds of the business and pushing the needle to the right side of the value meter.

It bears repeating that the first step in this courtship is for the in-house lawyers to learn and understand the business. It is impossible to provide value as an in-house lawyer if you do not understand the business of your only client. For example, how do you give advice about or draft a contract if you do not understand the underlying business model, that is, how does the company make money? Simply put, take time to:

a) read about your company's business (e.g., company website, public filings, press releases, industry publications, or analyst reports);
b) get demos of the company's products and services;
c) meet with your clients individually and ask them to walk you through the business and the challenges and opportunities they see; and
d) ask to participate in staff meetings, quarterly conferences, or any other gathering of different groups of your business colleagues.

Get out from behind your desk and get your hands dirty! Clients will love it when they see you are truly interested in how the business functions and how you, as a lawyer and trusted advisor, can use that knowledge to help the business meet its goals.

Next, always be practical with your advice. This goes hand-in-hand with knowing the business. Once you know the business, it is much easier to give advice that is useful and practical versus what some call "law review" answers. In other words, when you give legal advice, always think about the practical impact of what you are proposing. Will this advice work in the business world? Are you suggesting burdensome compliance with regulations that have little bite? Are you delaying contracts by fighting over word choices? Are you letting perfect stand in the way of good enough? If so, stop. For example, legally, it would be great if you could get away with not giving any type of IP indemnity in your contracts. But, if your business is selling software, sales will plummet without offering such protections. Instead, focus on the many different ways you can give an IP indemnity, yet limit exposure to the company, such as liability caps, conditions on how the buyer uses your products, and controlling the defense of any claims. Clients will trust (and seek) your advice when it makes sense to them and feels balanced, practical, and useful in the real world.[6]

In-house lawyers are not much good to the business if they do not have time for their clients. This does not mean you have to be working 24/7, but you do need to be available to your clients when they need to reach you. Just like any customer of any service, nothing makes them unhappy more than not being able to reach you or feeling like you are not keeping them updated. Here are some common-sense basics (many of which are discussed above as well under marketing—it is all intertwined):

- Be available during regular business hours, even if you are working at home or remotely.
- If you are out of the office, put an out-of–office message on your email and voice mail (along with an emergency contact number).

6 For more, see discussion *infra* at page 109 on how to get contracts signed quickly.

- Respond to emails and voice mail messages within 24 hours or less—even if it's only to let the person know you received their message, but will respond in more detail later.
- Keep clients updated on what is going on with their matter. Do not wait for them to contact you for an update. Be proactive. Even if it's to tell them that there is nothing new.

Finally, while not typically part of the bargain of being an in-house lawyer, sometimes you need to bite the bullet and be available at non-standard business hours: holidays, early morning (for clients outside your geographic location), weekends, nights, and other odd times. It happens. Learn to live with it. Additionally, lawyers tend to spend a lot of time working on things *they think* are important. But we must always ask ourselves this question: does *the business think* this is important? If not or if you do not know, stop and rethink what you are doing. Smart in-house lawyers spend time learning what motivates their key clients. Do clients have sales goals they need to meet each quarter? Are they trying to minimize the risk of a data breach? Do they need to find a way to get dozens of smaller contracts signed efficiently? Whatever it is, you cannot help your clients unless you learn what matters to them. The easiest way to do this is to ask them. Everyone appreciates being asked what they need to be successful. This can be at a meeting, lunch, or even just over some coffee. Another way to get feedback about what is important is through a client survey (which we will discuss later in this book). Just like the business, customers of the legal department need to see a willingness to constantly improve and evolve.

Another way to win fans (and reduce your workload) is to teach the business how to help you help them. Everyone likes to help. We have all experienced the business colleague who drafts her own contracts (typically a download from the internet) and claims she saved a ton of time. Usually, it is the opposite, and the contract that was downloaded is bad for many reasons. However, you can take advantage of the fact they are interested in helping and doing some—or a lot—of the contract legwork themselves. Instead of getting mad or frustrated, use this eagerness as an opportunity to teach them how to help. Consider preparing a playbook[7] or checklist[8] that sets out what the provisions of your standard contact mean, along with acceptable and no-go alternatives. Then let the business use these materials to help you write the first draft of a usable contract. Alternatively, a simple list of things they need to gather so you can start working on their matter can be effective too. Regardless of whatever or however, if you can turn business people into a deputized group of honorary paralegals, you can save yourself time and get the business more invested in the success of the legal process.

---

7 *See infra* at page 154.

8 *See* Appendix 2 for a sample checklist.

One of the best in-house corporate lawyers I ever met gave me a really good piece of advice once that I tried to use every day, "Always work to make the client look good." As an in-house lawyer, your job is to do more than give good legal advice, you also need to be a counselor. Counsel how the client can best succeed with their deal, presentation, solution, strategy, or whatever they are seeking to accomplish. This means helping them with the basics like spelling and grammar, how to organize thoughts, and presenting conclusions and options. Show them how to read their audience and how to package their ideas in a way that will not only have the best chance to gain approval, but also protect them from tanking their careers because they did not understand the difference between a highly polished presentation versus something that appears thrown together at the last minute. Offer to be a sounding board for anything, sit through a mock presentation, and or hold a question-and-answer session with them. Teach them what you know about how things work at the company. All in all, think about the *non-legal* things you can do to help your clients succeed and look good doing it. They will remember you for it, and they will be appreciative of the value you bring to the table. This does not mean do their work for them. It means finding a way to partner with your business client and help them understand you are a resource and someone they can count on to have their back and help them succeed.

When it comes to love, a bit of humility goes a long way with business clients. As a lawyer, you are used to being one of the smartest people in the room. You are also used to a certain amount of respect for the opinions of lawyers or the legal department. There are many ways to attain this respect. One of the easiest ways is to be humble. While your business colleagues will follow the advice and demands of a lawyer who is full of themselves, they will generally loath to work with them or include them voluntarily in what they are doing. This can lead to bad things for the company, i.e., boxing the lawyers out usually means that opportunities to avoid problems early get missed. On the other hand, if you are someone who answers their questions with a smile, positions legal advice not as an edict from on high, but rather as a partner with the business to achieve a common goal, then you have the makings of a great relationship. A relationship where the legal team is a highly valued and sought-after resource. While sometimes being in demand can be a pain, it is far better than the alternative. All it takes is a little humility and the ability to shrug things off that, in the end, really do not matter. They do not need to feel like they are imposing on you when they come to you for help. Keep the grimaces and exasperated sighs to yourself. You are a member of the legal department and you are there to help. If you keep this front and center, the business will love you for it.

As you get to know your clients and what is important to them and the business, you can level up by being someone who is constantly on the lookout for problems or opportunities and bringing them to the attention of the business—even if they are not legal issues. I called this "bringing them the mouse." Just like a cat will favor their owner by leaving dead vermin outside their door as a way of being helpful, you too can bring a mouse to your business clients. If you see something that could cause problems for the business or a particular deal or contract, speak up. For example, you see one of the company's key competitors has entered a new geographic market. That is worth bringing to someone's attention. Likewise, if you know of a small company with a great product that would fit into your company's business, find out who to talk to about it. It may be an opportunity no one has focused on yet. The key is to be more than someone answering legal questions. Not everything is something worthy of attention, so pick your spots and your issues. That said, you are part of the team, so be on the lookout for things that can hurt or help the business and pass those on to the right people. They will remember and love you for it.

Be the "Department of Yes"

One bogeyman that in-house lawyers need to bury deep in the ground is the perception that the legal department is the place where deals go to die. Almost all in-house lawyers have heard this comment, and most agree that generally, it is an unfair label. That said, sometimes the business does raise legitimate concerns about the legal team blocking deals. The thing to keep top of mind on this issue is that, ultimately, the department exists to serve the business. It is easier to focus on this concept when one focuses on the twin goals of in-house lawyers: maximizing value creation (yes) and minimizing value destruction (no). The challenge, of course, is in balancing these two goals, especially when it comes to things the business *really* wants to do or contracts they *really* want to sign—no matter how bad the idea or deal. This balancing act often leads to the hardest negotiations most in-house lawyers face—the internal ones. In the end, it rests on the shoulders of the lawyers to find ways to get to yes far more than they get to no. A legal department that accomplishes this feat regularly earns the respect and the gratitude—even the love—of the business; all of which are heavy thumbs on the value perception scale. Here are some things in-house lawyers can do to make the legal department the "Department of Yes".

At my first in-house job, I was fortunate enough to occasionally attend the weekly meeting of the senior management. I was a bench warmer for sure, but I kept my eyes and ears open and my mouth shut: two very good skills for any lawyer. I remember a meeting where one of the executives was explaining to the group why the company was not going to take some action. He went on and on about how legal said we could not do this, and legal said we could not do that, and this is why the plan died. The CEO, who was starting to fume, looked at the executive and very loudly said, "Legal doesn't run the [expletive] business. We do." I have never, ever forgotten that moment or that lesson. It is an important thing for all in-house lawyers to keep in mind. Our primary role is to advise the business on risk and legal issues. The business ultimately decides what it wants to do with that advice. It might follow it, it might ignore it, it might do something in the middle. But, unless there is a crime being committed or people could get seriously injured, your job as an in-house lawyer is to make your points, but then ultimately accept the decision, and do everything you can to make it happen. It is not personal. It is not that anyone thinks you are an idiot. It is not an affront to your legal prowess. It is just a business decision. Being a lawyer does not make you the boss. Be an advisor and a counselor. Let the business people run the business.

Email is a helpful tool but it stinks in terms of solving complex problems or tricky situations. If you have any type of deal or request that is not straightforward or simple, do not rely on email to get everyone on the same page. It will not work, and it will be a mess. Moreover, because email cannot convey tone or nuance, you can quickly find yourself in an escalating email exchange with the business. That serves no one's interest, especially that of the legal department. The only loser in an intracompany email firefight is, in fact, the legal department. Legal is a support group and a cost center, not the deciders. When issues are complicated or tricky (or simply getting out of hand), pick up the phone and talk to your business colleagues. Give them the floor first. Take the time to *truly listen*[9] to what they are trying to accomplish and what they need. In other words, hear them out fully. Only once you have listened, processed, and repeated back your understanding of what the business wants, then take your time to—calmly—explain the legal side of the equation and what you believe is needed to best protect the company (that is, maximizing value creation/minimize value destruction). Focus on the goal and not the wording or who wins—none of that matters. The bottom line is that the odds of the legal team and the business aligning on the path forward are much higher if you ditch email and pick up the phone.

The English philosopher Thomas Hobbes famously wrote that life is "nasty, brutish, and short." Well, it is. Just like your workday can be sometimes. Do not waste your time fighting every battle or battles that are not yours. Getting to yes requires letting things go. For example, you must be able to look at a draft contract (or redlines to a contract) and figure out if the business can live with the wording proposed by the other side. If so, do not wordsmith it. Do not argue about it. Just accept it and move on. Get to yes. Generally, good enough is, in fact, good enough. Be realistic about risk. There are risks to almost everything you do on the contracting side. But if the risk has a 0.1% chance of happening, think hard before

9 This is what is commonly referred to as active listening, a skill all in-house lawyers should master. *See, e.g., Five Active Listening Skills that Make Better Lawyers*, available online at https://attorneyatlawmagazine.com/5-active-listening-skills-better-lawyers, for a discussion of key active listening skills.

holding up a deal over it. Advise the business about the risk, but recognize it is their decision to accept it or not. As long as the decision is made at the right level of responsibility, get over it and get the deal done. Likewise, if the penalty for failure to do something is low (say one hundred dollars), and the effort to comply is large, think about whether it is worth fighting over whether or not the company must take immediate action. A dose of practicality will go far with the business and get you to yes with far less wear and tear. It also burnishes your credibility with the business, so when you do take a hard line on an issue, they know it is something material.

Of course, your ability to be effective in drafting, analyzing, and getting deals done goes up exponentially with your knowledge of the business. No matter how you go about it, everything you learn about the company will make you more effective and your ability to demonstrate mastery of the company's business gives your colleagues confidence in your abilities and your advice. All of which makes getting to yes that much easier.

Growing up, my mom always told me, "It is not what you say, it is how you say it." The right tone can go a long way in your working relationship with the business. Yes, there will always be a group of knuckleheads in the business who can barely tie their shoes, let alone negotiate a contract, but pointing that out to them gets you nowhere. Likewise, lecturing or coming across as the cranky old man telling people to get off your lawn is another way to go backward fast. Remember, the first rule in the legal department must be service with a smile. A positive attitude, a willingness to help the business understand the issues (even the non-legal issues) will all reflect favorably on you and the department. The Department of Yes is *always* ready to help, always keeps its cool, and even brings a laugh or two to the table.

Contracts are the grease on the skids of business, and in-house lawyers are the chief skid greasers. Stated bluntly, the highest and best value of an in-house legal department is ensuring contracts get done. If it has been awhile since the department has refreshed its contracts, make that a priority (and then calendar regular refreshes of your contracts going forward). The easiest way to get to yes with contracts is to start out with a fair and balanced agreement.[10] If your contract is one sided, with ridiculous asks, you will find yourself in long, painful negotiations with customers. And there is little the business hates more than long, painful negotiations. Look at what your competitors are doing with their contracts, talk to your business partners about what provisions cause them the most friction with customers, try to remove the superfluous and redundant language, and make your contracts shorter and easier to read and understand. Track and consider the clauses that are most frequently negotiated and what the company has agreed to in place of the standard language. Should you avoid the pain and

10 This concept is discussed in more detail *infra* at page 109.

make the landing zone the new standard language? All of these are things you can do to help get to yes faster.

Keep and maintain solid relationships with the various business units and business leaders you support. Talk regularly with your business clients and *ask* to attend meetings such as sales kick-offs, staff meetings, etc. Do not wait to be invited. Being present at such meetings in real-time is the best way to learn what the unit needs and also raise your profile within the unit so that they know their lawyers are on the team. Just being there and being a good listener goes a long way in developing a better working relationship with your colleagues, a better understanding of the issues (and new products and services), and the ability to influence the business *before* issues become harder to solve. All of which gets you to yes.

Never run from a challenging deal or problem. It is rare that the answer to a challenging problem is, "No, we cannot do that." If that is the limit of your imagination, then you are in the wrong job. Instead, the answer is more likely, "No, we cannot do it *that way*. However, here is an idea that might get both sides what they need." There are many paths that can take you to the place you *need* to be. Always lead with creativity and flexibility. Get in a room with the business team and/or other lawyers and brainstorm on how you can solve a particularly tricky contractual problem. While sometimes you fail, more often than not you can come up with something that works. And if you work directly with the business to find a solution, you not only get their buy into the idea (which makes them more motivated negotiators), but also you get their admiration and their belief they have a lawyer who is not locked into no, but is locked into how.

There are plenty of places where business deals can go off track. Among the most common is the failure to ensure all of the right people in the business are in the loop and have signed off on the contract. Sometimes the business folks think working with the lawyers is the only step in getting a deal done. It is not. Most deals require input from finance, tax, CTO, information security, customer support, delivery, and more. That is why it is a great idea to create your own checklist about who at your company needs to be looped into the contract review and approval process. And make sure your business counterpart knows in advance that there are usually a good number of other people who need to be involved in the contract process and who must agree to any non-standard provisions. That way there are no surprises. While technically it should be the responsibility of the business person to track down and obtain all the necessary approvals, be ready and willing to help. Knowing how to shepherd a deal through the review process is a required skill for an in-house lawyer and a sure way to get to yes much faster.

My philosophy is simple: if you give a man a contract, he can get that deal done. If you teach a man how contracts work, you can save yourself a lot of time! Seriously, and as discussed in more detail later in this book, one of the best things you can do as an in-house lawyer is teach your business colleagues how contracts work, what the different provisions are designed to do, and where the company has flexibility from its standard clauses. Start with creating as many form agreements as possible. To the extent the business can use templates that do not require additional input from the legal team you are well on your way to yes. Likewise, an easy-to-use playbook that informs the business users how the form agreements work, what the different provisions do and why they are needed, and acceptable fallback positions, that is, changes that are acceptable without additional legal input is invaluable. If the business team understands the why and you give them talking points to use with potential customers, they typically become advocates for the company's standard forms and positions. Otherwise, what you get is a salesperson who advocates solely for what their customer wants, giving you two parties to negotiate against. Ideally, teaching can be in a group setting so you get maximum value for your time. Sales orientation sessions for new hires are a great place to start. Look for opportunities to present at staff meetings or large gatherings of the sales team. Record these sessions so they are available to anyone who missed them or joins the company later. If one-on-one training is your only option, focus on the managers as they can pass the knowledge down to their teams.

Remember, the Department of Yes is open 24 hours per day, 7 days per week, and 365 days per year. Does this mean you need to work all the time? No, it does not. But, the legal team needs to be *available* at all times. This means that regardless of whether you and your team are out for the holidays, on vacation, or busy on other matters, whenever the business contacts you, there needs to be a response from the legal department. Silence is not an option and nothing upsets the business like not hearing back from the legal team. For example, the Christmas season is not a holiday in many parts of the world. How does your department deal with matters involving clients and customers for whom Christmas is just another work day? Smart in-house lawyers have a plan in place to deal with issues like this. Most likely this means working out expectations in advance with your business clients. It is far easier to let them know your availability than it is to have them frantically trying to track you down or stew in anger while they wonder why they are not hearing back from you. Likewise, whenever anyone is out on vacation or out of the office, be sure they include an emergency contact number in their out-of-office message. Odds are low that you will be disturbed but if needed, it is there. The general counsel has the ultimate responsibility to ensure that if the need arises, someone is covering legal issues, especially contractual issues—even if it is them. Usually, matters can wait until someone is available, but sometimes they cannot. These cannot-wait matters are usually high-profile CEO-level deals. And sometimes, the reality of in-house life is you have to work late nights and weekends. There is nothing unusual about this. Again, this doesn't mean you have to work all the time, but you do need to be available when the *real* need arises.

It is difficult to continually balance protecting the company and serving the demands of the business to get deals done. Everything starts with ensuring the business knows that the legal department wants to get deals done—just as much as the business, and that the in-house team is doing everything it can get to yes. This is where hearts and minds are won. That said, if the company wants to accept any and all terms the customer puts in front of them, they do not need a legal department, they just need a pen. Focus on the things you can control, keep pressing on with your plans to help the business get deals done, and, most importantly, keep the lines of communications with the business (and each other) open at all times. The Department of Yes keeps pushing forward no matter what.

Think and Act Like an Owner, Not an Employee

Do you know who business owners love? Other business owners. It is an interesting group, bonded together by many common issues and a unique way of looking at things. They thrive on risk, avoid regulation like the plague, and—for the successful ones—no job is too small and the clock does not matter. If something needs to get done, they do it. They are constantly worried about the bottom line and where the next dollar is coming from. Employees, for the most part, clock in and clock out. They do their job, look forward to getting paid but when they head home or go on vacation, they often leave *any* thought of the business back in the office. Lawyers often straddle the difference between the two extremes of owner and employee. They work hard, but generally like the comfort of sticking mostly to legal issues, happy to let the business folks worry about running business issues. Outside counsel worry about the next dollar in, but in-house counsel generally do not—they have all the clients they need. Most do their jobs competently, come and go on time, and will often take work home with them, or even on vacation. On average, however, if you put all in-house counsel on a continuum between owner on one end and employee on the other, they probably lean closer to employee. In my experience, if you want to win the hearts and minds of the business, start thinking and acting more like an *owner* and less like an employee. Owners tend to be indispensable to their businesses, i.e., the business is in trouble if the owner is not around or disengaged. Consequently, for in-house lawyers, this means finding ways to make yourself indispensable to the business.

For in-house lawyers, you must look to impress not only your legal department boss, but also your business clients. This is the minimum requirement to achieve indispensable status. For the purposes of this section, we will focus on making yourself indispensable to your business clients. Why? Because no matter how many hours you put in, how much your department colleagues love you, that you volunteer for company-sponsored charitable activities, or whether you chair the local chapter of the Association of Corporate Counsel, it will mean squat if your clients do not care or are not impressed. Remember, impressions matter as much as reality here. If they *think* you are valuable then you are in good shape. If not, you may have a tough row to hoe. Doing good work and putting in the hours are table stakes. But there is much more you need to do. To start, one way to boost perception is to not be the problem. This means that you are doing good work, meeting deadlines, keeping your word, cheerfully doing the administrative work that comes with being an in-house lawyer. You show up for meetings on time and prepared, not complaining about every little thing that does not go the way you think it should go, and so on. Valuable attorneys are the ones who are *easy* to work with.

I believe all in-house lawyers should be partial generalists. They should be able to deal, on the fly, with pretty much whatever comes up. Those who can do this are valuable lawyers. But, developing a level of expertise in an area of the law that is critical to the company will greatly increase your value. For example, there is little more valuable to a business than an in-house lawyer who is an expert on drafting and negotiating contracts. For commercial agreements, I would focus on being the expert on the more complex agreements, i.e., those agreements that are typically heavily negotiated and deal with issues not easily learned. Degree of difficulty matters, not the easy things that anyone can do. Likewise, if you can make yourself invaluable to a leader of the business, that is, be the person that leader turns to when she needs legal help, it can be a tremendous plus in your favor as they will inevitably be talking to your boss about how indispensable you are to them and their team.

Still, there is little that is special about showing up and doing your job. That is what you get paid to do. Unlike soccer for five-year olds, there are no participation trophies for in-house lawyers. To make the right impression, you need to think and act like an owner of the business, not like a cog-in-the-machine employee. Owners work their butts off and are constantly worried about all of the details and all of the things that need to get done. If they are not, then their business fails. Employees can—and usually do care—but only the rare ones go *above and beyond* the day-to-day requirements of the job. You can bet big that those sitting in the C-Suite have developed owner mentalities and that is why they are where they are. And they want employees around them who think the same way. For in-house lawyers, it starts with developing a service provider mentality, i.e., just like an outside lawyer seeking new business or looking to hold on to the clients she already has. If this is your filter, your actions will line up accordingly. In-house lawyers that go above and beyond, show initiative and owner mentality, and constantly strive to generate value (for the department and the company), are the ones with the most value and closest to being indispensable. Here are a few questions to ask when trying to think like an owner:

- ☐ How do I maximize productivity with a minimal number of resources?
- ☐ Am I spending the company's money in the most cost-efficient way?
- ☐ Am I thinking about the long-term and coming up with new ideas, or just dealing with the specific problem on my desk today?
- ☐ Do I prioritize my work properly and focus on what is truly important?
- ☐ Am I developing others?
- ☐ Do I delegate effectively?
- ☐ Do I tackle problems head-on and when they arise (or am I looking for someone else to deal with it)?
- ☐ Am I looking out for things to fix?
- ☐ Do I just clock in and out, or do I take action when things need to get done outside the 40-hour work-week?
- ☐ Am I using downtime to improve my skills and abilities, or am I playing games on my phone?
- ☐ Do I take the initiative, or do I need to always be told what to do and how to do it?

There is, of course, more to it than the above but, hopefully, you see the framework of thinking like an owner versus thinking like an employee. And, depending on how you answered these questions, you will have a pretty good idea of where you are on the continuum between owner and employee.

Encouraging feedback is also important to winning hearts and minds. Business owners always want to know how they are doing, so they can improve their service or products. It is the same with in-house lawyers. While generally you cannot control whether feedback about your performance is positive or negative, you can encourage clients to give you feedback simply by asking them for it. Literally, "Please let me know how you thought I did on this project and if there is anything I can do better." Make sure clients know you welcome their feedback, positive or negative, and that you want to hear both because that will help you improve. Getting feedback is the only way any of us can improve. And everyone has things they can work on. Proactively encouraging your clients to let you know the good and the bad and that you will take either in stride. With the right attitude, it will pay off.

Your clients will value you even more when you are generous with your time, concern, and knowledge. Again, this is the difference between being a worker bee and being something more than that. It can be as simple as just asking them if there is anything you can do to help them. It can be as formal as being part of a company mentoring program to help younger employees get a leg up. Sometimes it is a client with a request such as, "Do you know any attorneys who can help me with a will?" and taking the time to help them find one. Or offering to review a memo or PowerPoint with a client before their big presentation, to help them hone the document and practice their pitch. I will also put being inclusive in this bucket, because nothing makes a better impression with someone than an in-house attorney going out of their way to make sure everyone at a meeting is heard, introducing themselves to someone new to the company or who is otherwise attending a meeting of unfamiliar faces, or asking someone on the sidelines to join in with whatever is going on. Your willingness to make time to help others is a great way to expand your network at work. Being generous does not have to take a lot of time, but it does take a conscious effort. It will pay off in multiples as the goodwill you generate will build and enhance your reputation within the company.

Another way owners thrive is by learning new skills and honing those they already possess. Figure out what skills are underserved in the legal department today or will be needed several years down the road, and start developing or enhancing your knowledge in these areas. Ask clients (and your manager) what areas they think are underserved and/or will be important. This can help you find the right programs or materials and, hopefully, both will keep you in mind as projects or need arise. Still, do not fall behind in your own area of expertise. If you are a litigator, keep current with important cases and developments in the jurisdictions where the company is most likely to find itself in litigation. If you are a corporate attorney, keep updated on best practices for drafting commercial agreements. Most importantly, stay up to speed on the company and read everything you can get your hands on about the business, its financials, the marketplace, competitors, key customers, and vendors. Doing so will help you move beyond being only a lawyer and become more strategic in your thinking, something highly valued inside and outside the department—and something discussed in the next section below. Be proactive in finding the next need for the company, and capture that space for yourself first.

Finally, successful business owners generally are positive people. One of the easiest, least expensive, and least time-consuming ways to win hearts and minds at the company is simply to be positive. Find ways to keep your sense of humor and smile. Be friendly and approachable, someone your clients *like* to be around and work with. Embrace change and all those goofy ideas that rise to the surface every few years at most corporations. The easier path is to say something is stupid and shut down, or even be passive-aggressive about whatever the new initiative of the month is. The harder, but far more productive path, is to give everything a fair shot even if—on the surface at least—it seems like an utter waste of time and doomed to fail. It may be, but the higher-ups are going to be looking for the people who are at least trying to make it work (and for those who are overly negative or disengaged). Bring that smile to the office (or Zoom) every day. Keep complaining to a minimum. Be nice to *everyone*. And remember the basics: say please and thank-you, offer solutions when you raise problems, and always ask how can I help you? Positive people move up and stay on. Negative people usually do not.

Become a Strategic In-House Lawyer

Another way to win the hearts and minds of the business, to bring more value to the table, is to evolve into a strategic in-house lawyer. The reality of in-house practice is that it is no longer enough to be an excellent lawyer with deep legal skills and institutional knowledge. That just gets you in the door. The business wants more out of its in-house legal department, especially from the general counsel and senior members of the legal team. They want you to be part of the business and they want you to be strategic. Yet, no one teaches you how to be strategic in law school. Most figure it out as they go along in their careers. And some never figure it out. There is no magical incantation that makes you a strategic thinker, but there some tried and true things you can do to evolve into that role. And, if you can in fact evolve into such a role, you will be at the apex of the in-house lawyer value food chain.

For in-house lawyers, *strategic* can mean different things. While you need to be strategic about legal matters, the business is not really asking you for that when they ask you to be more strategic. Rather, they want you to think *strategically* about the company and its business goals and objectives while you work. By doing so, you can influence the business beyond just everyday legal issues. Here is a simple test: do people on the business side seek you out for advice about operating the business (and not just legal issues per se), e.g., "Should we do X?" or "What do you think about Y?" And, if so, are they often following your advice? If not, you must figure out how you can start helping to mold the discussion and the debate around business issues by weighing in with your own thoughts versus just looking to spot legal issues and engaging solely on that basis. A strategic lawyer does both.

As with many things, going deep to learn about the business you work for is the first step to becoming a strategic lawyer. It is impossible to think strategically without a thorough understanding of a) how your company makes money; b) its products and services; c) its important customers and vendors; d) its competitors; and e) its business plans and strategy. Ask yourself if you feel you have mastered all of these. Would you bet a million dollars on it? If not, you have some work to do. Here are some places to start (depending on your ability to gain access to these items):

- ☐ Read company strategy documents.
- ☐ Read company business plans.
- ☐ Read all press releases and public filings (if any). For more depth and insight, read the public filings of your company's main competitors.
- ☐ Read board slides.
- ☐ Ask for demos of company products and services.
- ☐ Meet with the heads of different business units and staff groups and ask them about the marketplace, their competitors, strategy, etc. (Most will be

flattered you asked for time). The same goes for meeting with senior members of the legal department who often have their finger on the pulse of the company.

- ☐ Read analyst reports about your company (if any).
- ☐ Identify industry publications, newsletters, blogs, etc., and add those to your daily reading.
- ☐ Ask someone in finance to walk you through the most recent financial statements (P&L, cash flow, and the balance sheet) and share their thoughts about how the company has positioned itself in the marketplace and what they think it should be doing to become more profitable.
- ☐ Be well-read generally, that is, read for fun and knowledge. Read books and general news magazines. Read several newspapers every day (not word-for-word, but at least to scan for stories that might be of interest to your business). You can use this general knowledge in several ways, including spotting non-legal opportunities to raise when the time is right and building and enhancing your personal relationships with your business colleagues (just by being a well-informed conversationalist).

If you are not sure how to go about getting access to company materials, ask your manager or others in the legal department. If they cannot help, then ask people in the business for what they can share and check with your corporate communications team, strategy group, and investor relations teams to see what they can provide. The resources are out there, you just need to be willing to get your hands dirty and dig around for them.

The language of business is numbers, so it is important that all in-house lawyers have a basic understanding of finance. There is virtually no way to be a strategic thinker in the business world without it. This does not mean you need to have an MBA, but you need to be comfortable around numbers and you need to understand your company's numbers, i.e., its profit & loss statement, cash flow statement, and balance sheet.[11]

Developing personal relationships with senior members of the management team is essential to learning to become strategic. Not only will you obtain updates and insight into the business, but it is also much more likely that—as your relationship becomes more personal—these colleagues will view you as a sounding board and collaborator in the business versus a lawyer they need to deal with on legal issues. Moreover, a lot of business gets done at your company *outside* of meetings and emails. To the extent possible, you should develop personal relationships with every member of the C-Suite or their equivalents at your level (as eventually these people will advance up the chain just like you, and building the relationships now will pay off down the road). A helpful trick is to find out who the CEO, CFO, or whoever relies on the most and develop a strong

---

11 *See infra* at p. 48 for a discussion on basic finance for in-house lawyers.

relationship with *that person* as they generally are in the know and an influencer within the company. Make yourself someone that person comes to and relies on. Ask company leaders if you can attend their staff meetings (regularly or on occasion). This is where you really learn about what is going on with their part of the business.

To become strategic, you need to move beyond the tactical day-to-day. There is nothing particularly strategic, in this context, about day-to-day lawyer work. You need to pull away from just ticking things off your to-do list and managing the operations of your team. The first step is to carve out time each day (or every other day) to think. Block 15 to 30 minutes on your calendar to churn on a new problem, something you have read, or whatever. You want to think about the business generally and about generating or protecting shareholder value. This matters because, in the messy ooze that makes up the typical in-house lawyer's day, we tend to rely on muscle memory when faced with whatever comes up, i.e., we stick to legal issues and we look to solve those legal issues in the same method and manner as we always have. This is the antithesis of being strategic. You need to start thinking differently. When a new issue or problem arises, making time to really think about it and its impact on the company (good or bad) is a critical step to being strategic. What is involved? Who is involved? What are all the options? What are the risks and benefits of any particular path? You are not confined by your job title here. You are always free to think about, and weigh in on, issues, problems, and opportunities in ways that go beyond merely legal. An obvious one is to speak up on non-legal concerns at meetings. You are a smart person and you likely have views and opinions beyond whether or not something presents a legal issue or not. Speak up! If you are a naturally shy person or intimidated by authority, you are going to have to figure out how to overcome that. And, you are always free to ask the business whether they can share any opportunities for you to engage in a more strategic manner. Ask, "What can I be doing to be more strategic in terms of helping the business meet its strategy and business goals?"

As you begin to hone your strategy skills, try to take yourself out of situations where you are only working on legal problems. That means seeking out roles in strategic projects underway at your company. Most companies have cross-functional strategic projects going on all the time, that is, important projects that involve persons from many different parts of the business. Get assigned to one of those at the next opportunity, focusing on finding a project involving long-term planning or strategy for the company. You will absorb a lot just being part of such a team. And if you can join one remember to work hard to go beyond your role as just a pair of eyes from the legal department there to weigh in on legal issues. That can—and should be—part of what you are doing, but you are also trying to get looped into the business discussion and strategy as well. Be prepared, diligent, and deliver on what you promise. This likely will mean some extra work on your part, along with a willingness to raise your hand and volunteer. But, if you do not make it known to everyone on that team that you are interested in more than just the legal role, all you will get is legal work.

Another important part of being a strategic lawyer is to talk like a business person rather than a lawyer. This means ditching the complicated and flowery language many lawyers love to use (both when talking and when writing). If you want your colleagues to think of you as someone other than a lawyer, then figure out how best to communicate with them. In a nutshell, you need to learn to keep things simple, to get to the point quickly, use visuals and graphs, and back up your thinking with numbers. And, most importantly, always be practical. Live in the world of what is doable and what is most likely to happen. The sky is rarely falling, and resources are not unlimited.

And now for the real secret of becoming a strategic thinker–create a checklist! Sound dumb? It is not. I created one a long time ago and literally used it every day. Basically, any time someone raised a significant issue at a meeting or in an email or when I was just mulling over things, reading a newspaper, or watching TV, I went through this list. It often helped me come up with better legal strategies, but it also spawned many other ideas that would fall under be more strategic, and I would share those as appropriate with the business:

Strategic Thinking Checklist

- ☐ Who does this impact/who is involved?
- ☐ What is the business trying to accomplish here? How can legal help?
- ☐ Does this maximize value creation/minimize value destruction?
- ☐ How does this fit into the company's strategy?
- ☐ What's the game theory here? If we do this:
  - ☐ What happens in the short term?
  - ☐ What happens in the long term?
- ☐ Is there a pattern behind this problem/issue? Can we fix or change it?
- ☐ What are the benefits and risks of doing this? How much will it cost?
- ☐ Is this something that will make customers or vendors upset? Will it bring on litigation?
- ☐ Is this something that if it becomes public or goes badly could damage the reputation/stock price of the company?
  - ☐ Even if we can do this legally, should we?
- ☐ Is this covered by any specific law or regulation?
  - ☐ Will any regulator care if we/they do this? How would we respond if they do?
- ☐ Can we use legal tactics/government affairs to *legally* advance our interests/stop this? Should we?

- ☐ Have our competitors/anyone done this or faced this before? If so, what did they do? What happened?
- ☐ What is the craziest "what if" I can come up with here? Why would/wouldn't that work?
- ☐ Who in the company needs to know about this?
- ☐ Is this something that could injure someone?

After some practice, this all becomes second nature at some point. It will help a lot if you are familiar with the basics of game theory. Game theory is the study of interactive decision-making, i.e., where the outcome for each participant depends on the actions of all (just like a group of competitors in the marketplace, for example). As a participant, when choosing your strategy or course of action you must take into account the choices of the other participants. But, as you consider their reactions, you must recognize that they are thinking about yours, and take that into account when thinking about their thinking. Sounds hard, but just watch the movie *A Beautiful Mind* and you will get it![12]

Here are some examples that show how in-house lawyers can think strategically:

- A company has a number of patents and consistently applies for and obtains new ones. However, there is no strategy behind the process, i.e., why does the company get them, and what are they going to do with them? The legal team could come up with a patent licensing program where it proactively seeks to generate licensing fees from the patents. The patents can also serve as a deterrent to anyone seeking licensing fees from the company. And there is value to use the patent program to maximize tax benefits for research and development or to provide additional value in the event the company is a target for purchase.
- A common question at many businesses is, "What is stopping us from signing more contracts?" The business probably thinks the standard contract is too long or too complicated. Rather than state all of the reasons why each provision in the agreement is needed for legal protection, the legal team could simply find a way to cut the length of the contract in half. It may not meet the goal but it will inevitably come up with a shorter, more customer-friendly contract, and that is what the business actually wanted.
- Few things are as wasteful and expensive as litigation. If a company is faced with numerous lawsuits, instead of spending all of its time simply defending and resolving each case as cheaply as possible, the strategic thing

12 *See also*, *Game Theory Explained* at https://www.pbs.org/wgbh/americanexperience/features/nash-game/.

to do is to try to figure out what is driving all the lawsuits. Look for the pattern in the data, and decide whether there is a way to make changes in the business that will reduce or eliminate the lawsuits. Also, a lawsuit can be an effective hammer to leverage in a negotiation, i.e., litigation as a business strategy in and of itself.[13]

- A company lawyer can keep her eyes open and look for opportunities to find companies the business development team may not be aware of, i.e., acquisition targets that fit nicely into the company's growth or marketplace strategies. This is only possible if the lawyer knows and understands the company's strategy and can fit non-legal pieces into that strategy.

There is obviously more, but the point is that if you have a framework to work against, over time, you will be able to pull in more and more of the concepts and concrete steps set out above. Start with looking at how to solve legal problems within the context of the company's overall business strategy rather than looking at the legal issue in a silo. And, the best thing legally (e.g., a lawsuit) may not be the best thing strategically for the business (e.g., suing your best customer). When a lawyer starts thinking like this, you are becoming a strategic lawyer, a real asset to the company, and winning the hearts and minds of the business.

A Crisis is Your Friend

The COVID-19 pandemic has provided a unique opportunity for in-house lawyers to demonstrate value by stepping up to lead during a crisis. I had a great mentor who used to say "Let's not let a good crisis go to waste!" What he meant by that was any type of crisis situation is an opportunity for the legal team to step up and lead. And that should be the case as lawyers are uniquely qualified to deal with the uncertainties, challenges, and general craziness a crisis situation presents to any company. The legal team should be the first ones raising their hands to help, including taking charge of the response process, if that is needed (or called for under a written crisis plan[14]). And, if not in charge, be good team members and reliable partners. Regardless, in-house lawyers should grab the lead on keeping the written record of the company's plans and response to the crisis. Not only are lawyers generally the best writers in the company, but they also tend to write in a low key, "just the facts" manner,which you will appreciate if there is ever litigation, and there is a good chance the documents may be subject to attorney-client privilege if properly tied to the provision of legal advice. Most importantly,

---

13 *See infra* at page 163 for a discussion about the strategic use of the law to advance the interests of the company.

14 *See infra* at page 216 for a discussion about preparing crisis plans.

the legal team can exude calm and reason, two things typically in short supply during a crisis.

To start, during a crisis, it is important to obtain truthful and accurate information about what is going on and what people should be doing. Stick to reputable written sources of information like major newspapers (*The New York Times*, *The Washington Post*, *The Wall Street Journal* and their international equivalents) and authoritative, neutral websites. Getting accurate information will: a) help you help the company and b) help you deal with those dealing in speculation and wild rumors.

A large amount of time will be focused on how best to help the company's employees (starting with your own team). Make sure the company is communicating frequently and accurately. Understand upfront that different employees will have different concerns about a crisis, along with different levels of ability to process the information. Do not act like everyone has a law degree from a top university. Bring things down to a basic level and do not judge when some employees seem to be going a little nuts. They do not live in your world. Respect, patience, and concern should underpin everything you and the company are doing when it comes to your employees during a crisis.

Next, start considering legal issues. Look at your contracts, both existing and *pending,* to determine what happens (or needs to happen) given the crisis. Pending contracts may need to be altered in light of the crisis or put on hold. For existing contracts, look at those with your most important customers and vendors first to see if they are impacted by the crisis (as those probably have the biggest impact on the company). An important clause is likely the force majeure provision, which excuses the performance of one or both parties under the right circumstances. This can either be bad or good for you—or a combination of both. You will need to analyze whether the crisis triggers the clause and, if it does, what does it mean? Is payment excused? Can either party terminate? Will supplies be disrupted? Also, do not forget about *Restatement (Second) of Contracts* Section 261 and the common law "Default Rules" concepts of "impossibility" or "impracticability" (along with "frustration of purpose") as these might apply as well. Next, look at your leases (as lessor or lessee). If you are in the middle of an mergers and acquisitions transaction, the crisis may impact your deal, including offsite due diligence and any material adverse condition clauses that could change the price or let the buyer out of the deal altogether. Similarly, review any loan or financing documents to determine if your actions during the crisis or those of your customers and vendors trigger anything. And it is always a good idea to speak with your lenders and key investors to make sure everyone is on the same page and understands the company's strategy to deal with the crisis. Finally, consider whether the issues the crisis caused lead you to rethink clauses and language in your contracts. Do you need to add or change language to better protect the company in the future?

That business continuity insurance policy sitting in the drawer may now be relevant. In fact, a crisis is the time to pull out *all* of the company's insurance policies and determine whether any of them provide protection against the problems caused by the crisis, e.g., you may need to become an expert in your company's property or health insurance policies. The company's insurance broker can be really helpful here. Even if you don't think there is coverage, double-check with the broker as you may be pleasantly surprised by what is covered.

A crisis will likely generate litigation, both by and against the company. When a crisis hits (if not before) take time to think through claims you may need to bring to protect the company, as well as potential claims that could be brought against the company.

Just about every company with in-house lawyers has shareholders. While many companies are publicly traded, most are privately held either by a small group of individuals or private equity. Regardless, there are things that must be done in the wake of a large crisis:

- Consider whether and how to hold virtual meetings of the board of directors.
- Do the company's bylaws or governing statutes provide for written consent for shareholders and board of director votes?
- For public companies, how are you disclosing risks and material matters related to the pandemic? You may need to file an 8-K instead of waiting until the next quarterly filing. And, whatever you disclose will likely be scrutinized heavily by plaintiffs' lawyers and regulators. So, use extra care to get it as right as you can.
- How will you update shareholders about company efforts to deal with the crisis? If your company is publicly traded, pay attention that you disclose anything material to *all* shareholders within the parameters of the rules.

Because the legal team excels at writing, a crisis is a perfect time to put those particular skills to work and help craft the inevitable, necessary communications. Someone on the legal team should be reviewing *every* piece of substantive communication that the company intends to send out. This likely means you'll be teaming up with corporate communications, investor relations (if applicable), and human resources. You will have two audiences that have different needs:

- Internal audience: This is primarily the employees (and their families) but also includes the board of directors and any onsite contractors. The keys are a) accurate information; b) sent in a regular and timely fashion; c) with clear guidance on the issues that matter most (policies, procedures, pay, benefits, who to contact, what to do in certain instances, and similar information). Ensure you have a way to communicate to/through non-company provided devices such as smartphones personal email addresses, and other channel so everyone receives updates.
- External:This is everyone else you need to communicate with: customers, vendors, public markets, social media, the news media, shareholders, and

regulators. As to the latter, consider reaching out to your regulators proactively to touch base and let them know how the company is dealing with the crisis. They will appreciate your reaching out to them and keeping them updated. For everyone in the group, the communication rules are pretty straightforward—keep it simple and honest. Have your facts straight. Ensure only authorized representatives of the company are speaking with the media, and that they are well prepared before doing so.

A crisis may require that the workforce not come into the office, such as a fire, earthquake, or pandemic. This means the legal team must check in with the IT team to insure there is a solid infrastructure in place to allow for the spike in remote workers. For example, video conferencing will likely surge—meaning Microsoft Teams, Skype, GoToMeeting, Zoom, and other services will be in high demand. You may need to obtain additional licenses for software, rework existing vendor contracts, including service level agreements, increased insurance coverage, and a host of other steps. Ensure that you protect the company's trade secrets. Instruct employees that any hard copies of company documents must be secure at all times and then shredded before being thrown away (or save them and bring them back to the office for proper disposal). If you have hourly employees working from home you will need to find a way to track their hours and, if triggered, pay overtime. Plan on working with HR on this point. Many companies will set up a website for employees where they will post the latest news and updates. The legal department should be reviewing those communications and helping to respond to any non-trivial issues employees raise.

Lastly, and sadly, a crisis provides the perfect cover for alarming emails and text messages (disguised as company communications or public service announcements) trying to fool employees into clicking on a toxic link. Make sure all employees are warned, have updated anti-virus and malware software installed, and know who to contact and what to do if they receive something suspicious.

Leading during a crisis is a key way for the legal department to demonstrate the value of its wide range of skills, many of which do not require a law degree. The goal (in addition to navigating the company through the crisis) is to come out the other side with the leaders of business saying, "Thank God for our legal department!"

Present Legal Issues Like a Business Person (Not a Boring Lawyer)

Finally, when it comes to winning the hearts and minds of the business, there is little more important than lawyers communicating with the business in a non-lawyerly manner. By this, I mean dropping the long-ingrained habit most lawyers have of making what they write or are presenting way too complicated, word heavy, overly dense, and equivocal. Instead, the in-house legal team needs to move much closer to the manner and methods of the business when it comes to writing and presentations. When was the last time you sat in on a business presentation where they referenced footnotes, had zero graphs or charts, took forty-five minutes to get to the point, and then had no recommendation for next steps? My hunch is never! So, why do in-house lawyers insist on doing these things? It is probably because it is hardwired in us from law school and law firm life. But to succeed in-house, you need to start thinking differently about everything you write and how you present ideas to business executives. If you do it the right way, not only with they get what you want to convey, they will recognize you are a different breed of lawyer. And in the in-house world, that is a good thing.

Writing

As general counsel, I saw a lot of writing. Emails, memos, policies, correspondence, and so on. Most of what my teams produced was well written. Some of it was not. Well, it was well written for a lawyer, but it was not well written for what the business needed. For example, lawyers love to write very long and exhaustive emails, with a very detailed discussion of the facts and the law, including case citations and citations to secondary legal treatises. And they like to sprinkle in plenty of Latin phrases, lots of wheretofores, and other legal jargon. At the very end, is a long summary of everything the reader has just read along with an unclear conclusion saying this on one hand, but that on the other hand, with no clear recommendation on what to do next or discussion about the most likely outcome given the different risks at play.

As an in-house lawyer, the first thing you need to do is forget almost everything they taught you about writing in law school and at the law firm. In other words, you need to stop writing like a lawyer and start writing like a business person. Once you start doing that, the business will see and treat you more like a partner versus a hired gun.

When it comes to writing, you cannot undersell the importance of listening to what the client is saying. What *exactly* is the problem and what do they need from you? Sometimes, we are so intent on getting started and jumping into the fray, we do not take the time to ensure we understand the assignment. Learn to resist the urge to get started immediately. Take a deep breath and start your writing by asking a lot of questions upfront and as needed going forward. Be sure you know the who, what, where, when, and how of the problem. Do you have all the facts? Are there key documents you need to better understand the issues? Is there someone else you should speak with to get more background? In short, this is the time to be a lawyer. While some may find all the questions annoying, it is better to be a bit annoying than to spend time drafting a document that misses the issue or does not help solve the problem. If the issues are particularly complicated, send a short summary back to the client setting out your understanding of what the "go do" is and ask them to confirm if your understanding is correct or off-base. Doing this has saved me many times from going down the proverbial rabbit hole.

Your business partners do not want to read through pages and pages of text to get to the answer. They want it now. Figure out the main point of your email or memo and put it right up front at the very beginning, in summary form. That is, get to the answer as soon as possible. If the answer is simple and clear, that is great, although rare. If the answer is not clear, note that and set out the most likely answer/outcome. After setting out the short answer, then you can give a detailed discussion of the facts and the analysis as needed.

Clarity is the goal of all written communication. Unfortunately, as lawyers, we frequently get bogged down in details, alternative theories, and "on the other hand" arguments. The most successful (and valued) in-house lawyers are those who can take complex issues or voluminous information and turn it into something simple and straightforward, using clear and concise language, all to enable the business to make better-informed decisions. Remember the basics. Who is your audience and what are you trying to tell them? What are your main points? Keep your sentences short and direct (think like Ernest Hemmingway). Lose the big words and the footnotes. For example, do not write, "The company, pursuant unto the common law of the State of Texas, unilaterally terminated Mr. Smith's situation" when you can write, "The company fired Mr. Smith." Edit your writing, then edit it again, if you have time. The more you edit, the tighter and clearer your writing will become. Use examples, descriptions, or analogies if those can help the reader understand your point, e.g., illustrating how a clause in the contract is supposed to work. If you have extra information that might be important, do not try to weave all of it into your document. Attach it to the email or the memo as an appendix, or just note to the reader that additional information about the issue is available if they need it or want to see it. Most importantly, be sure to make your writing understandable to outsiders. Could someone outside the company understand what you are trying to convey? This is important if your company gets into litigation where ambiguous or poorly written documents can sink the company.

No one likes staring at 3,000 words of text in block form. It hurts your eyes, and it is hard to read without getting lost. Break up blocks of text to make it easier to read and more interesting to look at. Use headings to transition to different sections or points, use bullets to quickly set out information, use **boldface**, *italics*, or <u>underline</u> to distinguish or emphasize things, try different margins for different sections, use a block quote now and then if appropriate. Your reader should be able to skim through the document and quickly get the gist of what you are trying to tell them. If the writing is easy on the eyes, you are more likely to engage the reader and have them grasp the key points.

Grammar matters a lot for in-house lawyers. You are being judged and measured every time you interact with the business, especially when interacting with the executive team. One thing they look for is how well their lawyers communicate. Your email may only be going to your friend in finance, but keep in mind that she may need to send it along to the CFO, who may, in turn, send it to the CEO or the board. While these people may or may not know if you have a great legal mind, they will know immediately if you can write well. Bad writers are far less valuable than good writers. Rule number one is to make sure you *always* check your spelling (and don't rely exclusively on spell-check). Be careful with the overuse of exclamation points. Be sure to use active voice (subject-verb-object). Using active voice makes your writing more direct and powerful. Many executives and board members look for this when they read memos or reports. An easy way to remember how to use active voice is to simply put the person or institution doing the action at the beginning of the sentence. It doesn't work all of the time but it works enough of the time. For example:

> ***Passive voice***: "The plaintiff was awarded $200,000 by the jury in damages."
>
> ***Active voice***: "The jury awarded the plaintiff $200,000 in damages."

The rules of grammar can be tricky. Get yourself a copy of a helpful guide, like Strunk and White's *Elements of Style*, still the best book on basic American English grammar available.

Another common mistake in-house lawyers make with their writing is using a lot of legal jargon, which is what they are taught in law school and at law firms. As much as in-house lawyers laugh at business jargon, understand that the business groans at the pomposity of their in-house lawyers (and what the business thinks of the lawyers is more important than what the lawyers think of the business). A common pitfall is the Latin phrases that seem to always pop up when lawyers write, such as *prima facie*, *ultra vires*, *dictum*, *a fortiori*, *res ipsa loquitur*, and so on. Unless you work for the Medieval Times restaurant chain, dump the "Ye Olde Middle English" phrasing when you write to the business. Keep things simple, plain, and conversational.

No one in the business cares if you have "Shepardized" the cases, or if you have properly capitalized a treatise. And they certainly do not need to see case citations. You are not writing for a partner at a law firm or the court, you are writing for business professionals. Cut out the legalese as much as possible. The exception to this rule is when you are writing to another in-house lawyer or the general counsel and you know they are looking for legal research on the issue.

No one likes to be wrong, especially lawyers. But, as we all know, the law is rarely black or white so a lot of lawyers like to fudge on giving a clear answer.

You see this when they write equivocating language. This drives business people crazy. They do not want to hear about how many different factors can affect the answer. They just want your best answer. Give them one. For example:

> "***There are a number of factors that can impact how the court will decide the issue. Based on what we know today, and in particular [Y], we think the most likely thing the court will do is [X].***"

Likewise, the business wants to know what its options are in any particular circumstance and, ultimately, what you think it should do. This often requires you, as the attorney, to set out and weigh risk.[15] You need to describe the type of risk(s) at issue, the range of potential consequences (e.g., worst case, middle case, or best case scenario), the probability of each, and then give a recommendation or conclusion based on your analysis. Could you be wrong? Absolutely, but business people deal with risk, unknowns, and probability all of the time so there is no pass for the lawyers.

Always be clear with your reader about the next steps. For starters, if your email is urgent with action required, put that in the subject line or in the first sentence or two. If you need immediate action, tell the reader. At the end (or in your summary at the beginning), tell the reader what steps are needed next, even if you are telling them nothing more is needed at this point. For example:

> "***The next draft of the contract is due on Thursday. We need to give direction to the negotiating team by Wednesday at noon. Our legal recommendation is we go with Option A. Please let us know if you agree, have a different preference, or if you need additional information.***"

Lastly, keep in mind that courts are becoming more hostile to applying the attorney-client privilege to in-house counsel communications, usually tied to the issue of whether the in-house lawyer is giving legal advice or business advice. Because the business wants the lawyers to be more like business partners, this is becoming a tricky balancing act. Two things you need to do: 1) take all the necessary steps to establish and protect the attorney-client privilege, including stating right up front you are providing legal advice and 2) be sure you are giving legal advice.[16] If not, write with that understanding in mind. If the document is "mixed," try to separate the legal discussion from the business discussion so the legal part can be withheld or redacted if necessary. And, always be professional with your in-house writing, even casual emails. Everything you write on the job as in-house counsel is a business document, treat it like one. You never know who might be reading something you write, be sure you write smart and keep it classy at all times.

---

15 *See infra* at page 176 for a discussing on analyzing and reporting on risk.

16 *See infra* at page 180 for a discussion of the attorney-client privilege.

Presenting Legal Issues

As if writing is not enough, one of the most difficult things for in-house lawyers to do is present legal issues to senior management. The first problem is usually the lack of experience in presenting to the C-Suite or the board of directors. These opportunities are rare. Second, it can be intimidating. Executives have little time to spare and legal issues generally are not high on their list of favorite topics. You can often feel their impatience when presenting. Third, it can be challenging to simplify complex legal issues or the decisions that need to be made. While it is not easy, it is critical that in-house lawyers learn how to effectively present before the senior executives of the company. Below are some of the basics.

Do not start preparing your presentation until you have a clear objective in mind. What is it that you want to accomplish? What is the ask you are going to make? If you do not know, figure it out well before you get in the room. There is nothing worse to an executive than sitting in a meandering presentation with no clear objective. You will almost certainly get a look that says get to the point and stop wasting my time. It is smart to check with your manager (or the general counsel) to ensure they agree with you on the goal.

Keep the presentation as simple and concise as possible. If you have fifteen minutes to present forty slides, you are in deep trouble. If you have more than a handful of bullets on a slide, you are in trouble. No one wants to see a slide jammed full of text. Just as we saw with writing, be sure to get to the point quickly. Avoid the morass of tangential issues, case law, and interesting asides. One way to keep things crisp is to start up-front with the conclusion. For example, "Today we are going to ask you to approve authority of up to $250,000 to settle the Jones Partners litigation. We are going to walk you through the analysis quickly and then open things up for your questions." If you sent the materials in advance, you can start by saying, "I know you received the materials in advance, so I am going to hit a couple of key introductory points and then we will go right into the discussion portion on slide 10 where we will be asking you for settlement authority." That is, assume they have read the materials unless they ask you to do otherwise. In other words, tell them the time, not how the watch works.

Unless you are the most amazing presenter ever, you must practice your presentation numerous times. Be sure you understand the legal issues and the facts front and back. Stumbling through the presentation, looking for notes, or admitting you don't know something too many times can be deadly. Find a quiet conference room and practice, practice, practice. This is especially important when you are not experienced with presenting to the top people in the company. If you are a nervous public speaker, you will be much more comfortable if you have gone through the presentation in practice mode a dozen times or so. Given the stakes, including how the executive team views you, i.e., rock star or dud, the extra practice is worth the time. Try to get a colleague or your manager to sit through one of your practice sessions. They will have feedback on the slides and on your presentation style that can make the difference between an awesome presentation or a meltdown. Finally, ask your manager or the general counsel what to expect. What is the seating arrangement? What is the dress code? Are there any special protocol issues you need to be aware of? Be proactive and take charge of your presentation.

Generally, if you are presenting on legal issues to senior management, the presentation is covered by the attorney-client privilege. This privilege is one of the most important tools available to in-house counsel. Here are three things to keep in mind:

- Ensure the subject matter is appropriate to claim the privilege. Opining on purely business issues falls outside the privilege. You must be providing legal advice to your clients for the privilege to apply. Draft your slides with that in mind.
- Properly label any presentation as "**Attorney-Client Privilege—Prepared for the Purpose of Providing Legal Advice.**" If the document has an attachment or a cover email/note, label those as well. Likewise, where appropriate in the presentation, write clearly that what is presented is legal analysis or legal advice. For example, "our legal opinion is..." Or "our legal advice is to..."
- Write the presentation as though a judge might decide it is *not* privileged and must be turned over to the other side. This is a scary thought, but it does happen. While you cannot leave out your legal advice, be careful about what you leave in. Do not use profanity, off-color jokes, or funny memes. Do not denigrate anyone, or use boastful, testosterone-driven language about crushing or dominating. Think about how a jury will read what you wrote. In other words, write smart.

As with your written work product, when you end a presentation to the executives, expect them to ask what is next? Anticipate this. The last slide of your presentation should be a call to action. What is it you need from the executive team? Is it the authority to take some step in litigation, or make legally important changes internally at the company, for budget to implement some technology, or key terms in a strategic transaction? Whatever the case may be, be sure you set out what you need or the next steps in clear, concise terms.

Expect and welcome questions. Questions mean the executives are paying attention and are interested in what you are saying. So, make sure you leave time for questions. If you only have 15 minutes, make your presentation 10 minutes long with 5 minutes for questions. Pause after a slide or a key point and ask if anyone has questions. The questions will likely be hard and you will need to think on your feet. The first rule of thinking on your feet is to not try to put anything over on the executive team. If you do not know the answer, simply say "I don't know but I'll find out and get back to you." That is the best you can do. You can prepare for questions in a couple of ways:

- Look at each point you are making and try to come up with questions you would ask if that point was presented to you.
- Ask a colleague or manager to read the presentation and see what questions they have.
- Talk to the general counsel or their deputies about what types of questions the senior executive team or board of directors usually ask, or if they know of specific questions that are likely to come up.
- Limit the things you put into your presentation that can drive questions. Less is more here. The more you jam into your presentation slides, the more likely it is you will be asked questions, many of which can detract from the conversation you want to have.

Be wary of acting like you are the smartest person in the room. When presenting to the executive team, your role is information giver (facts) and counselor (legal analysis) based on what you think the company should do. But, if the executive team decides to go in a different direction, do not be overly aggressive and insisting on your solution as the only path forward. They may have information that you are not privy to, or simply have a different risk tolerance or different priorities. While it is okay to point out any facts or analysis you think they may have missed, you do not want to continue to resist their decision because you think they missed the point. Accept the decision and move on. At most, go to your manager afterward if you truly believe the executive group made a horribly wrong decision that will put the company in serious jeopardy if not corrected. Realize that legal issues are like a foreign language to most business leaders. Be patient and take time to explain some of the basics so the executives know what is going on, for example, the discovery process in litigation. Finally, if you get a yes from the executives, shut up and get out of there. Do not keep talking—they may change their minds!

The business will appreciate it if you are evenhanded in your presentation. Do not try to exaggerate good facts or play down bad facts (or vice versa). Play it down the middle. Your role here is truth giver, and no executive team can make good decisions about anything, let alone legal issues unless they know the plain truth. Do not try to slant the facts to drive senior management to the action you want them to take. If there is an option that you believe superior to other options, that is fine. You can certainly relay that you think that option is the best course. But, do not forget to list the other options and, if they have merit, explain what the merit is, but also explain why you still think your recommendation is the best option. The executives run the business, not the legal department. Give them the evenhanded and complete information they need to make those decisions. They will recognize you are doing so.

Nothing makes you look sillier to the senior management than a glaring typo in your presentation. They may not understand legal issues well, but they do understand proofreading. Ask a colleague to proofread it beforehand as typos are an easily avoidable problem. Likewise, be prepared for having your time shortened. You may have had thirty minutes, now it is fifteen minutes. You may have had fifteen minutes, now it is ten. Prepare in advance for what you will do in this situation. Always keep a professional manner about you. Save the jokes for your friends, not the executive team or board of directors. You do not need to be a robot, but be professional, engaging, and brief.

The best slide decks contain minimal text (to the extent possible). Slides should guide the conversation instead of reading like a legal memo. The less content on the slide, the better. Dense text hurts the eyes and lulls people to sleep. A graphic or two helps a lot. But, do not use pictures or cute animation just because you can. Do not just read the slides verbatim. Once you flash a slide up your audience will begin to read it. If you read it aloud, you will never keep up, and you will bore your audience. Hit the highlights of each bullet and keep the conversation moving. It is, after all, a conversation. If you do have dense information you want to share or want to have available just in case, put it in an appendix.

Summing Up

To begin the process of creating an atmosphere where the business sees the value the legal department can (and does) generate, in-house lawyers should focus on these things in terms of winning the hearts and minds of their business colleagues:

- ☐ Market the value of the legal department every day. The key is constant communication with the business to ensure alignment around the right priorities and that they are aware of the accomplishments of the legal team.
- ☐ Do things that make it easy for the business to love the legal department. Being responsive, approachable, and practical will go a long way to accomplishing your goal.
- ☐ Focus on getting to yes (no is the last resort). No matter how weird or goofy the idea, your initial thinking should be based on how can we get this done.
- ☐ Think and act like an owner of the business, and what that entails from a mindset and effort standpoint. The math is simple, owners are more valuable than employees generally. Acting like an owner will pay off.
- ☐ Learn how to be a strategic in-house lawyer. Always try to think beyond the legal issues presented. Use your deep knowledge of the business to be more than a hired gun solving discreet legal problems. Use my strategy checklist to help you get started.

- ☐ Take advantage of opportunities to shine. A crisis or other challenging situation is your moment to bring all of your value to the table. Relish these opportunities to show what you can do.
- ☐ Write and present legal issues like a businessperson. When it comes to your writing and presentation skills, mimic the business because that is what they best understand. Get to the point, give a recommendation, and use numbers, charts, and graphs to convey information.

Act Like You Are Part of the Business (and Not a Bunch of Lawyers)

Lawyers tend to be herd animals, i.e., there is safety in numbers. They like to keep to themselves, honing their peculiar work habits and idiosyncratic ways of talking, writing, and thinking. That may work fine at a law firm, but within the confines of a business, it is a huge mistake. As I discussed in the last section, one key to showing value is to win the battle for the hearts and minds of the business. This occurs mainly through *how* in-house lawyers behave. Remember, most businesspersons will have little to go by to evaluate the quality of your legal work. But, by acting in ways that engage the business in a manner they are most comfortable with, in-house lawyers can build up the desired perceptions tied to showing value, e.g., hard-worker, practical, strategic thinker, available, excellent business writer, and so on. Lawyers have years of negative perceptions to overcome. Even something as tame as a well-worn legal joke can cast the department in the wrong light. Consider these two jokes about lawyers:

> "Legal is where deals go to die!"
>
> "First thing we do, let's kill all the lawyers!"[17]

They are both are kind of funny and, then again, kind of not. And neither has anything to do with legal skill. They both are responses to perceived lawyer behaviors, which is what you need to overcome. In other words, Marketing 101. However, to be truly welcomed into the tribe of business leaders, in-house lawyers need to go further than just raw marketing. They must be able to show the business that they think like the business. They need to show their math. Literally. This next section discusses why it is important for lawyers to stop acting like a bunch of lawyers, that is to say, standing off in the corner judging and talking amongst themselves about the minutia of the law and, instead, adopt the ways of the business. Put differently, they must develop and hone the inner business-

---

17 From William Shakespeare's *Henry IV*, Part 2, Act IV, Scene 2.

person that is inside every in-house lawyer i.e., the ability to seamlessly morph between lawyer and business person as the situation requires.

Understand Basic Finance

Let us start our journey with the most important subject, basic business finance. Most lawyers go to law school thinking there won't be any math. While in law school, they are generally correct. But, once you get into the real world, especially the in-house world, things change. Accounting and finance are the language of business, and if you do not speak the language, you are in trouble. You do not need to be a finance expert, but you should be able to recognize and navigate the basics of corporate finance. Doing so will help cement your place at the business table versus the much smaller and less cool lawyer-only table.

Everything starts with GAAP, at least in the United States.) GAAP stands for generally accepted accounting principles, which the Financial Accounting Standards Board (FASB) promulgated. These are the rules that the finance and accounting teams use to track, measure, and report the financial performance of the company. GAAP is especially important if your company is publicly traded because regulators want to ensure that investors have an accurate understanding of the financial condition of the company. GAAP financials are the subject of audits outside accounting firms conduct, another way to ensure investors/shareholders have an accurate picture of the company's financial health. Aside from this regulatory focus, the use of GAAP also gives company management an accurate picture of the financial health of the business and, most importantly, its viability as a going concern. Outside of the United States, companies use IFRS accounting standards, which the International Accounting Standards Board (IASB) promulgated. You may also hear of companies using non-GAAP measures to report their finances. This means the company's management feels there are other metrics to report to better show the company's true financial position. Generally, you see such measures with the word "adjusted" in front to indicate deviation from GAAP. For example, a company might exclude extraordinary one-time expenses because they are not part of the normal operations of the business. Companies that use non-GAAP measures must still include the applicable GAAP measures and if there are too many non-GAAP items in the financial statements, investors become very wary about the quality of the information and the health of the business.

There are two ways to keep track of money. The easiest way is to use a cash basis where you simply record money coming in when you get it and the money going out when you pay it. Unfortunately, for all but the smallest businesses, the cash method does not work well because it postpones recognition of revenue, and it does not match the costs of generating revenues with those specific revenues.

The answer is to utilize an accrual basis method. Under the accrual method, revenues are recognized in the period when the goods or services are rendered and the costs/expenses are recognized in the period in which those expenses helped generate the revenue. In other words, they are matched. Under the accrual method, it is irrelevant when cash is paid out or received. Not only does GAAP require the use of the accrual method, the method more accurately reflects expenses and revenue, and it gives management a better picture of sales activity in the relevant period. This is all part of double-entry accounting, which has been around for about 500 years or so. In sum, for every accounting entry in the books, there is an equal and opposite entry made as well, this is how the accounts balance.

There are three core financial documents you need to know about as in-house counsel. The first is the balance sheet. The balance sheet is a snapshot in time that shows what the company owns (assets), what it owes (liabilities), and what is leftover (owner's equity). The balance sheet is the product of the accounting equation:

Assets = Liabilities + Owner's Equity

Assets are things like equipment, cash, buildings, accounts receivable, pre-paid services, and supplies. It also includes intangible assets like goodwill and intellectual property. Liabilities are things like loans, salaries, interest, accounts payable, and deferred taxes. Owner's equity is simply the difference between the two and constitutes the stockholders' claim to the assets of the company, for example, common and preferred stock. It also represents the net worth or book value of the company. Keep in mind, the book value/net worth set out in the accounting equation is not the same thing as the market value of the company, which is typically much higher because everything is shown at cost in the accounting equation versus what a willing buyer will pay for the assets.

Next is the income statement (also called a profit-and-loss or P&L statement), which shows how profitable the company is over some measurement period, such as, a year or a quarter. It shows two things: revenues (money in) and expenses (money out). The difference is called net income. It is expressed as follows:

Revenues – Expenses = Net Income

Revenues are earnings resulting from the activities of the company, for example, the sale of goods and services. Under the accrual method, revenues are recorded when earned and not when actually received (this means revenues are *not* the same thing as cash receipts). Expenses are the costs incurred to produce the company's revenues, e.g., rent, salaries, costs of materials, advertising, depreciation, and utilities. Like revenues, expenses are accrued when incurred regardless of when the company actually pays for them. Under the accrual method, the expenses are matched to the revenues they generate. For example, Company X contracts to deliver 100 widgets in August for $1,000. The revenue from the contract is recorded for August, regardless of when the customer pays for the widgets. Company X also contracts to pay a vendor $100 to deliver the widgets to the customer in August, with payment for the delivery services due in September. The expense is still recorded in August and is matched with the $1,000 in revenue. The difference between revenues and expenses is net income or net loss if the company losses money. It is also often referred to as the company's bottom line. A multiple of net income is an established method to place a value on a business, e.g., ten times net income. For in-house lawyers, the business may assign the legal department its own P&L. This means the business is closely watching how the department tracks expenses versus its budget. This is, in my opinion, a good thing because legal departments that can show that they operate like any other part of the business build credibility with the finance team and the other business leaders.

Finally, the cash flow statement shows cash in and cash out over a certain period of time, a year, a quarter, etc. It is comprised of cash from operating activities, investing returns, and financing or borrowing. All companies need adequate cash flow to operate, e.g., pay bills, salaries, and so on. Companies can be doing well from a sales standpoint but be cash poor, meaning customers owe them money, but have not paid yet. Because companies still need to pay their debts, this sometimes requires short-term loans from a bank or the sale of bonds or stock to generate cash. Investors and potential buyers of the business are interested in cash flow because cash is king. A discounted cash flow analysis is another way to value how much a business is worth.

Every company has what is known as a general ledger. This is the database that contains all of the journal entries. Journal entries are the record of each company transaction, e.g., sales, expenses, cash in, cash out, loans, salaries, and everything else discussed previously. The journal entries feed into the big three financial documents. Ensuring the integrity of the general ledger and journal entries is a big part of the job of the internal audit function, as well as part of the work of the company's external auditors. The general ledger may have dozens and dozens, if not hundreds, of different accounts under which to make entries. It just depends on how much detail the company needs. Some examples include: cash, accounts receivable, notes payable, service revenue, wages, rent, and depreciation. The legal department typically falls under a general category, selling, general and administrative expense (SG&A). SG&A represents most of the cost of operating the business. When times are tough and the business is looking to cut costs, SG&A is one of the first places to look. This is why it is so important to operate the legal department like part of the business, with particular attention to expenses and budgets. A free-spending legal department is not likely to escape the cost-cutting hatchet and will generate questions about its leadership and ability to operate efficiently.

Speaking the language is important too. There are, however, too many key finance terms to set out here. To go deeper, simply find a good glossary and keep a copy nearby for when you run across terms you do not know or need a quick refresher. Here are a few finance terms to focus on that come up often during internal business discussions:

- EBITDA (Earnings before interest, taxes, depreciation, and amortization) – It is a quick proxy for cash flow and profitability of the business.
- Depreciation/Amortization – Both are ways of showing the lessening of the value of a company asset over time. For example, a truck or a computer will decrease in value over time, ultimately to zero. Depreciation is for tangible assets and amortization is for intangible assets (e.g., intellectual property). The portion of depreciation or amortization assigned for any one year becomes an expense of the business, and typically a tax deduction.
- CAGR (Compounded annual growth rate) – This shows the annual growth rate of an investment or line of business over some period of time. It can be backward –looking, forward –looking, or a combination of the two. It helps analyze an investment especially when year-over-year results are not consistent. It is calculated as follows:

$$\text{CAGR} = \left[\frac{\text{End value}}{\text{Beginning value}}\right]^{[1/\text{years}]} - 1$$

- Basis point – One hundredth of 1 percent and is used to measure changes in rates, usually interest rates, but it can be used for rate of return, and so on. It seems small, but it can add up to a lot of money over time. For example, if the interest your company must pay on a bond it issues goes from 6 percent to 6.05, percent it rose five (5) basis points, and over time that .05 percent can mean a lot of money out the door.
- Goodwill – Generally, this represents the premium paid for a business over its book value ("owner's equity"), usually because the business has created a favorable brand, has a large customer base, happy workers, patents, or other IP, and so forth. Goodwill is an intangible asset of the company and sits on the balance sheet.
- Close Process – There are times when your friend in finance cannot grab lunch or a beer, usually when they are in the close process. This means they

are closing the books on the measurement period (month, quarter, or year) and preparing the appropriate financial statements for management or investors in the case of a publicly traded company. In addition to simply balancing the books for all relevant transactions during the measurement period, the finance team and management are looking at different numbers and ratios to determine if anything is "out of sorts" that either requires the attention of management or, more problematic, some type of disclosure in the publicly released financial statements.

- Pro forma – In the finance world, pro forma typically means financial statements generated based on assumptions, projections, and hypotheticals. For example, if your company is looking to acquire another company, the finance team will create a pro forma P&L to show what the combined operations would look like if the deal happens. They will make certain assumptions about costs, overhead, sales, and other factors to come with the make-believe numbers.

In addition to getting a clear picture of the financial health of the company, the big three financial documents can give deeper insights into how the company is performing and where extra attention—good or bad—may be required. Management and outsiders will take data from the three documents and plug them into dozens of formulas, each of which reveals some important fact or trend about the business. Here is a handful of the most useful to know:

- Gross margin – This is the company's total sales revenue minus its cost of goods/services sold, divided by total sales revenue. The resulting percentage shows the total amount of sales revenue retained by the company after backing out the direct costs of producing those sales. The higher the percentage, the more of each dollar sold the company keeps. If the percentage drops, then it usually means it is time to cut costs.
- Net present value (NPV) – NPV is a way to evaluate the profitability of a future investment. It ties into the concept of the time value of money, that is, a dollar in the future is worth less than a dollar in hand today because you have different opportunities to invest today's dollar and make more money, for example, collecting interest in the bank. There are several variables used to calculate the NPV of a project. A project with a positive NPV should be profitable and one with a negative NPV will likely lose money. Companies use NPV to compare and contrast different options to determine the best way for the company to spend its money on investments in new lines of business or products/services.
- Contribution to margin – This formula allows you to calculate the profitability of a specific product or service by subtracting the variable costs (but not fixed costs like overhead) of producing a product/service from the price charged for that product/service. A high contribution margin means the

product or service is a moneymaker for the company. A low or negative contribution margin means the product or service may be a drag on earnings and needs attention. And when times get lean, the company will put its resources behind products or services with a higher contribution and may look to unload those with low contributions.

- Earnings per share (EPS) – If your company is public or thinking of going public, this is an important formula. EPS shows how much profit the company delivers per share of stock in the company. It is calculated by subtracting any stock dividends paid out from the company's net revenue and then dividing that number by the number of outstanding shares of stock. One way management and investors check the quality of EPS is to focus on the cash flow generated by the company for each share of stock. This is a good indicator of the health of the business and is helpful when comparing companies with a similar EPS.
- Debt/Equity ratio – This formula measures how much debt the company is using to finance its assets versus using owner's equity. It is calculated by dividing the company's total liabilities by owner's equity (total assets – total liabilities). The higher the ratio/percentage the more debt the company is taking on to finance its operations. While using some debt (leverage) to operate the company is smart, a high ratio can mean the company is having to borrow money to simply keep going, which is not a good sign.

In the accounting world, companies must set aside money in "reserve" to cover, among other things, impaired assets and potential payouts in litigation. While a necessary task, no one is happy about it because setting a reserve takes money away from other uses. As an in-house lawyer, you will be involved in setting dispute/litigation reserves. It is a challenging task. The governing rule in the U.S. is called ASC 450 (previously known as FAS5) and is a standard the Financial Accounting Standards Board (FASB) set. A company must set a reserve (or an accrual) for a dispute/litigation if (a) the likelihood of losing or having to pay out is probable, and (b) the amount the company would have to pay out can be reasonably estimated. As you can see, there is a lot of grey in this task. "Probable" in ASC 450 is defined as "likely to occur." With litigation, it is extremely hard to predict if something is likely. I used a rule of thumb of a 75 percent chance of occurring as being probable. Equally challenging is estimating any payout, especially if—as is often the case—the other side has not yet put forth any damages number or if the damages number you get is clearly garbage. Still, it is a task you may be called upon to undertake and you need to bring all of your judgment and skill to bear to assist the business.

Again, you do not need an MBA to gain enough finance skill to be a valuable asset to the business. A law degree, plus an understanding of finance is a killer combination in the in-house world.

Operate the Department Like a Business

High-value legal departments deliver high-quality legal services at lower cost and with better results. Typically, you can solve part of the equation, but only at the cost of other parts. For example, you can get lower costs but not always higher (or even the same) quality as more expensive firms or systems provide. Yet, there is tremendous value waiting to be unlocked, if and when a solution becomes available. Forward-thinking legal departments have embraced legal operations as a way to unlock this value and demonstrate to the business that the legal department runs just like any other part of the business. Along with data analytics and legal procurement (discussed later in this book), legal operations help form part of the big three best business practices utilized by savvy legal departments of any size. Importantly, a legal operations function is not just for megasize legal departments. The math varies, but somewhere between 25 to 50 percent of in-house legal departments of all sizes have created legal operations functions and that number continues to grow.

The legal operations group consists of a person (or persons) and typically sits within the legal function of a company. The group usually reports directly to the general counsel and is responsible for the operations of the legal department, ultimately looking to maximize the efficient delivery of legal services throughout the company. In many ways, an in-house legal operations team mimics those of outside law firms, who for decades have benefited from separating the lawyers from the day-to-day operation of the firm. For example, generally, you do not see partners at law firms working on technology implementations or setting up the billing process. They care about these issues and are involved as needed, but their skills and time are saved for a higher and better use—practicing law.

Operations, in the in-house context, is a broad term and can mean many different things. Most legal operations groups focus on financial matters because that is where the biggest benefit lies, i.e., getting the legal department on a firm financial footing with accurate forecasting and accruals of legal spending and identifying the right firm for the right project at the right price. However, that is not all that they do or can do. There are many tasks the operations group can perform. Smart general counsel realize this and—if fortunate enough to have an operations person or group—use the team to the fullest extent possible, from financial analysis to strategic planning to data analytics. All of these function as ways the legal department can show value numerically, so they are critical in some manner to the task of showing the value of the legal department overall.

The goal of legal operations is to take on all of the tasks that do not require a law degree and to free up in-house lawyers to focus on high-value legal work. By taking non-legal tasks off the plates of in-house lawyers, the value of a legal operations function crystalizes. It frees up time for lawyers to be lawyers. When in-house lawyers have time to focus on legal problems and not administrative problems, performance improves as more legal work gets does with more thought and attention, and with less need for outside counsel. That is a huge positive for the company, especially the bottom line. On a more granular level, a legal operations team focuses on things that drive efficiency within the legal department by allowing the legal team to operate based on data and metrics. Efficiency also rises when the work of the legal operations team allows the lawyers to do more with less, turning what is usually a budget-time slogan into reality. The efficiency enhancements in the legal department, in turn, tie directly to a company's primary goal of driving profitability.

Here are just some of the things legal operations can do to enhance efficiency in the legal department and thereby enhance the value the department provides to the business:

- **Strategic Planning**
    - ➤ Partner with the general counsel and assist with driving her/his strategic vision
    - ➤ Create key performance indicators (KPIs) and yearly goals for the department
    - ➤ Succession planning
    - ➤ Create a strategic plan for the legal department
- **Financial Planning**
    - ➤ Prepare and set budgets
    - ➤ Operate e-billing system
    - ➤ Accruals
    - ➤ Spending forecasting
    - ➤ Negotiate (and monitor) alternative fee arrangements with law firms/vendors
    - ➤ Manage outside counsel and other legal vendors (including outside counsel guidelines)
    - ➤ Financial reporting (within the legal department and outside the legal department)
    - ➤ Create legal department dashboards
- **Operational/Analytics**
    - ➤ Staffing
    - ➤ Data analytics and metrics
    - ➤ Find process improvements (including how to scale legal services delivery to meet the growing needs of the company)
    - ➤ Contract management
    - ➤ Knowledge management

    - Records management
    - Determine legal process improvements
    - Regulatory compliance
    - Legal project management
    - Create and send satisfaction surveys (business clients, internal to the department)

- **Technology**
    - Vet, test, and implement new technologies (and train individuals on how to use the various technologies used by the department)
    - Maintain technology used by the department

If you add up the monthly time in-house lawyers spent on the tasks identified above, the math becomes clear. There are huge efficiencies and cost savings available for the taking by any size legal department willing to make the investment in legal operations.

One hurdle for creating a legal operations role within a legal department is the naturally conservative nature of lawyers. Most in-house lawyers prefer the status quo. Acting on crazy new ideas is not the way most of them behave, especially in an environment where mistakes can reflect poorly on them and the legal team regardless of the often-mouthed assurances from senior management that failure is welcomed within the company as a learning experience. (Unfortunately, that is rarely how it works.) Additional challenges arise from the simple economics of creating such a role or group.

- Where does the budget come from, and is this the best way to allocate scarce resources?
- If there is money for an operations role, is that the best way for the legal department to spend those dollars as opposed to, say, another lawyer?
- Skepticism about the value of legal operations, i.e., does the math really work out?
- What if my department is small? Will I get the same value from legal operations as a huge department?
- Where do I find the time to work on setting up legal operations when I cannot get to all of the work I already have on my plate?
- Will the general counsel let go of many of these operational tasks, overcoming the feeling that if they are not "in charge of operating the legal department, they are somehow failing?

It is crucial to make the case to the CFO and CEO as to why a legal operations role is needed, how it can improve the delivery of legal services, and—most importantly—how it can pay for itself over a short timeframe due to generating cost savings, cost avoidance, and increased technology adoption. Most departments see at least a 5 -– 7 percent reduction in spending by adding or enhancing a legal operations function. Small legal departments can benefit from a legal operations role too, even if there is not someone dedicated full time to the role. The principles work regardless of the size of the department. Most likely, other parts of the business have an operations person/team. Consequently, there is no reason why the same logic for having such a role should not apply to the legal department. The business cannot expect the legal department to operate like a part of the business if it short-changes it on the same tools the other parts of the business utilize.

Know the Importance of Accurate Budgets and Forecasts

As discussed, any promise that there would be no math as part of your in-house career is untrue. Math and numbers are important, in particular in showing value. To show value, it is necessary to have the funding to do the things a legal department must do, day in and day out. This comes from the legal budget —a math-based exercise if ever there were one. Given the importance, all in-house lawyers need to know how to prepare an annual legal department budget. It is not a simple task. To start, you must try to figure out in October what you will be spending in August of next year. Still, everyone in the business is going through the same budgeting exercise at the same time. Meaning that somehow, someway, you are going to have to find a way to come up with a spending plan that accurately accounts for the knowns and unknowns associated with providing legal services to the company. And it is important to the business that you take the task seriously and are not complaining about it, proclaiming legal is different, and saying it is too difficult to create a budget. That attitude will not get you far, and it is a big step backward on the value continuum. On the other hand, being able to accurately predict and stick to a legal budget is a big positive in the department's favor. So, rather than fight it, legal departments should embrace the process and use it as a way to show the value they are providing to the company and to make the pitch for more resources to bring even more value to the table.

When starting to prepare an annual legal department budget you must understand and account for all of the different items that make up the spending. If you forget something, you can end up with some big, costly holes. So, it is worth sitting down and thinking hard about where all the money goes each year. Here are some typical high-level categories:

- Salaries and benefits – This number usually comes from human resources, but it accounts for salaries, benefits, bonuses, 401K matches, and anything else that goes into the fully loaded cost of each employee in the department.

- Allocations – This number comes from the finance team and accounts for the department's share of the rent, utilities, technology, copiers, phones, and any other costs associated with operating the company that is spread among the different business units and staff groups.
- Department-specific technology – Besides technology generally provided by the company, some departments may have their own specific technology such as a contract management system, e-billing system, matter management, etc.
- CLE/Training – Every legal department needs to keep its people trained and up-to-speed. This includes conferences, seminars, and so forth.
- Travel – Another must-have. Be realistic here. Travel involves a lot more than the cost of airfare. Spend some time thinking about each month of the year, who will travel where, and what will they will realistically spend per trip. Lawyers tend to chronically underestimate the cost of travel.
- Bar fees/legal memberships – This includes state bar fees, membership in organizations, certifications, and so on.
- Subscriptions/Books/Newspapers – These cover things like legal research tools and any subscriptions or books/periodicals, etc.
- Outside counsel fees/Contractors – Other than salaries and benefits, this will likely be your biggest line item.
- Team events – Having a holiday lunch, working a charitable event, or planning on an offsite? You need to account for it.
- Postage/office supplies – Unless you never use overnight shipping, or buy pens and paper, you must account for this line.
- Miscellaneous – Basically, everything else, like translations, notary public license fees, trademark watch services, corporate secretary services, mobile phone reimbursement, and more.

Next, look at spending for the current year and then project a run rate for the full year. For example, if you have spent $500,000 through September, divide by nine to get a monthly average spend of $55,555. Multiply by the remaining months of the year, three (3 × $55,555) to get your *estimated* remaining spend for the rest of the year: $166,665. Add everything together ($500,000 + $165,665) to get your estimated annual spend: $665,665. You can use this as a starting point for estimating next year's spending. Look at all your open matters and determine which matters will likely roll over into the new year. Work with outside counsel to estimate the fees for those matters in the coming year. Then look at your historical averages over the past several years (if you have that data). This will help you ballpark your expected range of spend. Be sure to discard any unusually high numbers (for example, a massive antitrust case) that are not likely to repeat. Finally, work with your team to use everyone's knowledge of what they see coming, trends, their gut, and their experience (i.e., chance + probability) to estimate the new types of matters that *might* arise in the new year. Without this frontline input, you will be guessing versus forecasting. There is a big difference between the two. Guessing is one step above useless. Forecasting means you have taken time to educate yourself about the likely scenarios and outcomes. It will not be perfect, but it will be in the ballpark. All of this becomes your data pool to draw from.

Focusing on outside counsel fees is easy because such fees are the most obvious source of spending by the department. However, you need to be sure to capture all the essentials. These are the things you *must* spend money on to keep the lights on. And they can add up, which means if you do not account for them, they can become a nasty surprise as you monitor legal spend over the course of the year. These include things like state bar fees, technology costs, and subscriptions. Comb over the current years' invoices and expense reports and interview your team to capture everything. Do not forget things like fees to maintain patents and trademarks, business license fees and secretary of state annual reports, fees associated with your registered agent, stock service agent (if publicly traded), occupation taxes, and a host of other fees and costs needed just to run the department and provide legal services. As you dig in, you may well find costs that have been paid year after year even though no one wants or uses the services anymore. They are just automatically paid every year because no one said stop. Likewise, you might find you have several individual memberships to an organization that can be consolidated into a less expensive group membership. The lesson here is not to focus only on outside counsel fees when you plan your budget.

Work in what you know about the company's business plans for the next year, such as:

- Is the company expanding into new geographies or new lines of business?
- Is a merger and acquisition on the horizon?
- Will new products be coming online that may need trademarks, copyrights, or patents?
- Do you need to prepare to go after a large number of accounts receivable that are way overdue?

Whatever it may be, you need to know about it now, because now is when you are planning your budget. There are two ways to get this information. First, as discussed above, you should be highly tuned into presentations and discussions at the executive level about the plans of the company. It is rare that, by this time of the year, there are not several stakes in the ground as to where the company is headed. Unless highly confidential, those plans should be shared with the department and especially with those involved in planning next year's budget. Second, ask someone. You should have unfettered access to the business unit leaders and their chief lieutenants. Ask them to share their plans with you and use those to determine what the department will be dealing with next year.

Finally, write out on a whiteboard or in a spreadsheet your main legal services categories: litigation, employment, IP, commercial, corporate secretary, real estate, privacy, regulatory and compliance, and so forth. Start to plug in numbers for each area based on your analysis of all the data above. Have your team take a look and help review and refine the numbers. Do something similar for the other essential costs discussed above. When you are finished you will have a pretty good estimate of your legal spend for the next year (even if next year is months away) and you will have built your budget just like the other parts of the business.

When you look at the budget process as an opportunity and not as a chore, you start to see the power of working through and building up a budget like any other part of the business. If the business sees you take it seriously and are bringing real projections to the table versus uninformed guesses, not only are you more likely to get the funding you seek but also you will leave the right impression with the finance team and the rest of the business. They'll realize legal is not special, it is part of the business—a very important part.

Use 2×2 Matrix Analysis

Business people have an analytical and numbers-oriented way of looking at things. Something that fits nicely with how most lawyers approach solving problems. One of their good ideas to port over to the legal department is the use of 2×2 matrices as a way to visually analyze a problem. A 2×2 matrix is a square divided into four boxes whereby each axis is a decision criterion, e.g., cost, effort, risk, complexity, urgency, importance, or whatever you want. You plot different tasks or options into one of the four squares, such as expense and complex versus low-cost and complex, and so on. You have a graphical representation that allows you to make decisions based on the criteria. For example, you will focus your budget on items that are high value and low cost, or however you wish. For purposes of showing value, walking into a meeting with a 2 × 2 matrix will automatically gain the legal department credibility with the business rather than coming in with a lengthy memo or speaking off the cuff. The information might be the same, but the presentation is vastly different and one the business is used to seeing. Remember, acting like businesspeople and not lawyers is a key part of showing value.

One of the best and most useful 2 × 2 matrices is a SWOT analysis. It is a great tool to look strategically at the legal department as a whole and how best to plan to add value to the business. The power of a SWOT (as with all 2 × 2 matrices) is in its simplicity, i.e., it is an excellent 30,000-foot view of the legal department or a particular legal issue (e.g., data breach readiness). It is not the plan, but it will help you create the plan. And it will help you explain to the business why the plan makes sense.

For this section, a SWOT analysis is a shorthand way to set out what the legal department is good at (*Strengths*), what it is not so good at (*Weaknesses*), where there are opportunities to add value to the business (*Opportunities*), and what you need to watch out for (*Threats*). While primarily used for strategic planning, a SWOT analysis is flexible enough for use in analyzing one-off problems or tasks, or even evaluating employees. Here is a sample SWOT 2 × 2 box:

(Positives)	(Negatives)
Strengths • Strength No. 1 • Strength No. 1 • Strength No. 3 • Strength No. 4	**Weaknesses** • Weakness No. 1 • Weakness No. 2 • Weakness No. 3 • Weakness No. 4
Opportunities • Opportunity No. 1 • Opportunity No. 2 • Opportunity No. 3 • Opportunity No. 4	**Threats** • Threat No. 1 • Threat No. 2 • Threat No. 3 • Threat No. 4

The chart above sets out the four core SWOT attributes. You can also see how the items on the left-hand side are positives, while those in the right-hand column are negatives— or to stay with one of the core themes of this book, value creation versus value destruction.

Preparing a proper SWOT analysis is not something you can throw together in thirty minutes and call it done. It takes time to do correctly. I prefer to use a whiteboard and erasable markers/sticky notes, but you can use paper, a slide deck, an electronic document, napkins, or whatever works best to capture your ideas. Try to be as specific as possible with your ideas. For example, you might put "Do not communicate well with each other" as a weakness of the legal department. A better (more specific) example would be "Rely too much on email to communicate with each other." Similarly, do not put "Department lacks technology" when the better input may be "Do not utilize collaboration tools to the fullest extent possible." Do what works best for you. You can sharpen your initial ideas into more actionable ones with a little extra thought and effort. Lastly, organize the ideas in each quadrant in their order of importance. This way the department can focus its time and resources on the most important things first.

You will want to get as much input as possible from as many sources as makes sense for your situation. In other words, you do not want the SWOT to be just you and your thoughts only. Involve the entire legal department in helping brainstorm suggestions and ideas for each box. You can do this in a group session or, if you think you will get more honest input, appoint someone to collect suggestions from everyone with a guarantee of anonymity. Next, reach outside the department into the business and get their input. To the extent the C-Suite will participate, that is gold. Getting input from other senior management and frequent customers of the department is just as good, if not better. Consider using a survey tool to gather input. Outside counsel can also be helpful. The key is to get fresh and honest input, not only things you want to hear or that confirm your own thinking. Keep a running list of items to put in the different boxes so when the time comes to create or update your SWOT, you have new ideas and thoughts ready to go.

The fun and easy part of a SWOT is listing all of the things the legal department does especially well, the strengths. It could be anything from completing sophisticated contracts with speed, to an excellent working relationship with the sales team, to obtaining patents. It can even be something like the high skill level or longevity of the legal team. This is also where input from those outside the department is critical. Consider things like writing skills, use of technology, staying within budget, creation of self-help resources, and so forth. A proper SWOT exercise forces you to think through *all* of the different attributes of the legal department (good or bad).

Speaking of bad, describing what you are not good at can be tough—and painful. The first thing to keep in mind is that you do not want filling in the weakness box to become an exercise in how much the department stinks. It is about identifying weaknesses that matter and if you can improve upon them will make the legal department more valuable to the company. And weaknesses need not only be things you do poorly. For example, a weakness can be a lack of budget or people, lack of needed technology (or poor use of what you do have), or a poor brand within the company. In other words, consider your resources, systems, processes, and people. Like strengths, input from outside the department—especially the business— is critical. In this vein, keep a list of complaints you receive from the business about the department to add to future or update SWOT lists.

Opportunities for the legal department are positive things that require some type of action to make them happen. For example, there may be a great opportunity to identify an artificial intelligence tool that can help review and draft contracts. You can mark it as an opportunity, but you need to take several steps to make it a reality. If your legal department is hiring, then an opportunity may lie in finding an attorney who can bring a skillset not previously available in the department on board. Reorganizing the department may be an opportunity. You may be able to find a training program that can allow your current team to develop (or hone) new skills and thereby become more valuable assets to the company. And, as you have probably guessed, all four boxes of the SWOT are linked and interconnected. For example, you can turn a weakness into an opportunity. A strength may be available to counteract a threat and so forth. Identifying opportunities is a part of the SWOT where the input of the legal team itself is the most important source of ideas. However, do not ignore what the business sees as an opportunity for the department, as it may be something really interesting, such as involving lawyers in monthly staff meetings of the sales or marketing teams. Opportunities may not be legal in nature, e.g., the new U.S. Senator for your state is from the same town where your headquarters is located. This may mean a terrific opportunity to raise the company's profile in Washington, D.C. Finally, opportunities do not need to be moonshots or game-changers. They can be small and/or simple, but still have a positive impact on how the legal department generates value for the business.

Your ability to identify threats to the department is a skill all strategic in-house lawyers have developed, i.e., the ability to look outside the department and spot issues, trends, and developments that can negatively impact the team (or even the company). For example, a change in administration in Washington, D.C. may mean enhanced antitrust enforcement or increased regulatory burdens. Likewise, the COVID-19 pandemic produced plenty of threats to legal departments, such as layoffs, budget cuts, litigation, bankruptcies, force majeure issues, and so forth. Remember, you can use a SWOT for one-off issues facing the department, too. For example, a change at the top of the company where new leaders may have a different view on the importance and value of the legal department, including changes they expect. Finally, while primarily outward looking, internal threats can arise to the department, such as the departure of key department members, lack of a succession plan, uneven workloads, or failures in processes that cause unnecessary delays in getting work done.

A SWOT can be the first step in a larger effort to create a multi-year strategic plan for the legal department. It can be the basis of an extended team meeting or part of a legal department offsite. It can be a marketing tool to share with the C-Suite and leaders in the business to show how the legal department is acting on feedback, using business tools and analysis to strive for constant improvement, and how it plans on adding value through strategic planning. A SWOT allows you to tick all of these boxes in a way the business leaders at your company will understand and appreciate. Here is a simplistic example of a completed SWOT looking at the legal department as a whole:

Positives	Negatives
Strengths • Positive "brand" – Department of Yes • Ability to quickly produce contracts • Present complex legal issues in easy to understand manner • Manage spending to within budget parameters • Longevity of team – repository of institutional knowledge for company	**Weaknesses** • Lack contract management tool (cannot quickly find contracts) • No internal competition law experience • Lack self-help tools for business • Asia office feels "left-out" and not part of team
Opportunities • Implement contract management tool • Use next hire to plug competition law gap • Reinvent department meeting and host yearly offsite to enhance teamwork and inclusion • Create training program for business around contract playbook • Create formalized "back up" plan to ensure bench strength and limit pain of regrettable departures	**Threats** • Potential recession will impact headcount and budget • Trade war with [X] impacting exports (need legislative solution or work around) • No back up for Jane Smith if she departs • Primary law firms have announced steep rate increase for next year (consider new firms)

A 2 × 2 matrix is a powerful tool and a SWOT analysis is one variation.[18] For example, many of you are already familiar with an Eisenhower Matrix:

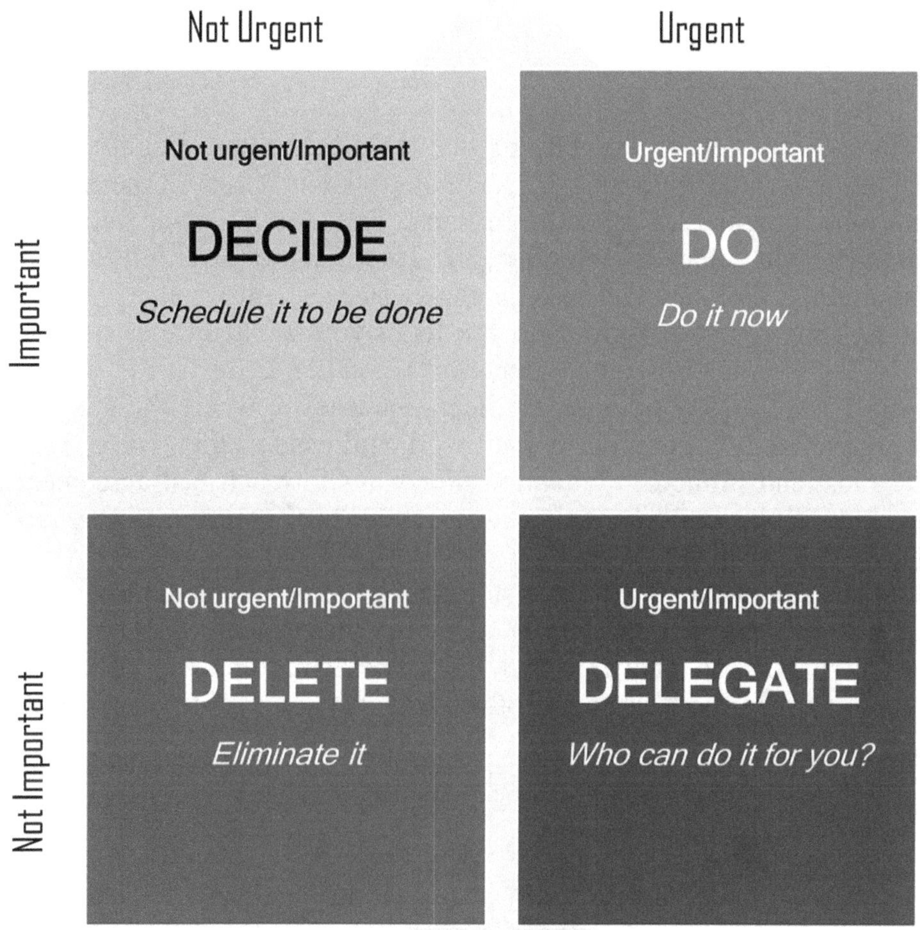

18 *See* A. Lowry & P. Hood, *The Power of the 2 × 2 Matrix: Using 2 × 2 Thinking to Solve Business Problems and Make Better Decisions* (Jossey-Bass Publishing, Hoboken, NJ, 2004). This book is considered by many to be the bible of how to use 2 × 2 matrices to solve a myriad of different problems. *See also*, R. Williams, *Exploring: Using 2 × 2 Matrices to Analyze Situations* (iUniverse Publishing, Bloomington, IN, 2007).

This 2 × 2 box helps the user focus on what is important and urgent versus that which is not important or not urgent. It also ties neatly into the "four Ds," i.e., with every task or email that comes your way you must decide whether to:

- Do it now.
- Decide to schedule for later.
- Delegate it.
- Delete it (ignore it).

Applying these to the Eisenhower Matrix, the tasks in the upper right (urgent + important) are those you do now or as soon as possible. Tasks in the upper left (important + not urgent) you schedule for later. Tasks in the lower right (urgent + not important) you delegate to someone. And tasks in the lower left (not urgent + not important) sit or are eliminated/deleted as have little value. While not perfect, an Eisenhower Matrix can help you focus your limited time on what the company values the most, urgent + important. You can use it at the individual level, or more useful in my opinion, the department level, where the department coalesces around the urgent and important work and ensures this type of work is getting the most and immediate attention. For ways to reach fast agreement on what the department should be doing now versus later, see the discussion on huddle meetings later in this book.

Another variation of the SWOT is a strategic value/process mapping analysis, which is just a fancy name for another 2 × 2 matrix that plots the strategic impact/importance of a task on one axis and the difficulty/complexity of the work necessary to complete the task on the other. It would look something like this:

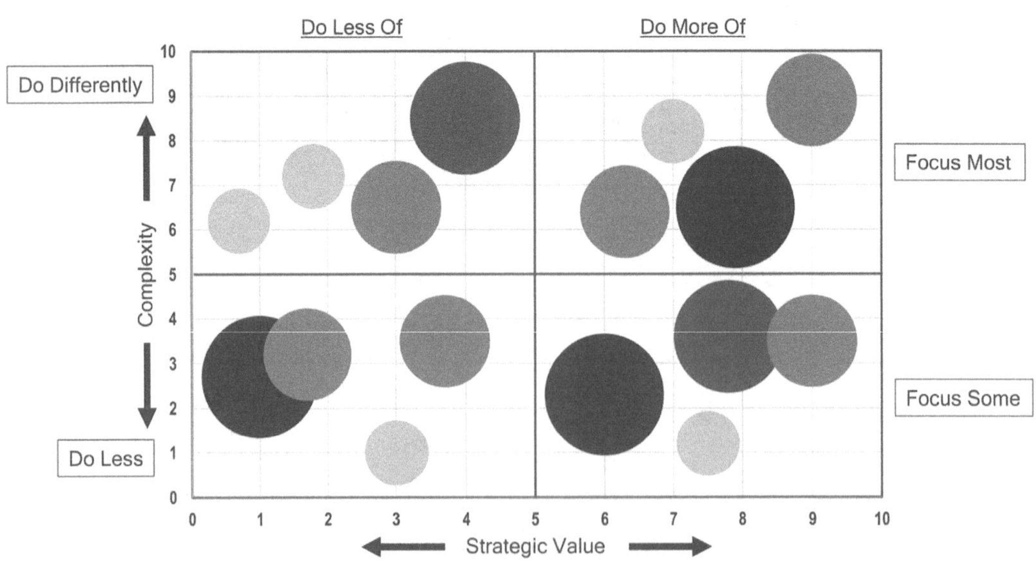

As you plot the different projects and tasks pending in the legal department, you get a snapshot of strategically important work (or not) on one axis, and work that is difficult or easy on the other. The answers reveal how you should deploy the resources of the department, in other words, what available resources should you utilize for the tasks in each quadrant. Complex and highly strategic work should go to the most senior in-house team members or your top-tier outside counsel. Low complexity and highly strategic work should go to mid-level in-house and outside counsel. High complexity and low strategic impact work can go to boutique law firms or even be a good learning tool for newer in-house lawyers as the stakes are low but the work challenging. Lastly, work that is simple and low-value may be prime for alternative legal services providers (e.g., India), single-person law firms, or even elimination. While nothing is in stone, a strategic value 2 × 2 matrix allows you to visualize the issues or distribution of types of work. From there you can better think through how to handle the work, if at all. Like everything I have described in this section (and elsewhere in this book), these are not decisions to make in a vacuum or alone. Partner with the business leaders and your legal department team to agree jointly on what work goes into which box and how best to resource it. When everyone is aligned like this, the odds of surprises or unhappy clients lessen dramatically. And, the fact you reached out for the opinion of the business and are using tools familiar to them will leave a highly favorable impression, underscoring the value proposition you are driving.

Get Comfortable with Data Analytics

It should be clear by now, business people love data. One reason is because of the insights into aspects of the business it can provide, including the overarching question of how are we doing? Indeed, most businesses spend significant amounts of time and effort analyzing data to answer this and many other questions regarding the value, health, and efficiency of the business. The data also drives decisions about ways to improve the business, including early warning signs when things are off and need attention before they become big problems. This process is known as data analytics.

Following this lead, legal departments should consistently ask themselves how they are doing,[19] While it seems like a simple question, it is fraught with multiple meanings. It could mean how are we doing against the budget? How are we doing with turning contracts for the business? How are we doing in the litigation? Or, how are we doing with our compliance efforts? Regardless of the what, the how has troubled legal departments for decades because they have historically lacked

19 If not, the business will.

the data to answer the different flavors of the question. Consequently, the legal department was often excused from performing or reporting with the same discipline and reliability as other parts of the business. Legal was special. Fortunately, or unfortunately, those days are long over. Businesses of all sizes expect their legal departments to work with, and report out, data the same way as the rest of the company. By doing so, the senior management of the company can look at the business holistically, including the legal department. Given this new scrutiny and the fact that data can demonstrate value, the ability of in-house lawyers to master data analytics has become paramount.

At a high level, data analytics is the process of creating, categorizing, and examining data sets to draw inferences and conclusions from them. Determine what the data tells the department and then use the data and conclusions to make better, more informed decisions or to increase operational efficiency. For in-house legal departments, this cuts across a wide variety of issues, from budgets and spending to litigation outcomes. If you consider that many legal decisions in the past were, and currently are, often decided on hunches or guesses, and that law firm relationships were usually based on who went to law school with the general counsel, you can see the appeal—and importance—of using data analytics to make and track those same decisions. Visibility and insight create actionable intelligence. If you couple that with better decisions and the evolving need for legal departments to operate and report like any other business function, there is an increasing demand by in-house lawyers for better data and better tools to analyze their data. Data analytics allows you to talk about legal issues with the business in a manner they can more easily comprehend, for example, with a decision tree. And, if you can use math to show the legal department handled 10 percent more contracts this year with the same number of staff you are on your way to being left alone. Legal departments that demonstrate they are operating like a business get a longer leash from management.

The core of data analytics is, of course, data. So, you start the process by identifying all of the data available to your legal department. This should come naturally to most in-house lawyers because it is part and parcel to what we do every day. Gather evidence so we can analyze it and draw out our legal conclusions. Data analytics is essentially the same thing, find the data and use it to make conclusions. Consequently, it is important to locate every piece of data you can find that touches or is touched by the legal department. Here are some places to start:

- E-billing systems (and if you are not using an e-billing system, gather data directly from invoices manually or ask your law firms and vendors to provide it);
- matter management systems (electronic or manually maintained);
- reports generated by the legal department;

- data available from legal-related tools the legal department utilizes, such as Thomson Reuters, Lexis-Nexis, Gartner/CEB, and so forth;
- data other departments at the company generated/created, such as finance, marketing, IT, compliance, human resources, etc.;
- publicly available data (free or purchased, e.g. benchmarking data);
- data shared between legal departments (creating your own data exchange with other in-house departments); and
- government data.

Next, categorize the data into four categories: 1) descriptive (what happened in the past), 2) diagnostic (why something happened in the past), 3) predictive (what is likely to happen in the future), or 4) prescriptive (actions you can take to affect events and outcomes). These categories help you determine the uses for the data. For most legal departments, especially those starting to dabble with data analytics, the best source of data is your e-billing system (or invoices) and matter management data (electronic or manual). From this core, you can start to grab some low-hanging fruit without much additional cost.

Once you understand and mine your data sources, you must determine what you want to measure. The what is the fundamental purpose behind data analytics. Coming up with the what may be hard or easy, depending on how your legal department operates. To start, think about the data you have. Then, think about questions where the answers could make the department run more effectively and/or efficiently, or reduce risk to the company. The process goes something like this:

- ☐ What do you want to measure and why?
- ☐ Locate and obtain the relevant data.
- ☐ If necessary, clean and structure the data.
- ☐ Run the analysis.
- ☐ Draw your conclusion, make decisions based on results.

Here is a simple example. The legal department sets a goal of reducing the average hourly rate it pays outside counsel by 10 percent year-over-year. This becomes the measure. Next, locate the relevant billing data for the prior and current year. In this case: hours billed by outside counsel and total payments to outside counsel. Run the analysis (payments divided by hours). Compare the results. Is the average hourly rate lower by 10 percent or more in the current year compared to the prior year? If not, take action to reach your goal. You can refine the measure and break it down by law firm to get more granular information.

The ways in-house lawyers can utilize data analytics are virtually endless. The only limit is the data you have on hand and your ability to imagine uses and questions. Here are some of the most common things that legal departments seek to measure using data analytics:

- spending efficiency or effectiveness;
- efficiency of outside counsel;
- structuring the legal budget;
- workload distribution in the department;
- project turn-around time by the department;
- contract analysis (e.g., which clauses are the most negotiated);
- litigation outcome analysis (e.g., when to settle and for how much);
- compliance (e.g., predicting compliance problems based on searching company data);
- e-discovery costs and effectiveness;
- legal analysis (review of contracts, legal strategies, opponent's briefs, etc.);
- department process improvements;
- measuring attainment of department goals or KPIs;
- benchmarking, see how your department stacks up;
- whatever the C-Suite wants you to measure; and
- ask your outside counsel to create analytics specific to the matter(s) they are handling for you.

Once you start to show the business your are using data analytics to derive some or all of the above, you will be on your way to cementing your place in the Finance Hall of Fame! Before you start planning the wording on your plaque, consider the fact that the presentation of the data matters almost as much as the results. One benefit of using data analytics in a legal department is that you can use dashboards to present the results. Dashboards are a common tool businesses use to give a visual summary of the status of a project, a goal (or goals), spending, IT systems, or whatever you would like to show visually. Many in-house lawyers sit in meetings where various groups roll out slick, highly visual dashboards that allow those business leaders to discuss key points in easily digestible snippets revealed via the dashboard. Many in-house lawyers are missing out on this whole dashboard trend. As you start to get your arms around your data, and start to ask and answer questions around how the department is operating (compared to its goals or benchmarks), you can capture those answers in a dashboard. It may be that the dashboard is only for use within the department at staff meetings, or it may become something you have whenever there is a cross-functional meeting where groups are reporting out on how they're doing. A basic dashboard for the legal department might include just four boxes on a slide:

Company X Legal Department
Legal Dashboard - March 2021

Spending/Budget	Commercial Agreements
A summary or graph of outside spending vs. budget (or age hourly rate or legal spend as a engage of company revenue).	A summary or graph of the number and type of commercial agreement completed.
Key Matters/Projects	**Intellectual Property**
Set or graph out status of key cases and/or legal department IT projects	A summary or graph of the company's intellectual property, e.g., patents, trademarks, licensing agreement, etc.

These are just examples. Your dashboard depends entirely on what information is important to you, the department, and the C-Suite. If you need help with creating a dashboard, Excel can create interesting charts and graphs, software like Tableau can turn plain data into attention-getting visuals, or you can buy pre-made templates from companies like Caspio. Alternatively, you can hire skilled independent contractors via an online job site to assist you.

I realize this can all be a bit overwhelming. If you are not experienced or comfortable with data analytics, start with the data you have on hand now, come up with some simple questions to measure, and get into a rhythm of generating basic, helpful reports. Before sharing with the business, share the results with the department so they can see the good and the bad. For example, if your average hourly rate for outside counsel is way out of whack, your team can help manage that number down through how they engage with outside counsel. Transparency is good for any in-house legal department, even if it hurts. Do not feel pressured to share the data outside of the legal department right away, unless someone has asked for it. Spend time refining your processes and making sure you understand the results. If things are not where you want them to be, make sure you have a plan to fix it. Showing up with a problem and without a plan to solve it is not smart. As you gain experience and as you figure out different data sources or different questions to ask, you can start to expand your use of data analytics, with the goal always being how can you use this data to make the legal department operate better and keep the company out of trouble. Making the department look good is just a bonus.

Develop Key Performance Indicators that Matter

The discussion above about data analytics dovetails nicely into a discussion about key performance indicators (KPIs). KPIs are all the rage at the moment, and businesses are looking to their legal departments to prepare and present KPIs as part and parcel to demonstrating value. Simply put, KPIs are metrics you track to determine if you are on target with some goal or benchmark. The only problem is KPIs do not work particularly well for in-house legal departments. Numbers and charts on pretty dashboards usually convey little of the context a KPI captures. Without context, you miss the nuance about the value an in-house legal department provides. KPIs, for example, rarely capture how departments think and react to prioritize on the fly suddenly urgent matters, what work gets pushed aside (or the extra legal costs incurred) because the CEO has another new, top priority. They also fail to distinguish between one in-house lawyer who may be stuck on one complex mega-deal or case, and others who are working on dozens of smaller, but important, matters. Nor do they reveal what risks, litigation, bad deals, costs, and other pain are avoided because the legal department was involved. In other words, KPIs stink at measuring intangibles, a big part of what in-house lawyers bring to the table every day. Unfortunately, intangibles are typically where much of the value the department provides arises.

Regardless, you can get value from KPIs, even if it is just to assure the C-Suite you are operating the legal department like any other part of the business. The right KPIs can help support the narrative you want to tell about the legal department by showing numerically where the legal team is adding value to the company. And, like it or not, KPIs can show you where there are potential problems that need watching or fixing. This is all valuable information.

The biggest mistake most legal departments make is trying to track too many KPIs. If you have more than ten you are in trouble and in danger of overanalyzing things. The process should work like this.

- ☐ First, figure out what you want to measure and why it is important.
- ☐ Second, determine what information you have that can allow you to make the measurement. Ideally, you will have data from previous years (or third-party sources) to compare/benchmark to and, if not, your best insights may

be a few years down the road once you have accumulated or obtained that type of data.

- ☐ Third, create a format that allows you to present the KPIs–and your progress against them—in the most straightforward manner possible but with a little flair. (A dashboard is an excellent idea here.)
- ☐ Finally, think hard about what you want to share outside of the legal department. There is no rule you have to share everything—or anything. Certainly, if someone in a position to ask wants you to create or share a KPI, then you must do it. But you may also want to use some KPIs to measure things that you are not ready to share, but about which you do want data and insight. Keep those KPIs close to the vest until you are ready —if ever—to share them.

Below are some key KPIs to consider tracking and that show value (and additional KPI ideas are set forth in Appendix 1):

- ➤ **Contract quantity**. This is a pretty simple measure: how many contracts has the legal department completed over the measurement period? It can be just a gross number, or better, a measure against some goal set earlier in the year, e.g., 500 contracts per quarter. One of the highest and best uses of the legal department is completing contracts as contracts are the grease on the skids of the company's business. If you want to get more granular, you can break out the number of contracts by type, such as commercial, NDA, vendor, complex, simple, by value, or whatever different types of contracts your department works on.
- ➤ **Contract quality**. This measure is more complex than quantity, but it also tells you a lot more. For example, consider creating a contract scoring process where you develop (with the business) a set of acceptable risk criteria for contracts. Your contracts are then graded based on how well they met certain criteria. The best contracts get an A and the worst a D (and low-scoring contracts must go on a separate approval track). You can then set a KPI around having one percent or less of the contracts completed by the legal department fall into the grade C or D category. You can also track quality issues like how many times the company's forms and templates are used, how many times you use customer paper, and by the level of redlines required to get to a deal, The understanding would be that the more effort spent on customer paper or deep redlines to the company's form contracts, the lower the contract quality in general.[20]
- ➤ **Budget versus actual spend**. This is a pretty core KPI as it shows where the legal department is in terms of spending goals, i.e., where actual spend is versus budgeted spend. This should be tracked on two dimensions,

20 *See infra* at page 112 for a discussion about reducing risks in contracts, including a contract grading process.

year-to-date (overall YTD spend versus over YTD budget) and for the most recent month, e.g., June actual spend versus June budget or forecast. Ideally, you are also tracking by type of matter, such as litigation, contracts, corporate secretary, intellectual property, etc. Also of interest are the average hourly rate for outside law firms (especially if you have a goal to lower that number) and how the department is tracking against any other savings initiatives you have in place.

- **Legal spend by business unit**. With some legal departments, this occurs automatically because all outside legal spending is charged back to the relevant business unit/staff group. Even if not, it is an important metric because it allows you (and likely the C-Suite) to see who are the big users of legal services and it can prompt you to investigate whether something is driving higher spend by one group versus another. The latter is easier if you are also tracking (within each unit's spend overall spending number) the type of matter. This is something you can easily track through your e-billing tool (or in spreadsheets.)
- **Legal spend as percent of revenue**. While somewhat misleading, consider tracking legal spend as a percentage of the company's annual revenues. This metric is dubious, in my opinion, because what drives legal spend at a particular company is subject to a wide variety of variables likely unique to how that business operates versus revenue it generates. This is a common metric and is one the C-Suite is likely to ask about or, at a minimum, is familiar with. You can use this metric as a target to help you manage down legal spending or, if you can find that right comparison/benchmark, show how on-target or off-target the department may be versus the benchmark.
- **Intellectual property development**. The company's intellectual property (IP) is often an afterthought. It should not be. It is a valuable asset that can really matter if the company is, for example, ever put up for sale, for tax purposes, or as collateral for a re-financing. At a minimum, the legal department should be tracking the raw number of patents, copyrights, and trademarks applied for and/or granted during the year. There is also value in knowing the gross spend on and the average cost to obtain each category of IP. And, if you calibrate spend by business unit to track IP, you will know which business units drive the biggest IP legal spend. For example, marketing may drive a lot of trademark spending, and this may be something ripe to discuss with them in terms of how to reduce the cost.
- **Litigation management**. After drafting contracts, the second most important function of a legal department is managing and preventing litigation, possibly the biggest waste of time and money most companies face.[21] Unfortunately, it is challenging to come up with one KPI to

---

21 *See* my discussion *infra* at page 163 on the potential value of litigation as a business strategy.

measure litigation management. What seems to work best are several metrics under the umbrella of litigation management. These include:

- Number of litigation matters over a certain amount, e.g., $100,000, $50,000, or $500,000. This lets you focus on reporting about the litigation that matters most. A subcategory to consider here is the number of risky litigation matters, meaning cases where stakes are high. These types of matters are usually of more interest to the C-Suite and board of directors than run-of-the-mill litigation.
- The average cost per litigation matter (tracked as both defendant and plaintiff).
  - o Outside fees/costs
  - o Settlement/judgment (paid or received)
  - o Fines (if you are including regulatory investigations under litigation)
- Percentage of cases won/lost.
- Percentage of cases resolved before trial.

➤ **Compliance management**. This KPI assumes the company's compliance function sits within the legal department, something still fairly typical. Like litigation management, it is difficult to set out one KPI to track for this area. Because the board of directors is always interested in compliance issues, consider tracking, among other things:

- Percentage of company employees who have completed mandatory compliance training.
- The number of compliance matters reported by channel, such as via a hotline, email, or other departments, like human resources, and so forth.
- The number of compliance matters resolved and the number of compliance matters open.
- The average time to close a compliance matter.

➤ **Strategic project(s)**. Typically, there is at least one strategic project or initiative going on inside a legal department during any given year. It may be a big technology implementation, it might be a cost savings initiative, preparing a succession plan or three-year strategic plan, and so on. Regardless of what it is, if it is important enough, it is worth tracking the progress via a KPI. For example, a KPI for tracking the implementation of a contract management tool where you track completion progress versus plan. This KPI allows you to quickly see if the project is on track or off track and, if the latter, ask why, and determine what needs to be done to get it back on track.

➤ **Legal department employee engagement.** When it comes to your team, one number to care about is the department's employee engagement score.

This is something most companies measure at least annually. Basically, it is a composite score based on the team's answers to dozens of questions. The higher the engagement score, the more satisfied people are with their jobs, the more willing they are to take on discretionary work, to tout the company, and so forth. It is also a great predictor of employee retention (or in terms of spotting problems that need attention). Finally, it is a good measure of the success of the department's managers. There are many available benchmarks/targets to track employee engagement scores against, e.g., the national average, the company as a whole, the different business units and/or staff groups, or the legal department's prior year's score. All of which makes this a fairly simple KPI to implement and track.

- **Customer satisfaction**. When it comes to demonstrating value, one of the most important things for a general counsel to know is how satisfied is the business with the legal department. While anecdotal information is helpful, the best way to understand this is via a legal department customer satisfaction survey,[22] which measures satisfaction across several specific items as well as generating an overall satisfaction number. The most straightforward KPI here is an overall score. For example, a target overall satisfaction number and a goal that 85 percent of the respondents will have the same, or higher, level of satisfaction with the legal department versus the prior year. You can also ask those taking the survey to assign a letter grade to the department (grades A – D) and shoot for a B average or better, or whatever makes the most sense for your circumstances.
- **Time spent.** There is one other KPI to consider, though it is a bit controversial. This KPI tracks what people in the department are spending their time on, e.g., administrative tasks, email, meetings, research, drive-bys, drafting, or whatever else you want to measure in terms of workflow. The reason it is controversial is because generally, in-house lawyers hate anything to do with tracking their time. If you start asking people to track what they are doing, you are going to hear about it. And even though the information would be extremely valuable in helping determine utilization, efficiency, the nature of the work getting sent to the legal department (and the level of difficulty of the same), and other important insights, it simply may not be worth the fallout from your team for trying to force something like this on them. That said, the overall pressure on legal departments to show value numerically may, someday, overcome the resistance to tracking time.

22 *See infra* at page 240 for a discussion on creating a customer satisfaction survey.

KPIs are here to stay, and savvy legal departments are figuring out the best ways to create and use them. While it is difficult to track the true value of the legal department via KPIs, there is value to extract from such a process. Not only in terms of valuable insights but, more importantly, the benefits from using KPIs to show value the department generates. Equally important is finding an impressive way to present your KPIs to the business. The right dashboard, slide deck, or spreadsheet can make a huge difference in how you and the legal department are perceived, regardless of what the KPIs actually show.

Manage Outside Counsel Spend Like it is Your Money

No in-house department is immune to cost pressure. Nor should it be. All parts of any business must deal with the reality of limited resources. Perhaps the biggest area for improvement for most departments lies with managing outside counsel spend. Aside from salaries and benefits, outside counsel (and vendor) spend is probably the department's largest budget item. Legal department spending often is highly visible to the entire executive team, especially the CEO and CFO. And given the business's natural aversion to spending money on legal issues, it is an area of intense scrutiny. The C-Suite will ask if the legal department leaders are being good stewards of the company's money. Are they managing their vendors properly? Are they applying modern techniques to find law firms? And so on. Demonstrating that you are paying close attention to costs and that you are thoughtful in what you are spending and why are key to demonstrating value.

In-house lawyers who run their matters, teams, and department like a business simply have more credibility at budget time and generally with the business. If you are doing this, you can generate a lot of trust with the finance team and the C-Suite. They will believe the budgets you submit are real and not numbers that need a significant haircut to bring back to reality. A legal department that keeps a constant and tight focus on its budget and spending, that provides accurate forecasts and accruals, and that treats the company's money like its own money, is highly valued. If you are not doing these things, the opposite is the case and you will likely find the budgets you submit and requests you make around money get a skeptical reception from the powers that be. Fortunately, this is one area where there are many tried and true methods of managing outside spending that you can and should adopt and use to demonstrate the department's commitment to good money management (i.e., enhancing value creation). Several of these are set out below. Above we discussed some KPIs and other metrics around spending. Now we will discuss how to drive success and how to meet those metrics. Once you can convince the business that you are the "master of your numbers," you will find budget and spending issues much easier to deal with on a day-to-day basis.

Managing Outside Counsel

As an in-house lawyer, you must be able to accurately forecast, predict, and control outside counsel spend. If you have an e-billing system, you can do this via features in that tool. If you do not have an e-billing system, you can create a spreadsheet that shows what was spent last month and the forecast for the current month. For example, at the beginning of May ask all of your outside counsel to tell you a) what you spent in April and b) what do you forecast we will spend in May? Then, capture this data over the course of the fiscal year (with a running total showing how you are doing against your budget overall). To increase accuracy (and to minimize surprises), go back mid-month and ask for an update. This will give you a very detailed (and accurate) look at outside counsel spending in the short term. It also provides a certain amount of precision and allows you to exercise proactive reductions in spending or shift spending priorities if necessary. Importantly, it forces you to talk more with your outside counsel about what is driving costs and how you can work together to manage the situation.

It is important to have a discussion with senior management about what is included in the legal budget and what is not. For example, the business may decide that merger and acquistions spend is not part of the regular legal budget and will be part of the project cost center and ROI on that deal. Likewise, you may want to charge trademark searches to the marketing department or immigration costs (e.g., H1B visas) to human resources or the business unit making the hire to help drive efficient behavior. To be clear, by doing this you are not abdicating your role as manager of all legal spending (whether it hits the legal department budget or not). You are simply making clear what does hit your budget, which gives you a better ability to manage the legal spend you are responsible for and measured against.

While the billable hour continues to dominate the way most outside law firms bill for their services, alternative fee arrangements are gaining steam and are worth discussing no matter the type or size of matter. The ability to negotiate alternatives to rack hourly rates is something to tout to the business as part of the value the department is bringing to the table (and you can measure it as a KPI). Considering some of the following alternatives to the hourly rate:

- *Discounted rate cards (from firms for the lawyers you use most frequently);*
- *Discounts tied to the average hourly rate for your city (Why pay New York City rates when your company is based in Minneapolis? You will need data on local rates for this one.);*
- *Retainers (a fixed amount paid monthly for a negotiated set of services from the firm);*
- *Blended rates (one fixed rate that covers both partners and associates);*
- *Fixed fees for specific projects (These fees provide cost certainty and most firms should be able to provide a fixed price for certain contracts and litigation, as well as patents, trademarks, and other legal services);*

- *A percentage contingency fee (the law firm is paid by receiving a percentage of whatever is collected by your company in the lawsuit. But consider building in safeguards to limit the "windfall" effect, e.g., have different percentages apply at different points in the case or have a cap of two or three times of actual billed time);*
- *Cost-sharing with other companies involved in your matter (joint defense costs, share expert costs, local counsel costs, translations, etc.);*
- *Cap on rates (hourly rates cannot increase by more than a certain percent in any year or over the course of engagement (For example, zero percent rate increase for first eighteen months, then the hourly rates cannot go up by more than three percent thereafter in any given twelve-month period.);*
- *Caps by phase (different phases of the matter are estimated and the law firm provides an absolute cap for each phase);*
- *Caps by project (similar to the above but the law firm provides an overall cap for the project);*
- *Volume discounts (discounts off the rate as you hit certain spend thresholds with the firm. Try to get the discounts to apply back to the first dollar spent vs. just the incremental spend over the threshold.);*
- *Get a number of free hours per attorney for them to get up to speed on your new matter (e.g., ten hours of "up-to-speed time" per attorney on the law firm's nickel);*
- *A number of free hours every month for one-off phone calls and quick questions (If your law firm gives you five hours of free consultation every month you will have the luxury of picking up the phone for a sanity check or quick answer and the firm will get the benefit of knowing that if the discussion turns into a real matter, it will likely go to them.);*
- *Limit or heavily discount the use of first-year lawyers (do not get stuck paying for learning on the job) If the firm thinks they need first-year lawyers on the case then either substantially discount the rate or, better yet, let the first-year tag along for free.);*

It is a difficult decision, but do not be afraid to move work to save significant costs. Nothing gets you cost savings faster than being willing to move work to a different law firm. If you are unhappy with the firm (or simply made a mistake in terms of sending a low-value project to a high-dollar firm), do not hesitate. Move the work to a firm better suited for what you need and/or offering cost savings that justify the move. You may wish to give the current firm a chance to retain the work if they can match the cost savings.[23] And, if you do move work, be sure to get free hours from the new firm to get up to speed on the matter.

23 Yes, this is called playing one firm off of the other, and it happens all the time in business. Do not be embarrassed, afraid, or timid about using this tool to save the company money.

Rather than moving work, be more thoughtful upfront as to which law firms you use for certain types of work. Sounds pretty basic, but you would be surprised how often in-house lawyers will send matters to certain firms without thinking about the match between cost and complexity or risk. Be sensitive to which work goes where and why. There may be reasons other than cost as to why you want to use a certain firm or lawyer.[24] Just be sure to discuss with your team which firm should get the work. Not only will you make a better decision, but also you start to train the next generation of department leaders about how and why to make such decisions. Consider creating a list of quality niche or boutique firms, and make an effort to push a certain percentage of your yearly legal spend to those firms. These are typically smaller firms that specialize in a particular area of the law and are usually staffed with lawyers who moved away from the larger more well-known firms. If you do not have a list, start to build one and simply use your contacts and networks with other in-house lawyers to get suggestions.

If you do not have an outside counsel billing policy, put one in place as soon as possible. It must go out to counsel with every new matter and to counsel you use most frequently yearly. This policy sets out, among other things, what you do and do not pay for. For example, consider not paying for online research, car services, or food unless someone from the company is present or it is cleared in advance. Reserve the right to reject any bills not received within three months of the work be performed. Nothing kills budget planning like getting a bill in November for work performed back in January. A policy will also help you in the event you did not get an engagement letter for the project.

If you have the time, run a request for proposal (RFP) process where firms bid on the project (discussed in greater detail after this). You will probably get better rates, and you usually get some free analysis of your legal problem as firms like to set out how they would attack the problem, especially when it involves litigation. Sometimes you can get a firm you prefer to match the rates offered by a competing firm. Still, there is not always time to go through an RFP process or you may have other reasons for not doing so. That is fine as everything depends on the circumstances at hand. RFPs are generally a tool and not a mandate. Likewise, get an engagement letter for every substantive project (or at least have a master engagement letter with your preferred law firms). Review their standard letter carefully, and do not be afraid to mark it up. The letter should spell out any discounts or alternative fee arrangements you bargained for, and be sure that your

24 For example, sometimes the situational optics require that you hire a big law firm instead of a boutique firm because with bet-the-company litigation you do not want to be seconded guessed by the C-Suite or the board of directors if you lose the case, despite that fact that the boutique firm would be able to provide just as good of legal services as the big law firm and at a substantially lower cost point.

outside counsel policy trumps anything contradictory in the engagement letter. Remember, if it is not in writing it may not be real.

If you ask outside counsel for something, they will typically move heaven and earth for you to get the answer. While nice, this level of service is pretty expensive. Sometimes you are perfectly fine with a little less service. Set your expectations upfront with your outside lawyers. It can be a cap on the amount of money you are willing to spend, or on the number of hours you are willing to pay for, or just making it clear you do not want a formal memo with the answer (an email or highlighted copy of the relevant case will suffice). You can also make clear that you only want so many lawyers involved on the project (or ask for a specific lawyer to work on your matter). Setting expectations upfront provides clear guideposts for outside counsel. And, of course, encourage outside counsel to come back to you if they think you need to spend more or get more people involved. Make sure they know you will expect them to justify why it is needed and that they ask *before* doing anything more than agreed.

Savings on outside counsel spend is generally measurable, i.e., tangible proof of value created. In the spirit of marketing the legal department, consider a monthly or quarterly report showing cost savings on outside counsel spend. A regular report will also keep you focused on the task at hand. You need to do two things: a) track monthly how you are doing against your budget or forecast (and if you are tracking over you know you need to start reducing spend somewhere); and b) create a short summary slide presentation or dashboard showing cost savings (monthly or quarterly is best). You need to be both creative and conservative. Meaning, turn over rocks to show you are saving money, but do not go so far out on a limb trying to gin up savings that you lose credibility. Keep things simple, and make sure you can reasonably support any assumptions or assertions you make in the report. The report can show the following:

- Spend vs. Forecast/budget. (If your report show you're overbudget, set out you're a plan to get back on budget.)
- Cost savings. Savings based on using lower-cost counsel or based on deals you struck to shave costs off standard hourly rates or savings on vendor costs.
- Costs avoided (legal). Cost savings because you won the case, settled a case quickly, or settled under settlement authority. Primary attorney's fees.
- Costs avoided (business). Cost savings when management does not have to prepare and give a deposition or attend a hearing/trial because of things the legal department did. If the CEO does not have to spend 20 hours in deposition prep, that is a huge cost saving for the business.
- Money in. Always a favorite because it highlights the legal department as a revenue generator rather than a cost center. For example, if you win litigation and the other side has to pay damages or other monies to your

> company, or pay your attorney's fees, or if you were able to avoid paying a tax or fine. (Avoided taxes are real dollars saved and that drop to the bottom line.)[25]

Your outside counsel can help quantify savings. Generally, they will be happy to show you ways they are cutting costs. And be sure to get the entire legal team involved. If your team gets excited about the process of saving money, the entire effort starts to snowball in a good way. Ask them for their ideas—both in terms of cost-saving ideas and how to measure and report the savings. Lastly, as cost savings are achieved, be sure to market those to the business. If you do not tell them, they will never know.

Use an RFP Process Whenever Possible

Way back during the in-house counsel dark ages, companies selected outside counsel based on things like relationships, reputation, tickets to sporting events, or fancy dinners. Those days are, fortunately, fading fast. That is not to say that the above are no longer important, but, more and more, the selection of outside counsel is based on the same principles and processes the company uses generally to select any vendor (and we will discuss this phenomenon in more detail in the next section). This includes the use of requests for proposals (RFPs) to search out and find the best law firm for the problem at hand. Like many things involving the business side of practicing law, most in-house lawyers are not particularly good at RFPs. Over time, however, they will get better because there will be many lessons learned from success and failure with the process. These lessons learned, along with the power of the RFP to drive better pricing and results, mean more in-house departments will get really good at it. That is a powerful development in delivering value, both to the legal department and the company. And, the resulting value generated can be fairly easily quantified, and thus filling in another important piece of the value jigsaw puzzle. All of this is attainable if you run the RFP process the right way. Here is how to do just that.

For our purposes, an RFP is a process whereby the legal department requests a number of outside law firms (or other vendors) to submit proposals to obtain legal work from the company. The proposals are in writing, usually via completing a template the in-house team sends. Legal departments send out RFPs for three different types of situations. Each situation operates somewhat differently from the others, primarily due to timing issues:

25 *See infra* at page 158 for a discussion of how the legal department can be a revenue generator for the company.

1. *Panel counsel.* Here, the in-house department is looking to create a panel or group of preferred law firms that can handle most, if not all, of the company's outside legal work (including specific types of matters or in specific geographies.) The RFP process for panel counsel tends to be longer and more involved because generally there is no urgent matter at stake and, once selected, panel counsel are part of the panel for several years and become deeply integrated with the in-house team.
2. *Specific project.* In-house lawyers sometimes use an RFP for one matter, e. g., a piece of litigation, a merger, or other types of projects. The RFPs may go only to firms on their existing panel or that the department has used before, or they might open up the RFP to new firms. Doing the latter is where more value typically can be unlocked. The process here tends to move faster, especially if the matter is urgent, and there is a need to get outside counsel identified and moving quickly.
3. *Specialty area.* This is a hybrid of the first two items in this list. In-house counsel is looking for a firm to handle certain types of matters, ones that may require the law firm to have a special industry or regulatory knowledge —knowledge that is not commonly found at most firms. Examples include tax law, competition law, ERISA, and so forth. The process can move quickly or slowly depending on the circumstances.

RFP paperwork can take on many different forms. The most typical is a Word document or Excel spreadsheet, though the former can be cumbersome if you have a lot of firms responding and you are trying to compare responses. Some in-house departments are using portals that counsel can sign into or special software that not only formats the RFP document, but also collates the responses into a report for ease of comparison, which can save a lot of time if there are more than a few firms involved. Whether such software makes sense depends on how often, how big, and how detailed your RFP process is. There is generally an introduction that lays out the goals or issues at stake. The more detail you can provide here will lead to better responses. For example, if it is an RFP for IP services, set out how many trademarks, patents, and copyrights you have, in what countries, and how many of each you expect (on average) to file each year. Likewise, provide some background about the company and the industry it competes in (if relevant). If it is an RFP for a specific piece of litigation, provide the complaint along with any other information or summaries you may already have prepared. Passing along such detail is the only way to get truly useful answers from outside counsel. Consider reasonable page and word limits for the RFP as, otherwise, you may end up with a firm sending you 200 pages of information, much of which is marketing gibberish.

Figuring out which firms to invite to the party can be a difficult task. If, for example, you are looking to reduce the number of firms you already use—but not looking to add new ones, then you send it to all your current firms. If you are looking for a panel that might include new firms, then you need to identify new firms to involve in the process. If it is a specific matter or area of expertise, you may need to identify only a few firms with those capabilities. The important part is to ensure you have enough firms involved to make the process work, i.e., generate quality proposals that give you value and a real choice in firms. You may need to ask around for recommendations from your team or other in-house lawyers (even outside counsel) on who to invite to bid. Asking for suggestions is a great way to identify firms you may not be familiar with. You can also do research online to figure out who are the right players, though this is likely to get you only the bigger law firms or those with bigger marketing budgets. And, you should strongly consider adding smaller, regional, or boutique law firms to your list as they can provide tremendous value with the same or better level of quality.

The heart of any RFP is the questions that you ask outside counsel to respond to. Limit the number of questions so you are not overwhelmed with information. Second, prepare questions crafted to get useful information and not generic marketing blabber. There are four core questions you need to ask about.

1. *Experience of the team*? You need to know the experience of the team that will actually be working on your matter(s). The firm may have tons of experience, but if those people work in a different country or will not touch your project, then it does not matter. You also want to know their experience with matters of the type set out in the RFP and, if applicable, for similar-sized companies in similar industries. Tell the bidders to skip providing copies of the lawyers' firm bios. Ask for a two-paragraph summary of why that lawyer is right for the team and what they bring to the table.
2. *Legal strategy*? You want to know their legal strategy for handling your matter or matters. This is more important when the RFP is for a specific matter versus a panel, but their general philosophy, creative ways they have handled similar issues, track record, and so on all matter. Plus, you will get a lot of insight that you can use in your project regardless of which firm you ultimately pick. Ask specific questions that require detailed, lawyer-prepared answers, such as questions about the team's record with the judge or success before the regulatory body questioning your deal.
3. *Staffing strategy*? In a billable hour situation, staffing strategy matters a lot. Require the firm to explain why the people on the team were selected and what they will be doing, what happens if more people are needed (and what is your ability to accept or decline lawyers?), and whether the firm will be using contract lawyers or alternative service providers to perform any portion of the work. How will the firm ensure that partners are not doing work that associates or paralegals or clerical staff should be doing? For blended-rate proposals, you want to ensure that you are not stuck with people who

are put on your matter because they do not have enough to do or whether work will consistently be given to less expensive associates who may not really have the experience to be efficient or properly handle the work. In short, an RFP process does not mean you should get anything less than the A-team for your matter.

4. *Project management strategy*? This matters less for fixed-fee proposals. Basically, you want to know how the firm manages legal projects, how often they will provide updates and status and strategy calls, how lawyers are brought on or off the project, how does the firm track important dates, how do they manage documents or depositions, and a dozen other tasks that come with any legal project. Ask for specific examples of the reports they prepare. For a billable-hour project, you want to know how they manage the budget and estimates, especially the process they use to ensure they stay on track.

Oddly, customer service is something that gets forgotten sometimes. However, how the law firm will treat you and your team is a very important part of establishing and maintaining the relationship between in-house and outside counsel. You can use the RFP process to lay the groundwork by asking some key questions. These questions work better when the RFP is for panel counsel or specialty area, but some of these questions work even when deadlines are tight. Here are some questions to ask:

- *Who will be the relationship manager*? This is the person you will deal with most often, especially if there are problems or concerns. What is their background, how comfortable are you with them and their "bedside" manner? Can you get references for other clients for whom this individual was the relationship manager?
- *What technology will you use to reduce my costs/do my work more efficiently*? Lots of law firms talk about technology, but can they put their money where their technology is when it comes to your specific matter(s)? Can you and your team have access to any of it? Ask them to detail how they use technology on your behalf, what technology they use, and for samples or examples of how they use it.
- *What is your data security program*? Data security is critical as law firms are now targets for hackers because of the nature of the sensitive and valuable client information stored by firms. How will they keep your data safe and confidential? Do they comply with any particular data security standards, are they certified or have they been audited?
- *How will you learn my business*? Any law firm that wants to develop a real long-term relationship will offer free hours to get up to speed on your business, the industry, and the specific matter. A law firm that understands your business is vastly better than a law firm that does not.

- *How will you handle conflicts*? This is a problem for the bigger firms who may represent a large number of clients. The RFP process is the time to figure out how ethical or business conflicts will be handled. In particular, what happens if a big client asks the firm to not represent your company in a matter simply because they do not like your company or the position your company wants to take? It is not a true conflict under the ethical rules, but it is definitely going to be a problem if it happens. Find out now if you are a top dog or if you will be fired by the firm (and consider the repercussions of that happening).
- *How do you manage diversity?* For some in-house departments, this is a core requirement. For others, not so much. Regardless of where you fall on the spectrum, the RFP process is the time to ask for (or demand) positions around diversity at the firm and on your matter(s).
- *What do I get for free*? Do not be bashful about this one, ask firms what they will offer you to sweeten the pot? This can take on many forms with the most common being:
    - ☐ Free hours every month to use for phone calls/short general advice issues.
    - ☐ Free CLEs and training for the department (and the business if needed).
    - ☐ Access to firm resources (online library, forms, Lexis/Westlaw/Practical Law, checklists, templates, artificial intelligence tools, etc.)
    - ☐ Industry development presentations to the business or the department. Law firms often have specialized knowledge about the industry your company operates in or developments in the law or with regulations, etc. Making that available to you—and their parts of the business—at no cost is a real value add).

Of course, in the end, the RFP process is about price, i.e., how can I get high-quality services at the lowest price? For years, law firms have been spending a lot of money and effort to sharpen up their side of this equation. And rightfully so, as they are a business and cannot take on projects that lose money. This means you need to be on your game as well. Most importantly, you need data about your legal spend over the past several years and data about what is "market" for your type of matter or your specific geography. If you do not have this data, it is difficult to tell if the price being offered is truly a good deal or not. Look for:

- *Fixed price*. This is the holy grail for in-house counsel because you get certainty around cost. To make this work you should expect to provide a lot of information to the bidding firms so they can correctly price the project. Ask what happens if the law firm guesses wrong. When you expect that you have a fixed price, you do not want a phone call from the relationship partner asking to redo the price. Simply put, "There is no crying in baseball," meaning the department relied on the firm to price it, and if the firm made a mistake, it must have a hard path to walk to get you to change the terms of the deal.

- *Blended rates.* These sound great in theory, but be careful that you understand how the project will be staffed and how much work will be pushed down to lower-cost attorneys who may not have the experience to do a good job (or do it efficiently). Blended rates can be tricky to manage, so make sure you have put guardrails in place to ensure you do not get screwed over.
- *Discounted rates.* Another thing to watch closely. First, be sure the discounts are off the regular rates of the people working on your matter(s) and not some firm average or rack rate that no one pays. Moreover, it is difficult to see the value of a rate discount unless you have data on your average hourly spend in the past and market data on what hourly rates others are paying. Additionally, get a freeze on rates for the duration of the project—or at least for several years or until the next panel review. Then seek a cap on how much rates can increase in the next go around. You never have as much leverage for the next round as you do when the firm is trying to get on your panel in the first instance. Also, watch out for the problem of lawyers who advance through the firm's pricing tiers. For example, you may have a young lawyer at a discount off at $400 an hour, but next year she becomes a senior associate and her standard rate jumps to $550. Is her rate still the discounted $400 or now a discount off the $550? That is a big difference.

Unless you are an old hand at RFPs, you will likely underestimate the amount of time it will take to complete the process. There are two forces at play here. The first is ensuring you give the law firms sufficient time to complete the RFP. The second is leaving yourself enough time to evaluate the RFP responses, select the firms you are most interested in, conduct interviews, and then make your selection(s). This is not a one-week process. Unless there is an emergency/urgency, plan on giving the law firms at least three to four weeks to complete their responses. Be sensitive to making RFP responses due around a holiday, as everyone gets pressed for time—including you. Leave yourself and the team helping you plenty of time to review and decide, but expect the date to slip when urgent matters that bust your calendar show up—as they inevitably will. Still, sometimes you have an emergency like a new bet-the-company lawsuit or a merger/acquisition where you really cannot wait four weeks to hear back from firms. When faced with this, you have three choices: 1) ask only firms you have used in the past to participate (thus saving time and questions— especially if you already have panel counsel); 2) streamline your questions to the essentials (e.g., ditch the customer service questions) and ask the firms to power through your timing; or 3) use who you always use and try to strike the best deal you can make with them.

Assuming you have the time, the ideal process for selecting the RFP winner flows as follows.

- Gather the responses and compile the information into a format that allows you to compare the firms in a head-to-head manner. If firms ignored your instructions or gave you a lot of marketing gibberish, strongly consider cutting them out right then and there because it means trouble ahead if they cannot follow the instructions of the RFP.

- Set up one-hour interviews with the firms you are most interested in, likely no more than three (unless it is a huge panel counsel effort). This is where you get to look them in the eye, ask hard questions about their responses, and get to brass tacks about price. Doing the interviews in person is the best method. Video a distant second. And by phone bringing up the rear, which is more of a last resort. Be sure the review team is part of every interview so everyone involved in making the RFP decision on your side sees each firm.
- Make the decision at a meeting of the internal team where you have asked everyone to rank their favorites and why.
- Document the deal like you would any contract. Do not leave out anything you agreed to because if it is not in writing, it is not part of the deal when crunch time hits.
- Do the right thing and contact all of the firms you did not select, either by a phone call or in an email offering a phone call. The reason for this is they will want to know why they were not selected. And you should be prepared to go through why with them. It may be a simple as you were 30 percent more expensive. Having this conversation is important because it is expensive and time-consuming for law firms to reply to an RFP. If they feel mistreated or that they did not really have a fair shot at winning, they are not going to play in the future. As a result, your feedback is important to them.

Your goal here, like that of the business, is to develop a repeatable RFP process and use it as often as possible for selecting outside counsel. This should become your new normal. You will most certainly get better pricing and services if your RFP process is done correctly. Lastly, measure the savings and value generated to share with the business as part of showing the value generated by the legal team day in and day out.

Develop a Legal Procurement Process

Technology is the hot topic of the moment for in-house legal departments. And it should be. As discussed later, it promises tremendous cost savings and productivity enhancements for in-house lawyers. Greater use of technology will almost certainly put the legal team squarely within the best practices of the business side of the company. However, there is something else out there that is equally exciting, but which rests on some pretty mundane financial principles long favored by the business. I am talking about procurement. Or, more specifically, legal procurement. While many in-house lawyers recoil at the thought of applying such a process to engaging law firms, it is worth considering. Not only because it is an easy way to show value creation (from using common business practices), but because it forces lawyers to think more closely about which firms they are hiring and whether they are truly the best fit and the best value for the project.

Most businesses have a procurement department, usually—but not always—separate from the legal function. Some of the people working in procurement may have a legal background, but generally, it is not a requirement. This is because procurement is largely about vetting, selecting, and negotiating relating to the purchasing of products and services important to the company. Therefore, it involves more than just contract drafting skills. It involves getting bids and putting in place an overall strategic purchasing process, from purchase orders to vendor payment to vendor management. Legal procurement is a subset of procurement dedicated to the selection and purchase of legal services from outside vendors, in particular, law firms. These people are professional vendor contract negotiators and they grind and grind until the right deal is struck. Noted legal procurement expert Silvia Hodges Silverstein states:

> *"Legal procurement focuses on buying legal services and managing the business side of relationships with law firms and other legal services providers. Buying and negotiations is their forte. They are based in the procurement department and report to the chief procurement officer. The majority of legal procurement professionals have a business/finance background rather than a legal background."*[26]

Importantly, what legal procurement is not about is replacing the judgment of in-house lawyers regarding which firm to ultimately hire for any particular matter. Rather, it is a process that replaces picking law firms based on relationships and hourly rates with data-driven decisions related to value.

Most in-house lawyers are not great at negotiating rates and services with law firms. Consequently, consider the improvement possible if someone outside the legal department helps you find the right law firms and negotiates the hourly rate, fixed fee, or whatever structure needed to ensure the best firm for the best value. If you are interested in breaking away from the long-dominant billable hour regime that consistently drives the wrong incentives for most law firms, a legal procurement process may be the best way to make that happen. Research shows that legal departments using legal procurement reduce outside legal spending by 15–20 percent.[27] Cost savings, plus the added benefit of allowing the lawyers to spend more of their time focused on legal work instead of dealing with

---

26 *See 7 Questions with Buying Legal Council's Silvia Hodges Silverstein on Legal Procurement*, available online at https://www.legalexecutiveinstitute.com/7-questions-buying-legal-councils-silverstein-legal-procurement/.

27 *See Lawyers Weekly, Legal Procurement Paving 'Profound, Lasting' Impact, Survey Says,* available online at https://www.lawyersweekly.com.au/corporate-counsel/23157-legal-procurement-having-profound-lasting-impact-survey-says.

negotiating rates and monitoring billing compliance of outside law firms, is another reason to consider developing a legal procurement process.

Depending on how involved your procurement team will be in your process, here are some things you can expect from them:

- *Pay less in legal fees.* For example, bigger discounts, better RFPs, and monitoring law firm compliance with fee agreements. Legal procurement can also help set up alternative fee arrangements (including fixed fees), success fees, contingency fees, fees by stage, caps, discounts, etc.
- *Use less in legal services.* Help with legal project management, efficiency improvements, and automation of routine tasks.
- *Find alternative sources.* Locate alternatives to your current law firm roster, from big law to boutiques to alternative legal services providers to one-person shops. The right firm at the right time at the right price, with no loss of quality.
- *Measure and analyze spend.* Assist with finding patterns or signs of problems before they become too big to deal with, and measure the value of the services your law firms provide. The lowest price is not always the winner, the best value is. Legal procurement can bring transparency to a traditionally opaque process and give you the tools to make an informed decision versus a gut decision. This, in turn, will allow you to demonstrate value and forward-thinking to the CEO and CFO as to how the legal department handles outside legal spending. It is not a black hole, there is rigor behind it.
- *Other vendors.* Legal procurement is not only about outside counsel relationships, any vendor used by the legal department can be something they take on.
- *Advocate.* Legal procurement can be an advocate for more legal resources internally. A professional group telling the CEO and CFO about the value of in-house lawyers versus outside spend. They can do the math the CEO and CFO want to see.

Letting procurement handle a key part of your law firm relationships is not something most in-house lawyers get excited about. For the most part, the purchase of legal services is left exclusively to the legal department. For some reason, legal bills and legal vendor relationships are treated differently than purchases made by the rest of the company. This is primarily because in-house lawyers did an excellent job of arguing that legal is different and that trying to apply basic financial principles to legal fees is a doomed endeavor. Actually, legal spending is not different. Most in-house lawyers object to a legal procurement function because:

- procurement can buy copy paper but not legal services—it is too hard;
- there is real risk in decisions made about law firms, and only lawyers are qualified to make those decisions;

- they believe they will lose autonomy and control over law firm selection;
- they will be stuck working with the cheapest firms, meaning lower quality legal services;
- long-term relationships will go by the wayside. Law firms will not wine and dine me anymore;
- they will have to teach new law firms about the company's business over and over; and they do not have time to engage with legal procurement over strategic purchasing decisions. It takes too long.

These are all (mostly) valid concerns. However, they are not necessarily true. For example, while legal procurement may be a relatively new tool for in-house lawyers, outside firms have engaged professional pricing experts for a long time. That is, most law firms have professionals dedicated to determining how to value legal services and how best to price them, including offering different (alternative) fee structures to clients. They study what's market, including public and private pricing surveys. In many cases, they also act as a buffer for the firm's lawyers, keeping lawyers out of the fee discussions and allowing them to focus on providing legal services. This is all fine, but it means law firms are ready for dealing with legal procurement. And, if you are not equally armed with your own pricing professional(s), how do you expect to appropriately evaluate the offers from firms? You are bringing a slingshot to a gunfight. Plus, there is value in having your own buffer to keep your lawyers out of the fee negotiations so they can focus exclusively on working with outside counsel on the legal issues and not the fee/business issues of the relationship.

To get started with procurement, you must go into the process with the right mindset, such as the relationship will be a partnership. This means you must sit down with your procurement partner and spend time teaching them about the specifics of what you are looking for in outside counsel and how you have historically conducted searches for law firms. In other words, embrace the situation. On the flip side, you will need to learn about the procurement process and how your partner generally goes about gathering information and evaluating potential vendors. From there, you must jointly develop a legal procurement plan. The process is looking for value, it is not a race to the bottom on pricing. And it is not about beating up law firms for lower hourly rates. Legal services are not commodities. Most importantly, it is not about giving up control, it is about gaining control over your law firm selection and management process. A sophisticated legal procurement function is involved throughout the entire engagement and helps you manage the business relationship with the firm.

One thing to understand clearly about the legal procurement process is that, ultimately, the legal department makes the call on which law firm to use for any particular project. The procurement team is there to partner with the legal department and help it analyze the different firms and the different value propositions, but in the end, the choice is made by lawyers as their professional judgment dictates.

Like anything worth doing, there is a lot of work on the part of the legal team at the beginning to make a procurement process successful. Here is a short list of what you will need:

- trust (you need to think of the procurement team as trusted advisors and act accordingly);
- benchmarking studies;
- internal cost and operations information, including details about your law firms and why you chose them;
- information about law firms generally, including peer reviews, win rates, etc.;
- analysis of your company's legal needs, including breaking down matters/matter-types as high risk, medium risk, and low risk. The outside counsel needs surrounding a high-risk case, for example, are much different than those of a low-risk case.
- willing to start small, i.e., do not feel any change must be an absolute commitment to 100 percent legal procurement. You can start with one or two projects, evaluate the success, and make changes as needed; and
- when there is a need for outside counsel, a detailed assessment of what you will need from them, such as a mini-project plan, is critical.

Your legal procurement team must understand the risks the matter presents, along with your goals, be it mergers and acquisitions, high-stakes litigation, a key commercial contract, or whatever. This can only come from the in-house lawyers and is a key part of working in tandem with procurement to find the best firm for the best value based on the specific needs and goals of the legal project.

Leadership and vision are required to adopt legal procurement. If you understand that legal procurement is not about who controls the selection of outside counsel, but rather a consistent and principled approach to engaging law firms and other legal services vendors, there is a path to better financial results for the department, with equal or better quality, and a lot less wear and tear on the legal team. They can spend more time focused on high-value legal work instead of haggling with law firms. And, if you have a procurement process in place, the odds of getting called on the carpet about legal spending go down dramatically as the process you use for purchasing legal services is the same type of process the business uses generally.

Perfect Project Management

If you have ever been involved with an important company project, from merger integration to tech implementation, you probably came across someone acting as the project manager. That is because the business figured out a long time ago that complicated and expensive projects require special management skills to ensure they stay on target and on budget. In fact, there is an entire business discipline dedicated to professional project management. Sadly, there is one group that consistently oversees expensive and complicated projects yet rarely, if ever, applies any type of disciplined project management to the project, let alone rely on anyone with project management skills. Yes, I am speaking about the legal department. Often, multiple-million dollar matters are managed primarily by in-house lawyers looking at outside counsel invoices every month, essentially shrugging their shoulders and thinking it is what it is. To put it bluntly, that is not good enough. Not anymore. And legal departments focused on demonstrating value and their business acumen know they need to up their game when it comes to project management.

If you are reading this book, you probably already know that managing a complex legal project is not an easy task. Not for in-house counsel, nor for outside counsel. There are too many ways for a project to go astray and turn into a disaster. Usually, the disaster has to do with cost/budget. While blowing the budget is definitely not good, a worse scenario is when the disaster results in the project failing, be it a complex contract, and merger or acquisition, or a high-stakes piece of litigation. A project fail can mean big problems for in-house lawyers. This is why in-house counsel and outside counsel must align early any time there is a legal project of material size or risk. In-house counsel cannot simply turn the project over to outside counsel and hope for the best. Those days are long over. Successful legal projects require substantial involvement and the input of in-house lawyers.

That is why legal project management has grown into an accepted and in-demand way to manage legal work sent to outside counsel. The good news is that in-house lawyers do not need to be experts in project management to make a big difference. Even a cursory application of project management basics will lead to better results.

To start, there is nothing fancy about legal project management. It is simply a structured way to manage legal projects, from litigation to mergers and acquisitions, to high volume transaction work. It borrows heavily from project management principles used for decades by the business, where on time and on budget are crucial. It works for projects that are sent to outside counsel or 100 percent insourced. Besides structure and cost control, project management provides benefits from a formal post-project evaluation, where in-house and outside counsel (and the business client) share what worked well and what did not work well with the goal of constant improvement over time. The process relies heavily on honest communication between in-house counsel and outside counsel. The more communication, the better the process. This requires that in-house counsel, and their outside partners, dedicate sufficient time to project management with every material engagement.

Every managed project starts with a kick-off meeting where the applicable stakeholders sit down in person and discuss the goals and objectives for the project. They also discuss what work needs to be done, by whom, and how in-house and outside counsel will jointly manage and communicate with each other during the project. The parties discuss how the legal work will serve a clear business objective, along with any concerns or special considerations that the team must take into account.

Next comes the scoping plan, the process where in-house and outside counsel document the following:

- goals to measure the project's success;
- the clear expectations of the client;the legal work that must be performed
- the steps that must be taken to perform the work;
- who is responsible for each task;
- the timeline to complete the project (broken down by phases);
- the budget;
- the assumptions (and any unknowns) that have gone into the plan and the budget with the goal being no surprises down the road;
- staffing and
- the reporting and tracking procedure.

This scoping process leads to a simple document called a BOSCARD which contains seven basic questions that are part of any scoping exercise: background, objective, scope, constraints, assumptions, risks, and deliverables. If you cover these items, you have the beginnings of a very good scoping document.

Any managed project requires a detailed project plan. The project plan takes the scoping document and puts it into action, i.e., it sets out the who, what, where, when, and how of the project. The three core elements involve 1) identifying the work activities, 2) allocating the right task to the right person, and 3) setting the budget. In-house and outside counsel must be realistic and honest about the work involved and the time required to get the work done. Hiding the ball, overly optimistic deadlines, or spending predictions will come back to haunt everyone involved. Moreover, it is important that in-house and outside counsel to get the business client to sign-off on the work plan, costs, and deadlines. If the business expectations differ materially from those of the legal team, it will not be pretty. This is where the Gantt chart[28] comes into play.

---

28 *See What Is a Gantt Chart?* on www.gantt.com.

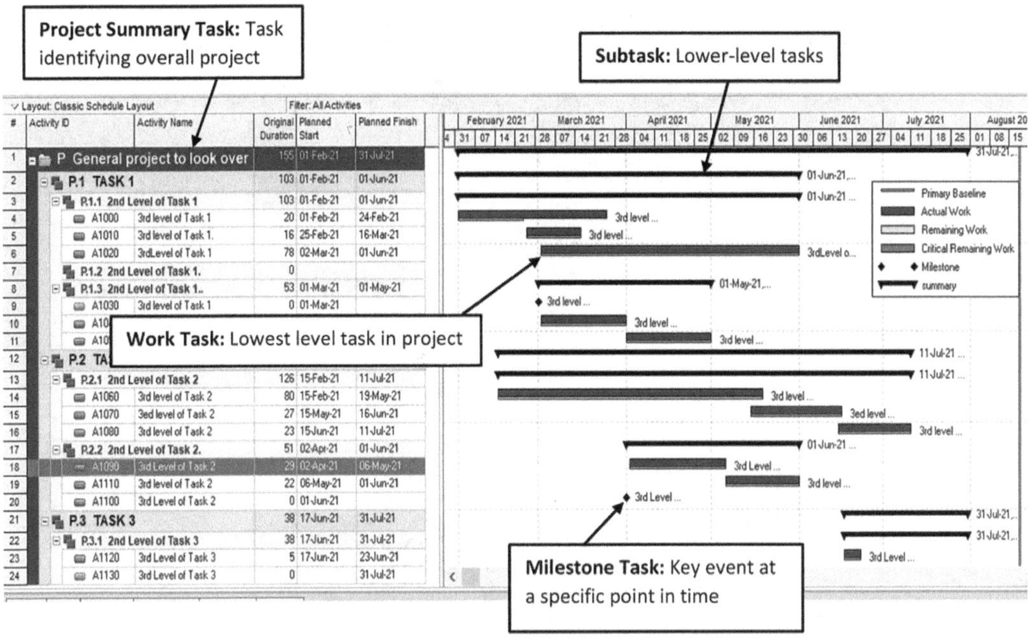

The project Gantt chart sets out the timeline for the project along with all of the key deliverables as well as dependencies, i.e., what has to happen to allow other parts of the project to happen. A related tool is the LACI chart, a roles and responsibility matrix for each task. The LACI chart sets out who Leads (is accountable), who Assists (must contribute), who must be Consulted, (approval/ input needed) and who must be Informed (kept in the loop) about each task. See chart below.[29]

29 Reprinted with permission. Thanks to Dallas-based Haynes & Boone partner Bill Kleinman for allowing me to share this chart and the next chart. Both are from his article "Using Team-Wide LACI Charts in M&A Transactions," available online at *laci_article_2015_bill_kleinman.ashx* (haynesboone.com). Kleinman is a widely noted expert on legal project management and is a contributor to the American Bar Association book, *Using Legal Project Management in Merger and Acquisition Transactions: A Guidebook for Managing Deals Efficiently and Effectively*, Second Edition (2018).

LACI Chart Designators		
Symbol	**Role**	**Explanation**
L	Leading	Each task should have only one leader.
A	Assisting	These people contribute to the work effort.
C	Consulted	Their approval or input is required.
I	Informed	Keep them in the loop.

Here is a sample of a LACI chart for a specific project:

Asset Purchase Transaction							
Task	**Participant**						
	CEO	**GC**	**CFO**	**Law Firm Partner**	**Audit Partner**	**Consul-tant**	**Invest-ment Banker**
Negotiate business terms	C	A	L	I	I	C	A
Draft and negotiate LOI	I	L	C	A	C	-	C
Determine deal structure	C	A	A	L	A	-	C
Due diligence and Schedule review	I	L	A	A	A	A	-
Arrange financing	C	I	A	I	I	I	L
Draft, negotiate and close purchase agreement and financing documents	C	A	C	L	C	-	-
Post-closing reporting	C	L	A	C	C	-	-
Integration	C	A	L	I	I	A	-

While Gantt charts and LACI charts can be helpful, they are not required for all projects. If you are just beginning to utilize project management concepts, there are simpler ways to set out the project plan deliverables and a basic to-do list. The idea is to have a written plan.

Every project plan needs project managers, i.e., the in-house and outside counsel responsible for the day-to-day planning and execution of the project. In addition to having the right expertise and legal skills for the project, the project managers must be able to:

- budget accurately and manage the budget;
- ensure the work gets done and gets done correctly;
- manage the team and coordinate work;
- innovate and adapt to changes in circumstances, resources, etc.;
- recognize when circumstances are changing such that a formal change to the plan is required; and
- communicate regularly to the team (legal and business) with regular updates and analysis of where things are in the process.

The most important task of a project manager is monitoring the project. In particular, focusing on the Gantt chart, LACI chart, or other project plan documents to ensure everyone is doing what they are supposed to be doing, that the work is getting done on time (and done correctly), that spending aligns with the budget, that the assumptions are holding true (or if not, understand what is changing), looking to flesh out any of the unknowns identified earlier during the planning process, and ensuring that communications are going out on schedule and to the right people. Monitoring the project is a daily activity and not something that can get a small amount of attention at the end of the week. In-house and outside counsel should speak several times per week, if not daily, regarding the status of the project and how things are progressing versus the plan. There will also likely be some type of steering committee set up that will set overall direction and strategy for the project and will be consulted for major decisions.

Communication is core to any project. With it, things move smoothly. Without it, things screech to a halt. Successful projects require: regular meetings/conference calls for the team to discuss the project, a process for updates between meetings, and development and utilization of standard reporting templates to communicate important information in a consistent and easy-to-follow manner. An important aspect of the communication plan is identifying who needs to know what information and when. Finding the right level of information delivered to the right person and the right time takes practice and flexibility. Lastly, do not overlook the need to ensure that all communications take into account the rules around attorney-client or work product privileges. Both must be preserved to the extent possible at all times.

It is unlikely all of the assumptions made in the scoping plan and project plan stay static. And, there were likely a number of unknowns when the project began. As circumstances change or facts become known, you must plan for and have a process to capture changes and to avoid/contain scope creep, that is, unapproved/unvetted deviation from the project plan. Through monitoring the plan and constant communication amongst the team, you should be able to spot changes well before they become a significant problem. Regardless of when you see them coming, material changes require that the team adjust the project plan and related documents to account for the change, and ensure that changes are communicated to all of the people who need to know and—most importantly—that changes are approved in advance by the right people. The hardest changes will occur around increasing the budget. The key, as always, is open and honest communication between in-house and outside counsel. Still, the more time spent up front with planning, the less surprises there will be down the road, especially as to the budget.

Finally, after the completion of any material legal project it is important for the team (in-house, outside counsel, and business clients) to sit down and discuss what went well and what did not go so well during project. Did we meet the plan objectives? What are the things that need to be fixed going forward? Is more training needed to avoid litigation problems? Did we create forms or templates that can be reused going forward to save time and money? Did the communications plan work? What caused us to miss the budget projections? What are the lessons learned—good or bad? A post-mortem meeting certainly is easier when the project went well rather than one that ended badly. But you can learn ways to improve, even from projects that exceed expectations. Real value is generated when the business and the lawyers meet together to extract lessons from the project and improve the ways to work together in the future.

Summing Up

If you have ever changed schools or moved to a new town as a teenager, you quickly found yourself adopting the lingo, culture, clothes, and mannerisms of your new surroundings. That is exactly what in-house lawyers need to do to be successful, that is to say, they need to act like they are a fully engaged part of the business. Adopting and perfecting the following business practices is the best way to do that. By doing so, you will be demonstrating value in a way that the business clearly understands.

- ☐ Learn and understand basic finance, especially how to read an income statement, cash flow statement, and P&L statement.
- ☐ Get comfortable with and utilize data analytics to make decisions (and when presenting to the business).

- ☐ Create KPIs that matter, and use dashboards to convey the results in a manner the business can best understand.
- ☐ Mimic the business's use of an operations function to ensure the legal department operates like any other part of the business and move administrative tasks off of lawyers' desks to allow them to focus on high value legal work.
- ☐ Use 2 × 2 matrices to analyze problems and to enhance strategic thinking within the department and as a way to convey your thinking about certain issue to the business.
- ☐ Managing outside counsel spending as if you were spending your own money (and provide accurate spending forecasts and accrual to finance when called upon).
- ☐ Adopt the use of RFPs and a legal procurement process to show you understand how to obtain the right legal services for the right project at the right price.
- ☐ Utilize legal project management to ensure material projects are set up for success, are managed on time and on budget, and that you capture significant learnings (good and bad) through a post-project post mortem.

Your Mission: Maximize Value Creation and Minimize Value Destruction

At one of my general counsel stops, the senior management brought in one of those big name consulting teams to help us. Though, I am not sure exactly what they were supposed to help us with. However, they showed up at my door one day with a list of questions. They started with, "Tell us your mission statement." My first thought was why in the hell would a legal department need a mission statement—but I was smart enough to play along. Without skipping a beat, I said, "To maximize value creation and minimize value destruction." They looked at me for a second or two and then they wrote down what I said so they could regurgitate it to me and the executive team in a month or two, so we would happily write them a check for putting everything we said into a slick slide presentation. Ahh, but I digress.

The real point of the above is that the mission of any legal department is simple: focus on the things that create value for the company and protect the company from the things that destroy its value. This simplistic statement ties nicely into every legal department's need to show their value. If the department can segregate its work into these two broad categories, it can find ways to report back to the business how its efforts added value for the business or prevented the erosion or loss of value. Consequently, it is important for the legal department to determine and focus on legal work that will add (or protect) the most value. If you can do this (and successfully convey what you are doing to the business) you will have the best possible chance of showing the value of the legal department.

Build Out A Value-Creation To-Do List

It has likely become apparent (or it will as you read on), the ways a legal department can show value are almost endless. Like a juicy law school exam question, it is easy to get stuck because there is almost too much to choose from. The key is to recognize the many different ways you can show value and then focus on the ones that matter the most to business, especially to leadership. One way to do this is to identify the issues that need yearly attention and then set up a to-do list for the department to focus on. While many of the items on the list can easily double as yearly department goals, that is a secondary benefit. Rather, the purpose of such a list is to institutionalize ways the department can continuously enhance value creation and minimize value destruction. Like many things in this book, it comes down to these simple points. Any item on your annual to-do list must satisfy one of these aims and, importantly, avoid single-point-of-failure issues when it comes to these critical tasks.[30] If not, reconsider whether the item is worthy of inclusion or not. More importantly, not only will this annual to-do list satisfy the critical purpose around value, it can also serve as a reminder to the CEO and other C-Suite executives that the legal department is proactively scoping and managing risk to the company and its various lines of business and taking steps to systematically and consistently deal with those risks.You will see that many of the items in the sample annual to-do list below are discussed in more detailed later in this book. Not all of these items will apply to every legal department, but you can use this list to customize your own or generate your own list based on the specific needs of the company.

Legal Department Yearly Value Creation/Protection To-Do List

- ☐ Work with human resources to review and update the following company policies/employee agreements or human resources issues:
  - ☐ Employee handbook.
  - ☐ Non-solicitation/non-compete agreements (ensure language meets standards for key states or countries where company operates).
  - ☐ Employee confidentiality agreement.
  - ☐ Intellectual property ownership agreements.
  - ☐ Exempt/non-exempt and employee/contractor classification health check.
  - ☐ Email/document drafting policy.
  - ☐ Create or update social media policies.
- ☐ Create processes and a set of legal operations metrics to effectively manage legal department budget and spend, including:

30 Single points of failure occur when there is a single person or place where if a breakdown occurs, the entire process goes off the rails. For example, contracts are stored on someone's laptop and if that laptop is corrupted or stolen, then all of those contracts are lost. The solution is to store contracts in a cloud service with appropriate disaster recovery protection. That way, the contracts are discoverable by everyone with access, and the odds of a catastrophic loss of all of the data is lower. Every critical process belonging to the legal department should be protected from single points of failure. A value-creation to-do list can serve just such a purpose.

- ☐ Create monthly report based on key operations metrics about legal spend:
  - ☐ Average hourly rate (year over year).
  - ☐ Average hourly rate by firm vs. market rate for similar work.
  - ☐ Partner/associate ratio (by project).
  - ☐ Spend vs. budget/forecasted spend (by project and overall).
  - ☐ Get outside counsel to help/buy-in with process.
- ☐ Increase use of data analytics to identify trends, problems, and opportunities.
- ☐ Create/enhance RFP process (including exploration of legal procurement processes).
- ☐ Identify smaller or boutique law firms to enhance ability to place outside legal work with right sized firm for the project or to reduce overall cost of outside counsel.
- ☐ Update (and enforce) "Outside Counsel Guidelines" and send to all current outside counsel yearly and at outset of every new matter.
- ☐ Create/update legal project management kick-off planning document and use to meet with outside counsel before the start of any material legal project to set cost and team expectations of both parties. At completion of the project, perform an honest post-project analysis of what worked,what did not work (for both the company and the law firm), and determine how the department can improve legal project management going forward.

☐ Perform compliance health check. Review and update key compliance-related policies, processes, training, and update/implement means to test compliance:

- ☐ Employee training process (how we teach employees about compliance).
- ☐ Anti-bribery policy (FCPA, and so on).
- ☐ Anti-trust compliance policy.
- ☐ Ensure compliance with export/import laws, OFAC, SDN list, and anti-money laundering laws.
- ☐ Sexual harassment training.
- ☐ Record retention policy/including legal hold process.
- ☐ Revise/update company business ethics policy.
- ☐ Update internal investigation plan and templates.
- ☐ Ensure all employees know how to report an ethics/compliance concern. Put into place andtest a hotline, compliance office email, and other mechanisms to allow employees to communicate concerns.
- ☐ Data privacy and security review of policies and procedures, audit use and security of personal data for compliance with contracts and

relevant law, perform tabletop exercise to test data incident response plan.

        - ☐ Ensure proper legal and/or contractual grounds exist for processing and transferring personal data pursuant to applicable laws and regulations.
        - ☐ Review/update employee training around IT security (password policy, phishing, malware, etc).
    - ☐ Work with internal audit to test key parts of compliance program and prepare metrics, including benchmarking.
    - ☐ Educate the legal department and the company management and employees about the proper use of the attorney-client privilege, work product doctrine, and how to write smart.
- ☐ Review company website:
    - ☐ User agreement review and update.
    - ☐ Privacy policy update.
    - ☐ Ensure links, pop-ups, etc. work and are current.
- ☐ Ensure basic company maintenance:
    - ☐ Review articles of incorporation and by-laws.
    - ☐ Ensure minute book and necessary resolutions of the board of directors are complete and current.
    - ☐ Update board on any changes in law or important cases regarding board oversight and duties.
    - ☐ Calendar (and complete) all important renewals of company licenses, registrations, and corporate filings.
    - ☐ Ensure board of directors is protected via proper indemnity contracts.
- ☐ Review processes and procedures around litigation or otherwise highly disruptive events:
    - ☐ Ensure company contract templates are reviewed and updated for ease of contracting and have well vetted dispute resolution clauses/procedures, including choice of law, arbitration, choice of venue, mediation, limitations of liability, indemnity, etc.
    - ☐ Update/create contract playbooks.
        - ☐ Train business on use of playbooks and basic contracting/negotiating.
    - ☐ Review procedures for the intake and management of new litigation.
        - ☐ Review procedures to keep the CEO and Board of Directors up to speed on material litigation.
    - ☐ Ensure appropriate crisis preparation procedures and plans are in place.
    - ☐ Ensure appropriate business interruption plans are in place, including working to identify and mitigate potential single points of failure that can materially disrupt business:

- ☐ Work with CFO and investor relations on quarterly and annual reports, develop a plan to deal with activist investors, ensure executive team is trained on Regulation FD, and ensure a process is in place to identify necessary 8-K disclosures (if company is publicly traded).

☐ Create and distribute a client satisfaction survey to company management and employees. Gather feedback about how your internal clients feel about the legal department and engage more closely with business.

- ☐ Distribute survey mid-year to get results in time for year-end review and next-year planning.
- ☐ Post results (or selected results) on department intranet web page so they are available for company employees to see.
- ☐ Create an action plan based on the results to improve the delivery of legal services to business.

☐ Place members of the legal department at weekly/monthly staff meetings of the businesses or business groups so as to help ensure enhanced cooperation with the business and that the department is knowledgeable about issues that concern the business and are able to provide guidance in real time.

☐ Meet on quarterly basis ask CEO and other C-Suite members and senior executives to tell you what concerns them about their area of the business, what opportunities they see in the short- and longer term, and ask how the legal department can better assist in mitigating issue or concern or attacking opportunity.

☐ Identify key government-related actions (domestic or international) that present either risk or strategic advantage to the company and create a government affairs plan around same.

- ☐ Identify any proposed laws or regulations (domestic or international) that are helpful to the company and design a government affairs campaign to support same.
- ☐ Identify any proposed law or regulation (domestic or international) that present risk to the company and design a government affairs campaign to oppose it.
- ☐ Identify key government/agency officials who can significantly impact your business and set get-to-know-you meetings with them over the course of the year.

☐ Review insurance policies to ensure the insurance the company has is what it wants and needs:

- ☐ Check specific policies:
  - ☐ D&O.
  - ☐ Cyber risk.
  - ☐ E&O.
  - ☐ CGL.

    - ☐ Business interruption.
    - ☐ Employee theft.
    - ☐ Other policies important to your company's specific lines of business.
    - ☐ For each policy, ensure the legal department and appropriate people in the business and staff groups understand the process of determining whether insurance might apply to a claim, along with when and how to provide notice of a claim to the insurer.
  - ☐ Take/update an inventory of the company's intellectual property such as patents, trademarks, copyrights, trade secrets, and other confidential information. Ensure proper policies and procedures are in place to protect the information.
    - ☐ Employee training on trade secret protection.
    - ☐ Agreements and procedures.
    - ☐ Exit interview process.
    - ☐ Onboarding process.
    - ☐ Securing the office (e.g., "clean desks")/proper sign-in and escort procedures for guests.
    - ☐ Develop/enhance patent harvesting program.
- ☐ Create/update a five-year technology plan for the legal department to increase efficiency and lower costs. Implement what can be implemented this year and set out a long-term plan to account for/budget for needed or improved technology over the course of the next five years, including:
  - ☐ E-billing system.
  - ☐ Matter management system.
  - ☐ Document management system.
  - ☐ Contract management/assembly.
  - ☐ Artificial intelligence tools.
  - ☐ Legal research tools.
  - ☐ E-discovery software (with state to the art legal hold management tools).
- ☐ Improve quality of life within the legal department itself.
  - ☐ Survey department members and hold 360-reviews of the department leaders.
    - ☐ Use survey results to create plan to increase satisfaction and engagement.
  - ☐ Improve the content and quality of staff and department meetings.
  - ☐ Plan for an off-site.
  - ☐ Find simple, but effective ways, to reward and retain your team members.
  - ☐ Help each lawyer create a development plan that provides opportunities for growth and responsibility along helping to ensure they can become successful in-house lawyers at your company.

- ☐ Ensure legal department is properly using document management tools to save key documents into single repository (no contracts on someone's hard drive and inaccessible to others).
- ☐ Create/update succession plan.
- ☐ Ask each team member to prepare a detailed checklist about one key facet of their job to compile into a booklet that will provide the tools and instructions needed if that employee leaves the company or is otherwise unable to do that particular task when needed.

☐ Create a calendar of action setting out the specific day or week during the year so that repeatable tasks set out in this to-do list so as to institutionalize it, and make it part of the legal department's normal yearly flow of activity.

While the list is long, there are dozens and dozens of other tasks, subtasks, and detailed descriptions that could be added to or layered on the above list. This is one of the interesting and fun things about being an in-house lawyer. Rarely is any one day the same as another, and rarely does anyone legal department face exactly the same issues as another legal department. The important thing is to create a framework of the key things that need to get done this year (and ideally every year) given the legal needs of your company. Make sure senior management knows about your list and agrees with the items,which is good for both focusing on the right things and letting the business see how proactive its legal department is. Equally important is assigning the work and tracking progress. All of the above can fit into key performance indicator metrics and be tracked in some manner by the department. In addition to tracking progress via KPIs for the business, keep the to-do list in front of legal team at meetings and with regular updates. Finally, with both the department and the business, use examples of how the different work or achievements of the legal department outlined above fit into the goals of the company and (more importantly) how they generate or protect company value.

In a Pinch—Focus Efforts on Revenue Generation

There are many ways a legal department can show its value to the business. If you asked me for the best way I would say focus on things that generate revenue for the business. I do not mean to minimize the importance of preventing value destruction, but it is so much easier to show the results of revenue generation than it is to show the results of preventing something. And, when push comes to shove, having tangible results you can point to is far superior to the sometimes nebulous discussion around problems avoided. What follows in this section are ways to help the company generate revenue, as well as a few ways to minimize value destruction. Many of these ideas came as a result of a checklist I put together many years ago when I was a fairly new general counsel., I started to focus on the question of value, as in how can the legal department help generate money? Nothing screams value like cold, hard cash. If you have followed my *Ten Things You Need to Know as In-House Counsel* blog series,[31] you have likely seen a lot of these topics discussed in detail. This list is where it all started for me and I will share it with you here.

Simple Ways the Legal Department Can Drive Revenue and Growth

- ☐ Increase speed of contracting.
  - ☐ Speed up turnaround time.
  - ☐ Simplify agreements—make contracting easier.
  - ☐ The right technology.
  - ☐ Make access to templates easier and train the business on use.
  - ☐ Staffing:
    - ☐ Maximize use of current resources/people.
    - ☐ Identify low-cost outside counsel for spillover.
    - ☐ Prepare checklist(s) and other self-help tools that allow business to avoid legal altogether.
  - ☐ Focus on current in-year revenue-generating contracts.
  - ☐ Focus on contracts/projects that drive or are the result of company innovation.
- ☐ Enforce contractual rights—do not leave money on the table without good reason.
- ☐ Help the business think through new business models.
- ☐ Protect existing and new business models:
  - ☐ The right contracts and clauses
  - ☐ Spot and maneuver around regulatory issues.
- ☐ Advocate for company, our industry, our customers broadly, drive company's leadership role, enhance loyalty and good feelings among company's customers, vendors, developer community, etc.
- ☐ Strategic use of litigation and regulation
- ☐ Develop business intelligence tools and data analytics for the legal department.
- ☐ Stay on top of new industry developments/business opportunities (core and adjacent)
  - ☐ Know who to bring opportunities to.

31 www.tenthings.net.

- ☐ Ask, "Would this make a good business for the company?"[32]
- ☐ Stay close to business partners, become part of their team.
- ☐ Read trade press and industry publications.
- ☐ Memorize company's strategy and goals (short- and long term).
- ☐ Align priorities of the legal department with those of the business.
  - ☐ What legal thinks is important may not matter to the business
  - ☐ Be the Department of Yes—focus on how.
- ☐ Treat department budget like our own money!

There you go. Not an overly complicated list but tremendously powerful, especially when it comes to value generation. As my legal department began to align itself around this list we become true partners with the business, driving revenue growth and constantly vigilant for anything that could enhance value and drive dollars to the bottom line.

Create Better Contracts Faster

You probably noticed a lot of items dealing with contracts on the above checklist. That should not be a shock by now given my position of their importance to the company and as part of the value generation calculus. All of the goodness legal departments, and their clients, can derive from contracts is multiplied when the velocity of contracting increases, that is, more is better. More good contracts are better still. Consequently, as part of the search for value generation in-house legal department should spend a significant amount of time figuring out ways to create better contracts faster. Below are some ways to do that.

Make Your Contracts Easier to Sign

I have been drafting contracts for a long time. Over time, I developed my three goals of contract drafting:

1. Clarity (everyone can understand the deal).
2. Get what you need (versus what you want).
3. Quick signatures (a short time frame from start to signature).

As lawyers, however, we often do everything in our power to undermine these goals, primarily by producing clunky, unbalanced, unreadable, overly long

32 That is, "Bring them the mouse."

documents that end up awash in redlines from the other side. This, in turn, frustrates the business, along with the lawyers. And it takes forever, so everyone involved in the process will be miserable longer.

I understand that sometimes it cannot be helped. Despite our best intentions, we may be dealing with someone on the other side of the table who refuses to work the contract process in a way that makes it easier for both sides, finding security in standing firm on Latin phrases, redundant wording, and complex sentences that require a codebreaker to decipher. Still, we can and should do better with contracts. If you believe that contracts are the lifeblood of any business and that the highest and best value the legal department can provide is getting good contracts done faster, then in-house counsel are, unfortunately, not devoting enough time to making their contracts easier to sign. Below are some ways I have used to correct this problem. Note, these are primarily for business-to-business deals, where lawyers represent both parties. It does not apply to boilerplate terms of use on a consumer-facing website or for a simple SaaS contract where the provider requires everyone sign up for the same thing (though even those types of agreements are sometimes negotiated as well).

- Buy this book. I am a huge fan of Ken Adams and his blog on contracting.[33] I am a bigger fan of his book, *A Manual of Style for Contract Drafting*.[34] Adams is a lifelong proponent of cleaner and clearer contract drafting, and he provides almost 500 pages of examples. If you truly want to learn how to draft better contracts that will meet the goals above, read this book.
- Make your contract balanced. There is little more painful (for me) than to sit down and start to review a contract that is so one-sided I burst out laughing. Most of the key terms of a contract, especially the boilerplate sections,[35] should be mutual—or as close to mutual as you can make them. Otherwise, all you are inviting are tons of redlines, to make them mutual. Put in fair time periods for termination rights. Do away with nine levels of escalation before either party can file a lawsuit. In other words, when preparing your templates or even a bespoke contract, put yourself in the shoes of the other side and ask if you would sign it as is. If the answer is no, then you have some work to do.
- Use plain language. Unless you are preparing a resume to work in the summer Shakespeare festival, lose the olde English and Latin phrasing. Write a contract like a normal person would write something. Avoid unnecessary complexity and shoot for short sentences (think

33 www.adamsdrafting.com/blog.

34 K. Adams, *A Manual of Style for Contract Drafting* (ABA Publishing, Chicago, 4th ed. 2017).

35 *See infra* at page 117 for a discussion about boilerplate provisions, and why they matter.

Hemingway). And always ask yourself if what you wrote down is clear. Could a judge or jury understand the section if there was ever litigation? If not, rework it. Be precise and concise!

- Stick with your definitions. If you go through the hassle of creating definitions for key terms, stick with those definitions throughout the contract. I suspect it is mostly due to laziness, but do not call it "Agreement" in section one and then "agreement" or the "contract" elsewhere. It also takes time for the other side to pick through your definition failures, slowing down the deal.
- Eliminate repetition. I realize contracts can be scary, but writing something once is enough. You do not need to repeat it elsewhere in the contract to be sure it is in there. Similarly, there is no need to use three words that mean the same thing. For example, "give, devise, and bequeath" all mean "give." Why not just use "give"?
- Do not send a PDF. If you are sending a contract over to the other side and asking for their comments and redlines, do not send a PDF. Send a Word version! Sending a PDF is like sending a big "Happy Screw You Day" Hallmark card to the other party.
- Redline all of your changes. It is hard for me to fathom this one sometimes but I now, out of habit, create my own redline version of the other side's changes. Why? Because I have lost trust in most lawyers to redline/show all of their changes. I do not think it is because they are nefariously trying to hide something (although sometimes it is). I think it is because they think it is helpful not to have so much red in the document, as if I will be insulted if they show that I missed a period or comma. The problem with being this generous is that if I find one change that was not in the redline, I now have no faith that all of the important changes are redlined. Dealing with this adds to the length of time it will take to get the deal done. If you change something, redline it.
- Keep changes to a minimum. If you want to get a contract off your desk and signed, stop making every little change that comes into your head. Do not change words over word choice issues. Do not add or delete punctuation that does not matter. If the way a clause is written works for the deal, leave it alone even if you could make it better with a good edit. Who cares? Concede it and move on. If the provision is clear enough, leave it alone. The single biggest delay in contract execution is the exchange of redlines. Do everything you can to keep redlines to a minimum and only revise or add things that truly matter.
- Explain yourself. If you have just made a material change in a document or added an entirely new section, put a comment in the document (or at least in the cover email) explaining what you have done and why. If I get a contract back with entirely new sections or a substantial rewrite of

something I wrote, it is difficult for me to know if I can accept it without any explanation of what the change is designed to do and why it is needed. I will either mark it up based on what I think you mean or I will try to schedule a call with you to discuss it. Neither of which is efficient.

- Check out the competition. If I could get a copy (properly) of my competitors' contracts, I would pore over them to see how they handled certain issues, and to see whether our boilerplate was in line with their boilerplate, what types of limits or caps they used, warranties, and so forth. I did this to understand what was market and to be able to intelligently discuss with the business where our contract templates sat with respect to the competition. That is to say, I was not going to blindly accept an accusation from the sales team that our competitors' contracts were easier to sign than ours were. But, if they were in fact easier in some material way, I was not against adopting that language into our agreements in some manner. Also, if I have an understanding of our competitors' contracts I can politely refute the well-known refrain from the lawyers for customers who say, "Well, your competitors have agreed to this language."
- Review your contract templates regularly. Every year, the legal team and the sales team should sit down together to walk through all of the existing contract templates. The purpose is to discuss what issues have come up that may give us reasons to change our templates. Our overall goal is to make contracts consistently easier to sign. So, over the past year, what wording, clauses, behavior, have slowed the contracting process down? Work on fixing that, and contracts will flow faster and more smoothly every year.

Given the importance of contracts to the company, I guarantee that if the legal department is proactively looking for ways to make the company's contract process go faster (and is reporting on those ideas and actions to the business/senior management via KPIs and business-savvy presentations), the business will see these actions as a huge department value add. The above is a great way to start this process.

Reduce Risk in Contracts

The most common question asked of in-house counsel typically involves commercial contracts and whether it is okay to sign this. There are multiple parts to this seemingly simple ask, but the core of the question has to do with risk. More specifically, if we sign this contract, are we taking on an unacceptable level of risk? Risk too, is subject to multiple meanings. Are we talking about commercial risk, legal risk, financial risk, reputational risk, or something else? It is typically the in-house lawyer's job to come up with the answer. Unfair or not, because lawyers are trained issue-spotters, the analysis of risk in commercial agreements and the process of minimizing that risk usually falls in the lap of the in-house legal department. Unfortunately, the process of spotting and analyzing risk is rarely black and white. It is highly subjective, and you are not always right. Still, next to creating a speedy contracting process, the legal department adds tremendous value if it is systematically finding ways to minimize risk in signing contracts.

A simple way to reduce risk in commercial agreements is through technology. More on this below, but start with implementing a contract management tool. Using technology over a manual process almost always reduces risk. Leverage technology for two key tasks. The first is centrally storing all your contract templates and executed contracts (including amendments) in a single repository where the legal team (or anyone else with access) can easily find them when needed. Most companies have executed contracts and templates sitting in multiple databases or worse—on someone's laptop. Being able to locate all of the company's contracts and relevant amendments in one place at any time without significant effort is a big accomplishment. Second is the management of the contract from negotiation through termination. Often referred to as a contract lifecycle management (CLM) tool, a CLM not only provides a central repository, but also allows the company to actively manage contracts, tracking such things as renewal dates and price increases for example. For the legal department, such tools provide a centralized place for contract negotiations, redlines, e-signature process, and storage. The more sophisticated systems can provide self-service modules where the business can prepare their own contracts from standard templates and even make changes using approved fallback clauses/language, and avoid involving the legal department at all in their deal. I like to call this the "value of non-engagement."

Another proven way to reduce risk with commercial agreements is developing a process to score potential contracts based on the risk tolerances of the company. By doing so, you can quickly determine if a contract meets the company's parameters for signature or if it fails. Failing contracts can be abandoned or be subject to further review. To create a scoring process, first determine which issues (legal, commercial, other) make a good contract in terms of acceptable risk to the company. Then select a scoring scale. It can be anything from letter grades (A-F), to high risk-medium risk-low risk (H-M-L), to numeric (1–10 scale, where 10 is the highest risk). For each issue/contract clause create different scenarios and assign a score to each. For example, you might determine that a limitation of liability limited to one times annual contract revenue is a 1, one limited to three times is a 5, and unlimited is a 10. Anything 5 or under is acceptable, but 6 and over is rejected or must go through a separate review process. If scoring is developed across issues affecting different parts of the business (and not just issues the legal department is interested in), you can quickly create a table that scores contract risks across a variety of important company issues. Scoring also provides a high-level view of contract risk across the company overall, which can be turned into KPIs. For example, 80 percent or more of our contracts are 5s (low risk) and no more than 5 percent of my contracts are 1s (high risk), which tells you the legal department should focus on the 5 percent instead of the 80 percent.[36] Here is a sample of what one page of such a chart might look like:

Contract Issue	Score	Score	Score	Score	Score
	5	4	3	2	1
Issue 1 (LOL)	[criteria]	[criteria]	[criteria]	[criteria]	[criteria]
Issue 2 (Indemnities)	[criteria]	[criteria]	[criteria]	[criteria]	[criteria]
Issue 3 (Warranties)	[criteria]	[criteria]	[criteria]	[criteria]	[criteria]
Issue 4 (Termination)	[criteria]	[criteria]	[criteria]	[criteria]	[criteria]
Issue 5 (Governing Law)	[criteria]	[criteria]	[criteria]	[criteria]	[criteria]
Issue 6 (Term)	[criteria]	[criteria]	[criteria]	[criteria]	[criteria]
Issue 7 (Payment Terms)	[criteria]	[criteria]	[criteria]	[criteria]	[criteria]
Issue 8 (Arbitration)	[criteria]	[criteria]	[criteria]	[criteria]	[criteria]

Scoring 5 = Best

Next, is building out a contract review committee. Many companies have these committees to review contracts over a certain financial amount, such as any contract over $250,000. The problem with using a number only is the committee's mandate is often limited to financial issues. While important, there is much more that may require review and debate, including legal and operational risk. The solution is to broaden the mandate of an existing committee or create one if none exists. While lawyers often understand the many different types of risks a contract presents, including non-legal, it is unfair to place the full burden of rejecting contracts on the legal department. When the legal team says no to a contract, they quickly develop the unwarranted reputation of being deal killers, which runs completely against what the Department of Yes stands for. A contract review committee spreads that decision among several different groups, such as finance, sales, operations, and others in addition to the legal department. Consequently, if

36 Systematically scoring the company's contract can also be a value add in the event of a merger or acquisition of the company, i.e., you can document the quality of your contracts and highlight the risk-management process the legal department utilized to generate acceptable contracts. This type of certainyt around quality can enhance the value of the company in the eyes of the purchaser (i.e., a high price) or, at a minimum, reduce the time spent in due diligence and thereby reduce the cost of doing the deal.

a deal is turned down it is because the contract review committee killed the deal after allowing multiple points of view to weigh in whether the contract was acceptable or not. A contract review committee ties nicely into the contract risk scoring chart above. The company can decide deals meeting certain risk scores can be signed without further review, while deals that do not meet the minimum scores go to the review committee. Here is a sample chart of a page of the contract review committee guidelines. Across the top are ranges of contract value. but you can use other criteria. The left side would set out different issues (e.g., legal, financial, etc.) and the key tells you what happens:

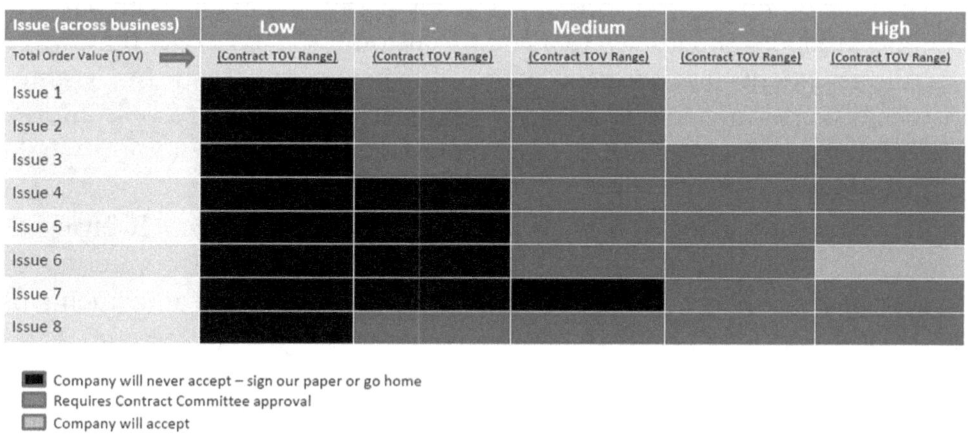

Risk is also reduced when you utilize standard templates. In fact, the solution to scrambling around looking for an old contract you can use as the basis for a new contract is to develop templates for all of your company's core agreements, and use those templates as the starting point for all deals. If you keep the templates updated yearly, it eliminates time wasted trying to locate the right form and provides a template tailored to the company's business and risk profile. Equally important, deals get done faster using templates, especially when the alternative is working off of a customer's standard procurement agreement which will need a lot of redlines and will take substantially longer to negotiate. Ideally, the contract review committee should make the decision to use customer paper, not the sales team. Just like the decision not to use customer paper should not lie solely with the legal team.

Another simple way to manage contract risk is preparing a contract signature policy, i.e., a policy that sets out who is authorized to sign which contracts the company enters into. It ensures that contracts of a certain type or certain amount are presented to someone at the appropriate level within the company to enter into such an agreement. Who signs a contract can depend on such diverse issues as tax planning, maturity and size of the business, or location of the customer. A well-drafted contract signature policy typically ties into the company's delegations of authority, a core document related to corporate governance. A contract signature policy also sets out the process that contracts, or certain contracts, must go through before being presented for signature. This is another way the company can ensure important issues are vetted and understood at the right levels before contracts are signed.

A contract playbook (discussed in detail later) is a document that breaks down the company's standard contract terms, sets out an explanation of each term/clause along with fallback clauses (that is, variations of the standard clauses that the company will accept if the customer wants to negotiate a standard clause), and notes when the company will walk away from a contract. While companies want to sell their products or services to as many customers as possible, they will only do so to the extent the contract makes financial sense and fits within the company's risk parameters. A properly prepared contract playbook allows the legal and sales teams to stay aligned and close contracts faster (or know when it is time to walk away).

Version control is another key to contract risk management. It ensures that everyone (sales, lawyers, and so on) starts every deal using the correct template. Using old agreements is dangerous, primarily because existing agreements likely contain negotiated terms and the company probably gave on certain issues — depending on business leverage—to get the deal done. If you use an old agreement, you have already negotiated away those terms without ever talking with the other side. Having template version control in place also limits the unfortunate situation of having the other side mark up the wrong contract, wasting time and goodwill. Proper drafting version control maintains a record of how the contract evolved over time, which can be a lifesaver if there is a dispute or litigation. Finally, if there are a lot of negotiations and edits, always run a compare of the contract you are about to sign compared to the version you agreed to. While rare, there are times when doing this will save the day, and a simple task generates huge value (value you can track).

If you want to be a hero to the business, work on a program to increase the chances that the company will get paid for its services. Oddly, many companies fail to focus on this fundamental issue, until it becomes clear they are about to get stiffed over an invoice. By then, it is usually too late to do anything about it other than prepare for litigation. And then, only if the amount is substantial enough and if the legal team believes there is money available to satisfy any judgment. If not, the business will just need to write off that balance due as a loss. The easiest way to minimize financial risk with your contracts is to understand upfront whether your potential customer is a credit risk or not. The finance department should handle this task. Additionally, your contract can require that all payments are due annually, before services are provided for that year. This is a good reminder that what is often referred to as boilerplate clauses in contracts are anything but. These clauses are where you can really beef up the protection of the company as things like limitations of liability, indemnity, choice of law, dispute resolution, collection of attorney's fees, notice, and many other core contract terms reside in these pages. Finally, at the first sign of financial trouble with a customer, the company should aggressively seek payment and not let the situation drag on. The longer a customer is in arrears, the more likely it is that you will not get paid. Be sure your contracts include a clause entitling the company to collect its attorney's fees in the event it must undertake collection efforts to get paid.

Even if the legal team has created wonderful contract templates, a cutting-edge playbook, and implemented a fantastic contract management system, it will mean little if the business team does not understand utilize what is in place. There is value to unlock and track via KPIs by constantly training the business on how to reduce contract risk. Consider the following:

- New hire training. All new sales hires get a standard 60-minute legal overview.
- Sales kick-off training. Most companies have an annual sales kick-off meeting. Legal team members should attend and should present classes on legal issues and ways to get contracts done faster.
- Sales-person playbook. Prepare a short and concise playbook for the business, one that explains to them how the different pieces of the contract come together and their role in helping negotiate smart deals.
- Super users. Identify several top salespeople and convert them into super users, that is, salespeople who get it and can help spread the word about how best to negotiate contracts and how to use legal services.

Reducing company contract risk is not easy, but it is doable. It requires focus and constant attention. By utilizing some fairly basic practices, in-house lawyers can substantially reduce contract problems and help the business sign-up to consistently good commercial deals. The legal team can lead the effort to reduce risk and improve contract quality. If more, and better, contracts get signed, that will reflect well on the legal department.

Teach The Business About Contract Boilerplate

Previously, I touched on the importance of boilerplate—the language tucked in the back of a contract that many lawyers simply skim over (a big mistake). While it is critical for lawyers to focus on these clauses, you can dramatically improve the businesses' ability to work with you and negotiate contracts faster by taking time to teach them about these critical clauses. Why? Because this is where the action is in a contract. Get it wrong, and bad things can await down the road. Get it right, and the company is well protected (or as well protected as the circumstances allow). The important starting point comes with recognizing that contracts tell the story of an agreement between two parties. How the story turns out depends in large part on who is doing the writing and, more importantly, who is paying attention. In-house lawyers can add tremendous value to the enterprise by teaching the business how to craft the best story possible, i.e., teaching what key clauses mean and why they are important. Here are a few important clauses to focus on:

Term/Termination

Surprisingly, one of the most litigated parts of any contract is the term and termination provisions. The term sets out how long the contract will be in effect. It can be a fixed term, e.g., three years. Or an "evergreen" term, meaning the contract remains in effect (or keeps renewing) until either party gives notice of termination. A key component of the term is the effective date, the day the contract starts to run. It can be the day of signature, a specified date in the contact, upon delivery or acceptance, or some other mark in time. It is important to always be clear when the contract will start and when it will end. Additionally, it is important to spell out any conditions for renewal such as price escalation rights. On the other side is termination, that is, when the contract ends. In the agreement, it can be on a fixed date (it simply expires), so many days after notice is given (often called *termination for convenience*), upon a triggering event of some nature, upon an uncured breach (material or otherwise), or a failure to make payment. Like the start date of the contract, being clear on when the contract ends can limit contract heartache.

Dispute Resolution

While entering into a new contract is the fun part, no contract lasts forever and the business must always plan for the divorce. The time to do that is at the beginning of the relationship. Dispute resolution clauses can be short or an entire exhibit to the contract. Here are the essential items for a good provision:

- Choice of law. Which jurisdiction's law will apply to disputes?
- Forum. Where do you want disputes heard? Ideally, your choice of law will match the forum.
- Arbitration. If the parties want to arbitrate you need to state that clearly and in the proper manner.
- Jury waiver. Do the parties want to waive the right to a jury? This sometimes makes sense in a commercial agreement.
- Dispute escalation process. Many parties like to build a formal dispute escalation process written into their agreement. This allows problems to be

escalated to a series of executives with set time frames to reach a resolution or pass it up the chain. Only when the process is exhausted may a party file a lawsuit or seek arbitration. This is all fine and good but be sure to keep the time frames short and do not include mediation as a mandatory step before either party can sue. Mediation can take a long time to set up and complete. The parties can always agree to mediate at any time.
- Fees and costs. Most dispute resolution clauses include a provision that the prevailing party in any dispute is entitled to have the other party reimburse them for their legal fees and related costs. A loser pays clause makes spurious litigation under the agreement less likely.

Force Majeure

The pandemic of 2020 made force majeure clauses cool. A force majeure provision covers situations that will excuse one of the parties' performance. Generally, they start with broad language about circumstances beyond the reasonable control of the affected party, which can let one party out of the contract simply by claiming something is beyond their reasonable control. To limit this, lawyers usually add a list of specific events that constitute an excuse of performance. Most clauses cover, at a minimum, acts of God such as a hurricane, fire, flood, earthquakes, and so on. Some include situations specific to the business, e.g., internet outage. Many clauses include a time frame trigger whereby if the force majeure event continues past a certain time frame (for example, more than 45 days), the contract will, or can be, terminated with both parties excused from further performance.

No Assignment

Unless there is a specific provision to contrary, either party to a contract may—with some exceptions—assign their rights to a third party. They may not, however, transfer their obligations under the contract to a third party. This can all get quite messy in the event of an asset sale or the desire of one party to subcontract some of their obligations under the contract. Generally, subcontracting is permitted because the party to the contract remains obligated to the other party for services. The parties to a contract need to spend some time thinking about the assignment clause and how they want their relationship to operate. For example, it may be appropriate for one party to subcontract some of its obligations. Or agree that the contract may be assigned to affiliates, successor organizations, or in the event of a sale or merger of one of the parties. Likewise, the parties may want no assignment rights. Regardless, the contract should provide for what happens in the case of an assignment made in violation of the terms, including stating that such assignments or transfers are null and void. And if consent is required for an assignment, add language that it may not be unreasonably withheld or delayed. That will save a lot of headaches.

Notice

It is important to set out how notice must be given under a contract. For example, if the parties have a termination for convenience right, to whom must they send notice of exercise of that right? Equally important is how the notice must be sent. Is it in writing, signed, via regular mail, email, certified mail, FedEx, facsimile, telegraph, courier, phone call, or some other method? What address must be used? Do multiple people receive the notice, e.g., the head of marketing and the legal department? A well-prepared notice provision puts an obligation on each party to update the identity of who must receive the notice and where. As is too often the case, there will be fights about whether notice was properly given. As in-house counsel, an easy, but important job, is to make sure any notice under any contract is properly given to the right person using the right method.

Entire Agreement

This is sometimes also called an integration clause or a merger clause. It usually says something like this: "This Agreement constitutes the entire agreement between the parties and supersedes all previous agreements, understandings, and discussion between the parties . . . " In other words, if it is not written into the contract, it did not happen. This means the business and in-house counsel must carefully review the agreement before signing, to ensure it covers everything discussed and agreed to by the parties during the negotiations. The entire agreement clause is designed to provide certainty that the written agreement the parties signed includes everything they agreed to and should limit any post-signing claims that the agreement between the parties contains additional terms and obligations.

Severance Clause

This is another one of those sneaky clauses that will be missed if the right circumstances arise. Simply put, litigation is a risky business. There is always a chance a clause in the contract will turn out to be illegal, invalid, or otherwise unenforceable. For example, a court may find a non-compete clause to be onerous. Without a severance clause (sometimes called a savings clause), a voided clause may cause the entire agreement to fail. A severance clause, however, sets out that if a court or government agency/legislation finds any provision of the agreement to be void or unenforceable, the parties agree that the rest of the contract remains intact. This clause can save the day!

Confidentiality

If you do not designate your agreement (or discussions and materials exchanged over the course of the agreement) as confidential, the other side is free to disclose the agreement terms and any information (price, trade secrets, etc.) the company shared. Consequently, it is a rare commercial agreement that lacks a fulsome confidentiality provision. Typically, the parties deem the agreement and its terms confidential, along with a provision for how confidential information will be exchanged by the parties during the agreement (including how any confidential information may be used). A non-disclosure agreement (NDA) usually covers confidential information exchanged before an agreement is reached and is then folded into the definitive agreement. The clause should also include a catch-all phrase making information confidential if it should—by its nature—be considered confidential (even if a party failed to mark it as such). Lastly, include provisions stating that when the agreement terminates, each party must return or destroy the other party's confidential information.

The Big Three

The most critical parts of any commercial contract (from the legal angle) are the sections dealing with indemnification, limitation of liability, and warranty. Or, as I call them, the "big three." These tend to be the most heavily negotiated clauses in the entire agreement. Why? Because they shift and cap/uncap exposure when things go wrong under the contract, something the business needs to understand.

- Indemnification. An indemnity provision requires one party to take on the defense costs —directly or through reimbursement of legal fees and/or damages—for losses the other party incurred for something arising under the contract. For example, third-party claims for IP infringement. Keep the clause expressly limited to third-party claims. There should also be a detailed process for how claims for indemnity must be tendered, who controls the defense, hires counsel, timing, settlement, etc.
- Limitation of liability. This clause sets limits for each party's liability under the contract. It could be unlimited or it could be capped, either a fixed amount (say, $500,000) or a formula (e.g., three times the amount the other party paid under the agreement). In the end, it becomes a balancing act. For the amount paid and the type of service or products provided, what is a reasonable level of risk for either party to assume? There are also carve outs (or different/higher caps) from the liability caps, typically around things such as a data breach, personal injury, gross negligence—whatever the parties negotiate. Lastly, this section is where you typically exclude all damages but direct damages, i.e., consequential, punitive, lost profits, indirect, and so forth.

- Warranty. The parties to a commercial agreement usually warrant several things to each other, such as that they are authorized to enter into the agreement, they have employees competent to perform the services purchased under the agreement, and so on. Additionally, there may be standard warranties about the product purchased, i.e., it will work substantially as described in the documentation, that it does not infringe anyone's intellectual property, etc. The types of warranties given depend on the type of contract. Equally, if not more, important to the warranty language are the disclaimers of warranty, i.e., disclaiming any implied warranties such are merchantability or fitness for a particular purpose.

The above will help familiarize the business with some of the key boilerplate clauses common to most commercial agreements in the United States. There are, of course, many other boilerplate clauses that may be important. It all depends on your company's business and what the legal department and the business find most important. So, be flexible in determining the clauses to bring forward to the business in an exercise like this. There is always value when the legal department acts as teacher, not only in the eyes of the business, but also in the reality of reduced risks and an enhanced ability to strike better deals quickly.

Implement Technology to Create Value

I have helped buy and implement a lot of legal technology over the years. I was there when fax machines were cutting edge and when e-mail was new. I helped build a home-grown document management system and spent time looking at uses of artificial intelligence to review contracts. Moving from typewriters to AI, yellow pads to iPads, is a pretty healthy span of technological change for any lawyer. The one thing that has not changed, however, is the importance of finding the right technology to solve your problems and then ensuring that technology is implemented properly. However, if the technology does not solve a problem (or make life easier for the in-house legal team), or if you skimp on implementing it properly, whatever you buy will likely sit there unused and unloved. Because there is so much value that can be unlocked or unleashed by technology, an in-house legal team is foolish not to spend the time and resources needed to get it right.

To start, you must accept that the right technology can make an enormous difference in productivity, accuracy, timeliness, and many other virtuous benefits. If you do not believe this, you can stop reading, get on your dinosaur, and head back to the Dark Ages of in-house counsel. For the rest of you, technology holds the promise of something better than you have right now. This is why the rest of the company invests in technology to run their part of the business. The legal department is no different, nor should it be. In-house lawyers are expected to be strategic partners in operating the business. To do this, you need timely, accurate information on-demand. Likewise, no one is looking to throw money and head-count at the legal department, year in and year out. Instead, most departments face a steady refrain of "do more with less." If you want to get more work out of the same size legal team with less money to spend on outside counsel, the only path forward is with technology; if you get the right technology and you use it properly.

The paradox of technology, especially legal technology, is that everything looks great, but only a few things are useful. If you buy software because it looks cool, you are in trouble, unless having it look cool and unused is your goal. Accordingly, the first step is to understand the business case for purchasing the technology. In short, what problem are you trying to solve? What are the department's biggest pain points? Is it not being able to meet the pace the business needs out of its legal team? Lack of visibility into spending? More or better reports? Reducing costs? Or are you trying to reduce the amount of drudge work so your team can focus on higher-value work? Whatever the reason, you must understand the problem inside and out. If you do not have a meaningful problem to solve, buying technology is not helpful. Here are the steps to walk through as you develop the business case.

- ➤ Identify the problem.
- ➤ What is the current process to solve the problem?
- ➤ Is there technology that will replace this manual process and solve the problem?
- ➤ What will it cost and do you have (or can you get) the budget?
- ➤ Will the benefits of the technology outweigh the cost? And how soon will those benefits pay off the cost? What is the return on investment?
- ➤ Do you have the support of management inside the legal department as well as the CFO, CTO, etc?

Once you figure out your business case, you must prepare a requirements document. This sets out exactly what you are looking for regarding technology, including a list of features necessary to satisfy your use case. Prioritize what you *need* vs. what you *want*. Need is the key, as focusing on need will keep you from falling prey to all the shiny baubles that are slick (and expensive), but do not solve your problem. Take your time when preparing this document, rushing it will not be helpful. Ask anyone who will use the technology, inside and outside the department, to contribute their thoughts and ideas. The document does not have to be long, one page is fine. It is basically a checklist that will be your guide as you analyze different software or products.

Here are a few items to consider including in your document, but tailor your list to your needs.

- ☐ Overview (A summary of what you're trying to accomplish, what problem will it solve).

- ☐ Must haves (A list of all the features the product must have).
- ☐ Should have (A list of nice to have features, but not critical).
- ☐ Does/does not (What the technology will do, and what it will not do).
- ☐ Cloud/local (Will the technology be cloud based or installed locally)?
- ☐ Budget (Target cost).
- ☐ Must connect to . . . (What other systems/products in the department must it connect to)?
- ☐ Support (What level of support are you looking for—internally and from the vendor)?
- ☐ Scale (Will the product easily scale to meet your needs, now and in the future)?
- ☐ User platform(s) (Where can people use the technology, e.g., smartphone, tablet, laptop, etc)?

Once you have defined your problem and written your requirements, you will survey the landscape to see what legal tech products are out there that can solve it. There are many places to find legal tech, and you can start with a basic web search. Just type in the problem you are trying to solve and add "technology" and "legal department" to the search and you will get some good results immediately. If possible, get a free trial for any products you are interested in. If that is not possible, get a full demo via webinar or in person. Multiple demos are better in this case. Ask in advance if you can supply a sample contract or problem for the technology to solve, a problem that is real to your needs versus a made-up problem the vendor might use. Keep your requirements document handy during the demo, check off the matches, and note the short-falls. Be flexible. It doesn't matter if the product does not solve your problem exactly the way you envisioned. The real question is does it solve it? If it does, it should go on your list.

Always undertake due diligence of the vendors you are considering. Ask for references from each vendor and reach out to other in-house lawyers or a community for opinions. Look for software analyst reviews, too. While no vendor is perfect, you must be able to determine which vendors stand by their products and will be a true partner in the implementation process. If you have a procurement department, they are your friend here. You can likely turn much of the vendor selection and contracting process over to them, so you can focus on the requirements and product review. Focus on these questions as you move through the process:

- ☐ Who needs to be involved in the decision to buy? You will likely need procurement, security, IT, and several other groups to all be aligned on a major technology purchase.
- ☐ Does the product have lots of users or are you one of the first? Products that have a large user base and have been around are more likely to be the

better choice. That said, every product was new at some point, so this cannot be your sole criteria.

- ☐ Spend time with the vendor's implementation team. Sales people are nice by nature, but you want to speak with the folks who will be working on getting you up and running with the product.
- ☐ What is the true cost of using the product? What does support cost? Future upgrades? Is training included? What is the cost to run the product on your systems? Will you need to customize it (versus off-the-shelf) and what will that cost? How many users are included, and what does it cost to add more? Do you need any special hardware? Is there a cost to transfer data if you want to port it to other systems?
- ☐ Make your decision based on what is available today. Do not rely on promises that products will solve your problem in the next release. It needs to solve it now.
- ☐ What happens when the contract ends? How easy is it to get your data back? Will the vendor help you transition away?

Once you buy the product you will need an implementation project plan, that is, the document that outlines step-by-step how you will implement the product. If the product is small and easy to implement, you may have a short project plan (if there is one at all.) Sophisticated products will require a plan. For large projects, it will be the IT department's job to manage the implementation, especially any technology that will touch company systems. You may need a steering committee to oversee the project. Your plan should cover change management and list critical milestones. Lastly, no matter how awesome the technology is, it will fail miserably if no one uses it. This is why user acceptance is among the most critical tasks in your project plan. User acceptance is the process to ensure the technology is presented, and works, in a way people will want to use it, along with the training program on how to use the tool. Always go with a clean, simple interface over lots of bells and whistles. And consider developing a handful of super users, i.e., people you train extensively on how to use the product with the plan that they will become champions of the new tool and encourage others to use it (and can answer questions and teach other users).

Legal department technology can be a tremendous time-saver and problem solver—faster, better, and cheaper. Get it right, and you are on your way to better productivity and happier lawyers. Get it wrong, and you have wasted a big chunk of your legal department's budget and time. Technology is great. People are better. Technology cannot replace the one-on-one connection between lawyer and client. And it never will. If you come to rely on technology 100 percent of the time, it will be a disaster for the legal department. Find the right tech for the problem, but never forget the value of the human touch when it comes to client satisfaction and overcoming obstacles or misperceptions. Pick up the phone, walk down the hall for a chat, get on a video call, and listen carefully to what is being said and why it is being said. Context matters, and technology is not always very good with context, but people are. Following are several in-depth discussions about specific technology that can add value to the entire company and are worthy of your focus.

Focus on Technology that Matters

Technology that Matters: The Core

If you are going to implement technology for the legal department/company, you should start with what I call "the core." The core technology is technology every legal department should have in place or be planning to put in place. This technology allows the legal department to provide the highest and most valuable return to the company for each technology dollar it spends. And will allow the legal team to be more efficient and able to focus more time on higher-value matters.

Number one on your list should be an e-billing system. With an e-billing system, you can do away with spreadsheets and paper invoices and get instantaneous data about where you are spending money and on which matters. This data can flow seamlessly into reports, dashboards, and KPI trackers. Virtually every law firm can connect to such systems so access should not be a barrier. And there is a wide variety of tools on the market, meaning one with just the right level of sophistication for your needs will be available. This is one tool that will definitely make your life as an in-house lawyer easier.

Second, as noted above, if you have ever been asked to locate a certain contract in a hurry, you know the value of a contract management system. Not only is it a central repository for all the company's contracts, it also allows you and the company to manage those contracts, in terms of price increases, termination, and to slice and dice contract information whenever asked. Additionally, many contract management systems also can create contracts allowing in-house counsel to work faster, or in many cases, create portals providing access directly to the business to create contracts themselves within pre-defined parameters, meaning they do not have to involve the legal team at all. A contract management system can, therefore, be an extension of the value added by the legal department in terms of a) risk reduction, i.e., ensuring compliance with key contract terms by both sides and by standardizing the contracting process; b) profitability, i.e., reduce the cost of contracting, speedontract delivery, reduce drag on and diversion of legal resources, manage contracting compliance; c) operational efficiency, i.e., contract visibility and insights (analytics, including self-service analytics whereby business leaders can obtain information about contracting without asking the legal department), locating contracts, managing contract obligations, e-signatures, version and template control, and automating the approval, renewal or termination of contracts process; d) business alignment around the contracting process, including contract ownership clarity and speedier internal conversations and collaboration (especially if groups outside of the legal department with contracting responsibility also utilize the tool, e.g., procurement); and e) enhanced company value, i.e., a company with a fully operational contract management and life cycle tool is more valuable to a potential acquirer, as it is evidence that the contracting process is state-of-the art and the numbers around contracting are valid. I like to think of it this way: if a contract management system can save one attorney-hour per week in time, that is fifty-two hours a year in time savings, which is a free week of full-time attorney time if not more.

Third, while related to a contract management system, a document management system is bigger and broader. It allows the legal department to store and locate all of the documents the legal team creates, from memoranda to board documents to policies, templates, checklists, and so on. Part of the value of a modern document management system is generally, it is cloud-based, which means it can be accessed by anyone on the team using any internet-connected device anywhere in the world, at any time of day. It should allow the team to easily find any document anyone created (except for documents that are restricted to certain individuals.) The legal team should adopt a standard naming and filing convention so all documents are saved into the system in a similar matter. For example, we used the following: Year-Month-Day [Full Name of Document]. It looked like this, "2021-05-13 Plaintiff's Response to First Set of Interrogatories" or "2020-04-28 SmithCo. Agreement for Purchase of Procurement System Software". By starting with the date in this order, the documents automatically sort in chronological order. By including detailed descriptions for the title, the documents are more easily found when using keywords. If someone just saved "SmithCo Agreement" into the tool, you can see that it would take longer to determine if you have found the right document. Additionally, the documents saved in the legal department document management system would be a goldmine to a third-party hacker. So, ensure that the database is as secure as possible. Your system must have top-shelf security and encryption and require strong passwords and two-factor authentication.

Fourth, governance, risk, and compliance (GRC) software is quickly becoming a must-have technology for many legal departments. GRC software helps legal, human resources, and others create and manage governance and compliance policies and procedures, codes of conduct and business ethics policies, and a host of other functions related to minimizing compliance and governance risk.[37] For many companies, it is impossible to stay on top of the global compliance and governance issues without software. To try to do it manually is like trying to fight

37 For example, online training materials, hotline incident management, third-party monitoring and screening, regulatory updates, data privacy, data security, disclosure and conflicts of interest management, and more.

a forest fire with a squirt gun. Moreover, most GRC platforms also provide reporting analytics and benchmarking tools which are becoming table stakes with the C-Suite, internal audit, and the audit committee of the board of directors. The platforms generally allow any employee anywhere in the world to connect and find answers to ethics and compliance issues or questions. GRC software becomes even more critical as more and more companies have different (non-legal) functions roll up to the chief legal officer. Having a systematic process and method to managing compliance can also help when regulators come knocking. One thing they look for is how much attention and resource the company devoted to compliance, and they will substantially reduce fines if they believe the company is taking the right steps to spot and minimize problems. For more on GRC generally check out LegalGRC.org, a not-for-profit dedicated to GRC issues.

Fifth, every in-house lawyer will need to do some legal research at some point. It might be on a specific legal issue or may be trying to find a sample contract template to use for a deal. There are many choices out there including, Bloomberg, Lexis Nexis, Wolters Kluwer, and Thomson Reuters.

Sixth, if you are serious about KPIs and data analytics you need to utilize some type of business intelligence (BI) software. BI software allows even a novice to gather and analyze data in a manner that was previously the exclusive regime of data specialists. It provides you with multiple ways to look at data and, thereby, provide insights into what the data is telling you. The analysis can be used as part of your KPI process or even as an early warning system where certain data trends about business or legal issues trigger legal department action. And, most BI software allows you to create dashboards and user-friendly charts and graphs—all things the business loves to see. There are dozens of BI tools on the market. The easiest place to start is to use whatever everyone else in the company is using because there will be support and guidance already available. Two of the most common BI tools are Microsoft BI and Tableau. Within five years, I believe legal departments will be expected to use BI software. Time to get on the train or get left on the platform.[38]

Technology that Matters: Electronic Signatures

No one in the business spends a lot of time thinking about the process of signing documents, especially contracts even though they are the critical value generator for the company. For years, contracts required so-called "wet" signatures, i.e., people physically signed multiple copies which were exchanged between the parties so each had an original for their files. Eventually, businesses began to

---

38 For more insights into how to use BI in the legal department, *see In-House Legal Data Analytics for Beginners* and *Best-In Class Legal Reporting: Audience, Content and Cadence* available for free at www.xakiatech.com/legal-data-analytics and www.xakiatech.com/best-in-class-legal-reporting, respectively.

accept faxed signatures, and then PDF copies of signatures. All of the PDFs were signed separately, then joined together to form a signed and valid contract (of course lawyers worked out wording to make this amalgamation of signatures acceptable). Finally, we have ended up with electronic signatures which are "expressions" of someone's intention to sign versus a wet signature (or even a copy of their handwritten signature.) Intuitively, you know it is all valid. But, is it really? The COVID-19 pandemic caused many in-house lawyers to contemplate this question, as well as finding ways for the business to sign legally binding contracts when no one was in the room and scanning a PDF was not a solution. E-signatures turned out to be the perfect solution for such a situation, and many legal departments have added value to the company by implementing an electronic signature process.

Humans have been officially signing documents for a long time. At least as far back as the ancient Egyptian and Persian empires. Though manually signing one's name did not start until around the second century AD. Before that (and even for centuries thereafter), the most common expression of officially signing a document was in the form of a seal or stamp. More often than not, it was a ring worn by someone important who would stamp that ring into a wax seal to ensure the authenticity of a document. This simple method of signing documents persisted well into the Middle Ages, where kings, and other members of the aristocracy, used signets (rings) to stamp documents to prove authenticity. Starting in the 1600s, signing one's name by hand became acceptable throughout Europe (and its various colonies). This led directly to the requirements of the 1677 Statute of Frauds, whereby a written signature became necessary for certain contracts to be formed. Over time, what constituted a signature got looser, anything from signing an "X" for your mark (which evolved from the practice of signing documents with the sign of the cross), to using a rubber stamp to the elaborate use of notaries to authenticate signatures on documents. For most of us, we simply sign with an ink pen (a wet signature), and move on.

Electronic signatures, however, are any type of non-handwritten expression of a person's intent to sign a document. This covers a wide variety of signatures, including:

- typed, printed name;
- email exchange;
- text message exchange;
- faxed signatures;
- scanned signatures;
- copy of signature pasted into a document;
- clicking "I accept" on a website;
- use of signing tool software, like DocuSign (more on this below); and
- a thumbprint affixed via an authentication device.

There is a second type of electronic signature that is tangentially important; and that is a digital signature. This is a signature based on cryptographic technology called a PKI (public key infrastructure). These authenticated signatures rely on encryption keys issued by a governing body (either as a digital certificate or a physical token) and a pin number to prove the identity of the signer. They are highly secure, but probably more work and expense than most businesses want to take on for everyday contracting purposes.

In the U.S., states figured out the need to boost electronic commerce back in the 1990s, culminating in 1999 with the Uniform Electronic Transactions Act, which was designed to give effect to electronic contracts (website terms and conditions) and electronic signatures. Forty-seven states and Washington D.C. have adopted some version of the UETA, while New York, Illinois, and Washington State have their own versions that do the same thing as the UETA. In 2000, Congress passed the E-SIGN Act,[39] which provides for the validity of electronic signatures and preempts any state law that is inconsistent with its provisions. Note, however, that certain agreements fall outside these laws including wills, trust documents, powers of attorney, and many real estate transactions. Similarly, certain regulatory agencies, as well as courts, have specific rules around what may be filed with an electronic signature. Outside of the United States, approximately fifty countries have electronic signature laws of varying degrees. Of course, as mentioned, parties to commercial business agreements can simply contract that electronic signatures are acceptable.

Under E-SIGN, a signature does not need to look like a handwritten signature to be valid. However, you must be able to authenticate in some manner the signature to the individual e-signing the document. E-SIGN also requires that the record of the contract be capable of being retained and reproduced. All of this is why (i) clicking I Accept, (ii) ticking a box, (iii) typing your name into a blank field, (iv) those weird-looking signatures many e-signature tools spit out when you click on the blank, (v) thumbprints, (vi) signatures in PDFs, (vii)) faxed signatures, and (viii) signatures traced with your finger on a smartphone or tablet can constitute as valid signatures (and satisfy the Statute of Frauds).

There are many benefits to your company adopting electronic signatures, including a) no need to track down people for physical signatures (and the delay this can cause); b) contracts can be signed literally anywhere;[40] c) eliminating or reducing the need for physical storage of contracts, as well as saving mailing costs; d) the ability to set up the routing process so the signatures are obtained in the proper order and a fully executed copy comes back to the legal department; e) the ability to monitor of the status of the execution of the contract in real time; f)

---

39 15 U.S.C. §7001, et. seq.

40 That is, on a smartphone, laptop, tablet, with no need to scan, fax, or send overnight. This means getting contracts done faster, a top goal of every legal department.

most of the solutions are simple and intuitive to use; and g) it has been the perfect solution to getting contracts done during the COVID-19 pandemic (and other emergency situations that may arise in the future).

Of course, there are some downsides to using electronic signatures. First, not every country/jurisdiction accepts them. Second, they cannot be used for every type of agreement. Third, not everyone will agree to use/accept electronic signatures regardless of the legality. Fourth, it is more difficult/more time-consuming to notarize an electronic signature (but it can be and is done in many places). Fifth, it is not foolproof. Like any signed contract, the other party can contest whether the e-signature is real or not. For example, scanned/pdf signatures are no more secure from forgery than a wet signature. Even the use of name-brand electronic signature software can be challenged in court, which is why you should have an electronic signatures clause in your standard contacts (see below). Ensure that any electronic signature software can provide an audit trail and other documentation to prove that the person clicking and "signing" their name was, in fact, the right person. The use of encrypted digital signatures can reduce a lot of these risks, but the cost and hassle factor may not be worth it to most in-house legal departments.

There are dozens of electronic signature vendors out there. Who you choose probably depends on what you need. For some, faxed and scanned signatures are good enough and there is little reason to change. For others, they want a provable signature audit trail and/or password features that only allow a signature with the use of a password. Some want the full scope of protections the digital signature experience offers. As in-house counsel, you should find a company that has an impeccable reputation and that can scale with the needs of your company.

If you think your company is ready to adopt electronic signatures (or enhance an already existing program), here is a to-do list to guide you.

Electronic Signature To-Do List

- ☐ Know the applicable law for your jurisdiction(s).
- ☐ Go slow. If you are just starting out, don't feel you have to hurry to implement electronic signatures. Start small, work out the bugs, then scale the process.
- ☐ Get help. The legal department should not be the lone department when it comes to implementing an electronic signature program. To do things right, it will take a cross-functional team including IT, human resources, sales, finance, and other impacted groups. Like any major tech project, you will need to do a lot of investigating your

options on the front end, and then create a project plan to implement and roll out the program.

- ☐ Create a company-wide electronic signature policy with rules and guidelines.
- ☐ Use a reputable electronic signature tool/vendor. (Decide whether or not you need a digital signature tool as well.)
- ☐ Build an electronically signed contract repository, and ensure that you keep and maintain the audit trail to prove the signatures for each contract should that ever become an issue.
- ☐ Add electronic signature language to your contracts. Here's a sample clause I like because it pretty much covers everything:

"*This Agreement and other documents to be delivered pursuant to this Agreement may be executed in one or more counterparts, each of which will be deemed to be an original copy and all of which, when taken together, will be deemed to constitute one and the same agreement or document, and will be effective when counterparts have been signed by each of the parties and delivered to the other parties. Each party agrees that the electronic signatures, whether digital or encrypted, of the parties included in this Agreement are intended to authenticate this writing and to have the same force and effect as manual signatures. Delivery of a copy of this Agreement or any other document contemplated hereby, bearing an original manual or electronic signature by facsimile transmission (including a facsimile delivered via the Internet), by electronic mail in portable document format (".pdf") or similar format intended to preserve the original graphic and pictorial appearance of a document, or through the use of electronic signature software will have the same effect as physical delivery of the paper document bearing an original signature.*"

Anything that helps get contracts done faster and with less friction is exactly the kind of achievement legal departments should be proud to brag about and use as a way to show value. Implementing an electronic signatures tool is one way to do just that.

Technology that Matters: Artificial Intelligence

Artificial intelligence (AI) is beginning to come into its own in terms of uses by lawyers. While there is more noise than real achievement at the moment, we are on the cusp of a revolution in the practice of law, which the adoption of AI technology is leading—in particular by in-house lawyers. Much like email changed the way we do business every day, AI will become ubiquitous, an indispensable assistant to practically every lawyer. That said, the term artificial intelligence can be a bit misleading, at least when it comes to application in the legal field. Perhaps a better description, and one that is catching on, is "cognitive computing." This means computers learning how to complete tasks people do traditionally, where the focus is on looking for patterns in data, testing the data, and finding/providing results. Put another way, a research assistant who can sift through an incredible amount of data and tell you what it found. The ability of any human to review and comprehend the same level of data without help is, to be blunt, impossible.

AI is the science of teaching computers how to learn, reason, perceive, infer, communicate, and make decisions like humans do. The initial goal is called machine learning, where a computer begins to make decisions with minimal programming. Instead of manually writing rules for how the computer should interpret a set of data, machine learning algorithms (i.e., instructions for solving particular problems) allow the computer to determine the rules itself. Ultimately, computers become better at their tasks with experience. Cognitive computing requires three core processes: 1) gather information, 2) analyze and try to understand the information, and 3) make decisions based on this understanding. As all lawyers know from experience, this process is iterative. We become better the more times we undertake the task, especially if we are corrected and guided in our work by someone more experienced (just like being a young associate at a law firm). It works exactly the same way with AI. This matters for in-house lawyers because AI has the potential to solve two huge problems all legal departments face: 1) lack of budget and 2) lack of manpower. If the use of AI can provide less expensive legal services (either used internally or purchased through a law firm), the value-add for the company is immediately apparent. In fact, if the use of AI can free up current legal staff from spending time on run-of-the-mill transactional tasks, the value is exponentially greater than merely paying less for legal services. Freeing up in-house attorney time gives the business more access to better and more involved legal services (i.e., in-house attorneys who can dedicate more time to thinking through problems and advising clients). The combination of these benefits will allow in-house legal departments to actually deliver on the persistent CEO/CFO demand of doing more with less.

Currently, the AI technology most in-house lawyers are familiar with involves e-discovery. Originally, the use of AI here was pretty simple, looking for keywords in megabytes of data. Doing this saved in-house lawyers an amazing amount of time and money that would otherwise be spent paying other lawyers to find relevant documents. Later, AI was used to eliminate duplicate documents and connect strings of emails, again doing in minutes that would take days if people did it. Finally, AI is now capable of searching discovery documents for context, concepts, and tone with what is known as predictive coding, going far beyond simple keyword searches. You still need lawyers, but you no longer need an army of them. The bigger impact, however, comes from how in-house legal departments use or will use AI for other tasks. The incentive for in-house legal departments to find the lowest cost way to do things is greater than the incentive for law firms to find ways to offer lower-priced services (i.e., quantity of billable hours versus quality of a billable hour). As a result, in-house legal teams will likely lead the way in finding and demanding new and better uses of artificial intelligence products. Here are some of the things AI can do (or will do) for in-house legal departments that will disrupt the legal market for years to come:

- Due diligence reviews. Due diligence reviews for a corporate transaction typically involve a large group of lawyers going through documents (hard copy or in an e-room) looking for litigation issues, key contract clauses, corporate governance, intellectual property, etc. Generally, it takes many hands (usually outside counsel) and many hours/days to complete. AI can do this in a fraction of the time.
- Prepare contracts. The Holy Grail for in-house lawyers who draft contracts is the ability to create and use a form agreement, meaning one that has standard terms and conditions and allows limited changes/customization. Form contracts are huge time savers and allow the company to have a consistent set of agreements. There are AI tools that can create contracts, using whatever set of parameters the legal department feels important. Moreover, the tool can be set up as self service for clients, i.e., the client can log onto the system, select the type of contract they need, enter in a few variables, and the system will produce a standard form agreement ready to go. The bigger step forward will be when these AI contract tools can (1) prepare the initial draft of redlines when the legal department is forced to review the customer's form contract to make the sale; or (2) review and analyze redlines the other party made and tell the in-house lawyers (based on a playbook or set of programmed parameters) whether the redlines are acceptable and, if not, what they need to change.
- Contract management. Historically, contract management is done manually. Someone either creates a spreadsheet and tracks everything by hand, or enters the data manually into a system that manages the key terms and dates automatically. AI has progressed to the point where the entry of the key information, such as parties, terms, dates, and other information can be done by the computer—without the need for human intervention (other than initial set up and fine-tuning). In fact, contract management—including an electronic signature process—can be managed as part of the same tool that creates the contracts, meaning an automated process from start to signature to storage.
- Legal spend/legal operations analysis. Most legal departments have or are moving to e-billing systems. There is an incredible wealth of information

in the e-billing system, but many in-house lawyers are not good at extracting the information in a useful manner. AI provides the capability to analyze what work was done, how it aligns with other work done by that firm, how that firm's work/efficiency compares with work provided by other firms, and how your firms' work/efficiency compares to the market generally. Imagine being armed with this information the next time you want to discuss billing rates with your law firms.

- Litigation analysis. There is an amazing amount of data in the U.S. court system's public records. Opinions and orders of courts, jury verdicts, and other valuable information generally are fully available. AI is providing technology to extract and analyze this information and providing predictions about the outcome of litigation (or even motions).
- Wrong doing detection. Taking the concept of predictive coding further, it is now possible to utilize AI to search company records (documents, emails, and even unstructured data) to detect bad behavior before it can bubble to the surface. AI is being used to sniff out bribery, fraud, compliance issues, even potential litigation—all based on the content of the company's own documents and data. AI can summarize conversations, the ideas discussed, note the frequency of the communications, and even the mood of the speakers.
- Legal research. In-house lawyers generally shortchange the research process because they don't want to spend the time or money to do a complete job. Or, they overpay either in terms of time they spend on a relatively mundane task or by paying a law firm to flail away on the question. AI tools will soon allow you to ask legal questions in plain English, and get an answer back. An answer that includes research of regulations, case law, secondary sources, etc.[41] Moreover, it may be possible to use AI as a talking FAQ service (chatbot) that can answer basic legal, human resources, and compliance questions from your in-house clients, yet be smart enough to know when to defer the answer to a live attorney. This will provide the ultimate in self-help—and value through disengagement![42]

It is somewhat unsettling to think about how AI will impact jobs in the legal industry. The most likely outcome is some job losses (and some job gains), but the value-added benefit of many lawyers freed from the mundane task of data gathering for the value-added task of analyzing results, thinking, and advising their clients. These are roles that will always require the human touch. AI will help lawyers do this better, faster, and more cost effectively.

---

41 In fact, this is already happening with Thomson Reuter's Practical Law product.

42 *See infra* at page 136 for a discussion about adding value through disengagement by the legal department.

Matthew Francke wrote about several reasons why people should/will never entrust a computer to provide legal advice:

> (1) Good lawyers (like good doctors) will—and need to—take the time to understand their clients, what they are seeking, and why. Judgment is needed as part of providing any legal advice. Computers cannot do this in the same way humans can;
>
> (2) If you have practiced law for any length of time, you already know that there is no Big Book of Law that contains all the answers to legal questions. Many legal issues can rarely be solved by simply looking up a provision in the law. Instead, most of the law is built on precedent where every case had someone arguing the exact opposite of how the case was decided (and it may have been a close call, hinging on one key or obscure fact or other twists). Meaning, things are not black and white and everything needs to be put into context, something computers are unlikely to handle;
>
> (3) Successful business people want to talk to a person, a counselor. This personal relationship cannot be replaced by a computer, and;
>
> (4) It is human nature to try to engineer the answer you want to get from a question. Asking if I can do [x]?" versus should I do [x]? How a question is framed usually puts things in the best possible light to get the desired answer. A human can look at the circumstances, the body language, and other intangibles, along with teasing out the relevant details so that you get not only the answer, but also help with understanding it so that you can accept it and implement it.[43]

Self-Help: Increasing Value Through Non-Engagement

This may be a bit controversial, but I have been thinking about it for awhile now. I propose that the legal department can generate tremendous value for the company by being less involved in the company contracting process. Before you call the men with nets to come and get me, hear me out. I am not suggesting the legal department stop working or check out completely. Rather, this is something else entirely. Something that falls well within the established value of self-help tools that more and more businesses are providing to their customers already.

If there is one thing that the recent pandemic has proven, it is that in-house lawyers and clients do not need to be in the same building together to get things done. This is due, in part, to the many new ways available to collaborate and work remotely. Given the success of this forced separation, it is time to rethink the

43 *See Why You Should Want a Lawyer (and not a Robot)*, available online at https://www.besthooper.com.au/Insights-library/why-you-should-want-a-lawyer-and-not-a-robot/.

historic separation of work between the legal department and its clients. Generally, the business negotiates the contracts and the legal department does the drafting. This has worked well for decades, though the legal department often ends up negotiating contracts along with, or in place of, the business. Nothing wrong with that, if it is the highest and best use of the legal function and the leaders of the business agree that it makes sense. While this separation of duties has worked well for decades, now is the time to rethink it and to align the legal department and the business around a new level of self-help, where the legal department adds value by not engaging (or at least not engaging all the time).

The technology exists today to permit the business—not the lawyers—to build contracts that fit within established contracting parameters and rules (a system the business and the legal team built jointly). When combined with the contract creation technology discussed above, such rules allow anyone with the right permissions to create compliant contracts using standard templates, clauses, and fallback positions. As long as the business colors within the lines there is zero need to come to the legal department for assistance. The legal team only gets involved if the other side wants to negotiate the contract outside of the established lines. The technology handles the creation, review, approval levels, e-signatures, and storage/management of the contract post-signature. The value the legal department creates comes from preparing the templates, clauses, and fallback provisions, training the business on how to use the tools, preparing a negotiation playbook for the business (critical), and staying out of the way (also known as non-engagement). And, once set up and proven, the legal team can refocus its efforts on higher-value and more complex work, work that generates even more value because 1) it is not sent outside to costly outside counsel; and 2) such issues receive more time and attention, driving better outcomes for the company.

On the flip side, the legal department spends a significant amount of time reviewing contracts and other documents that are, in fact, fine to sign as is. The problem is that it takes a good bit of time to determine that a contract is fine as is. And a low-dollar value contract can contain just as many issues as a high-dollar contract. Still, simple math tells us that the better use of legal department time is to focus on the high-dollar value contracts. Yet, the legal team must still review the low-dollar contracts, clogging up resources and usually meaning everything takes longer as there are only so many hands and so many hours in the day. The solution to this problem is fairly straightforward, that is, the legal department creates a checklist that the business can use to review low-dollar contracts. The checklist is designed to spot common problems such as indemnity, lack of limits on damages, confidentiality, data ownership, etc. If the business is properly trained on how to use such a checklist, they can review low-dollar contracts themselves and spot any problematic issues. If the contract has none, they can check the right boxes on the checklist, then the agreement is okay to sign and does not have to go through the legal department. If the business spots an issue on the checklist, then the contract comes to the legal team, but only for review of the limited issue and not the entire contract—a faster process than getting the entire contract to review cold.

To pull this off, the legal team has to invest upfront in creating the checklist(s) and the training program. The checklist can be a paper checklist or technology that automates the process.[44] The business must commit to building up and training the right cadre of individuals authorized to review and sign contracts via this process. And everyone has to get comfortable with a higher level of risk as it is always possible (even when lawyers are involved) that something will get missed. But, the cost-benefit analysis will likely show that the time saved, the ability to divert legal resources to higher-value and higher-priority work, and the consistent training and regular updates of the checklist and training materials will lead to better results and, most importantly, faster contracting due to the legal department not being involved. Additionally, a spot audit process will help increase the quality of the reviews and reduce the risk of serious problems.

Moreover, the business must get on board with the idea that not everything involving a contract requires someone with a law degree to review it. If you can read and write and you understand the company's business, you can handle pretty much most of what goes into preparing and negotiating contracts. The legal department, on the other hand, must get comfortable walking away from the process to some extent, letting the business handle more of the duties around contracts, and living with more risk than it may have historically been comfortable with, but which is at a level acceptable to the business. And the department must demand technology and tools to automate the process, including artificial intelligence and simple, user-friendly interfaces that are self-explanatory and will not scare the business away. This could mean an entirely new market for legal tech vendors as their audience is not just the lawyers, but the business as well.

A sample self-help contract checklist is included in Appendix 2.[45]

Be a Teacher

In the United States, one of the most admired professions is that of a teacher. Good teachers are as beloved as they are hard to find. Smart school districts do everything they can to hold onto such resources. The same is true for businesses. If you are an in-house lawyer who also has the skill and patience to teach things to the business, you have automatically increased your value and that of the legal

44 For the latter, *see* www.summize.com.

45 Huge thanks to London-based Alexis Alexander, general counsel of Liberis, for allowing me to share a version of a contract review checklist we worked on together. Any sensitive or competitive information was removed or changed.

department. Why? Because teaching the business how to avoid problems, how to get deals done, how to stay in compliance with various laws and regulations pays off on the company's bottom line. There are big cost savings you can tie directly to such teaching (and you can quantify the number of teaching sessions, the topics, and, with some thought, the impact). One of the most popular presentations I ever developed for the business was on writing smart. I set out the basics of that presentation next. I think the reason it was so popular was 1) no one had ever talked with the business about the problems with emails and other poorly drafted documents, so my audience would typically realize quickly that they were guilty as charged, and 2) I used real examples from our company's files to show the errors and the problems dumb documents cause (deleting any names or identifying information as I was not out to embarrass anyone). Within one or two examples, people were laughing but they were also learning—and that is what mattered most. All of this is a long-winded way of saying you can show the value of the legal department by getting out among your business colleagues and teaching them how to avoid problems. It is much more effective than yelling at them after a problem has arisen. What follows are some examples of things you can do to be a teacher.

Drafting Smart Documents

Pretty much during any given week you can read a newspaper and read about some trial or investigation turning up damning documents. Usually conveyed in emails, though more frequently text messages, instant messages, or collaboration channels.[46] As in-house counsel, you already know that poorly drafted documents, especially emails, can hurt your company, e.g., litigation extended or settlement on worse terms than if the document never existed. Labels such as "confidential," "company private," "restricted," and "proprietary" will not protect documents from being obtained through the discovery process. Document requests in litigation or government investigations are broad, typically calling for a variety of correspondence, such as handwritten notes, agreements, drafts, emails and email back-ups, calendars, spreadsheets, voice mail, text messages, calendar entries, and so on. I am convinced that if a nuclear war ever does break out, the only things left will be cockroaches and every stupid email you thought had been deleted. Once you write it down, it never truly goes away. Consequently, for any legal department, it is important that their business colleagues understand the importance of properly prepared documents, be they emails, text messages, or whatever.

Little demonstrates the value of the in-house legal department like a well-planned training session. The business not only learns about a problem and how

46 Such as Slack or Teams.

best to solve it/avoid it, but they get to see their lawyers in action. If done right, it is a powerful reinforcement of the department's value message. Teaching the business about how to write smart is the perfect marriage of solving a serious problem and in-house lawyers as teachers. As you develop your program, below are some key messages that you can incorporate into your materials, which will help limit—but not eliminate—problems that can arise from poorly prepared documents. I will focus on emails, but these rules apply to pretty much any written communication, as well as voicemails.

- To start, the business needs to understand that emails are business communications and they must treat them as if they were writing a formal business letter. Many employees and managers are under the false impression that an email is vapor, and once you send it and the person reads it and deletes it, it is gone. Obviously, this is not true. Once you send an email you have no control over whether the person receiving it forwards it, deletes it, or saves it. Likewise, even if deleted, it can reside on backups, in sent files, and even trash on your computer. In other words, it is hard to get rid of something you write electronically. This means the legal department should partner with human resources to prepare and circulate an email and document preparation policy. This policy will explain the problems that can arise from poorly drafted documents and spell out what is expected from employees when preparing any type of work-related communication (emails, Slack, PowerPoint, social media, etc.). Once this policy is prepared and circulated, it is important to get buy-in and reinforcement from the C-Suite.
- It is helpful to convince yourself that all emails and documents company employees prepare (even the legal team), may someday be seen by (hostile) third parties and/or published on page one of *The New York Times*. Consider this when you start to type. Another way to look at it is to pretend that every email you write starts with "Dear Company Suing Us," and then think about how that affects what you write down next. Similarly, do not write emails when you are angry. Take time to cool off. It may feel good at first, but you will inevitably regret firing off an email in the heat of the moment. President Abraham Lincoln used to have a process where he would write down exactly what he felt about something in a letter and then hand it off to his secretary and wait until the next day to revisit the issue. He almost always rewrote the letter with different language and a different tone because he knew that sending the first draft would only make his problems worse. This is still true today. You can adopt something similar with email by typing what you feel and saving it as a draft. You can come back to it in several hours or the next day. Odds are ninety-nine percent you will reconsider what you wrote and put your points into calmer and less angry words. Doing so will serve you and the company well. I have seen way too

many people try to recall a sent email, only to find that there is no such thing as a real recall button. Once it leaves, it is too late.

- If something is a draft, mark it clearly as "Draft: Subject to Revision" on every page. Delete drafts as soon as the next version is ready or, if it's necessary to keep prior drafts, delete drafts when the final version is prepared. First, marking something as a draft gives you the ability to argue that whatever is in the document was not the final decision or action of the company. It was a starting point. If a document is not marked as draft and you try to make this argument, a jury, judge, or regulator may have a hard time believing you. Likewise, avoid absolute or dogmatic statements. Things are rarely black and white in the world of business, or the world generally. Use words like "usually," "sometimes," "mostly," "apparently," and so on to show nuance and that circumstances matter. Slide presentations in particular, lend themselves to short, declarative sentences. When the document is flashed on a big screen in front of a judge or jury or the Department of Justice, it is difficult to now say you meant sometimes. That may have been what you meant, but it is not what you wrote. Give yourself some wiggle room if appropriate.
- Do not speculate on legal issues unless you are a member of the legal department or you are writing to a member of the legal department. Let the lawyers be the ones to draw legal conclusions. The business team should stick to facts. For example, do not write, "We clearly breached the contract here." First, you may not be aware of all of the different contractual obligations between the parties and how to correctly interpret the agreement based on the facts. Second, you may not have all of the facts. Third, there is little you can do to walk that statement back in a deposition or at trial and you will look foolish or worse trying to do so. Do not play amateur lawyer. If you need legal advice, ask the legal department directly. Be sure it is clear in the body of the email you are seeking legal advice to best maintain any applicable privilege.
- Unfortunately, one of the hardest lessons for business people and in-house lawyers to learn is that no matter how funny you may be in real life, regulators, judges, and juries will not appreciate the humor in your emails, texts, and so on. These are business documents. Everyone must treat them like it. The same thing goes for humor and funny pictures in presentations. These can and will be taken out of context by the other side in a dispute and you will be left explaining what you meant. If you are explaining in litigation, you are losing. Boring is always better when it comes to business documents. This is why you should also avoid gung-ho statements such as, "dominate the market," "destroy a competitor," "leverage our dominant position," or "impede a competitor/competition" to give a few examples. These types of statements may get the testosterone pumped up at a meeting

but they can and will come back to bite you in court. The same goes for project names, which, for some reason, business people think need to be funny or convey some hidden meaning. The problem is, if there is litigation, that hidden meaning will be used like a club by the other side regardless of what you intended with the project name. For example, "Project Pitbull" may be funny to you, but will not be funny to the jury. I preferred it when project names were simply year and number, e.g., Project 2021-01 or Project 2021-16. Remember, boring is better when it comes to business documents.

There are plenty of ways to mess up a business document. Perhaps the absolute worst is to send an email that includes asking the recipient to destroy or delete emails/documents after reading. Including this language will likely lead to things far more damaging to the company than whatever was in the email you were trying to have deleted. (Also, ask yourself why you are sending an email that should be deleted.) To be blunt, there is no walking back from telling someone to destroy a document. No matter how hard you try to explain what you meant, it will only sound like you are trying to weasel out of responsibility for what you wrote. Almost as bad is sending a document containing attorney-client communication outside of the company. Once this is done, the privilege is likely waived for that document. It becomes fair game for the other side and, potentially, doing so may open up other privileged documents to discovery. If so, congratulations, we have now moved from merely dumb to disaster. The only cure for this problem is to spend time teaching the business about how privileged communications work. Here is a checklist of the key issues when it comes to writing anything related to the business.

Smart Document Checklist

- ☐ Stick to facts.
- ☐ Be boring—everything is a business document.
- ☐ No off-color jokes or profanity.
- ☐ Do not disparage customers or vendors.
- ☐ Do not disparage coworkers.
- ☐ Never tell anyone to delete or destroy documents.
- ☐ Do not speculate on legal issues or liability.
- ☐ Assume anything you write will never be deleted and will be used against you and the company in litigation.
- ☐ No gung-ho statements.
- ☐ Do write emails when you are angry.
- ☐ Mark draft documents as draft.

Despite your efforts, people will make mistakes in documents and emails. It does not mean they are bad people. More likely, they were not thinking about what they were writing and how it may be perceived down the road. As in-house counsel, you need to stay vigilant and keep working with the business to make sure they understand how harmful bad documents can be to your company. Communicate regularly with them about this issue, do live training at staff meetings or large gatherings of employees (webcasts work, too). Use real examples from the headlines or company documents to bring home points.[47] The business will value the help and advice—especially once they understand the litany of bad things that can happen. And you will sleep better knowing the quality and tone of your company's business documents will improve.

Help Them Get Contracts Through Legal Quickly

A common question you will hear as in-house counsel is "Why does it take so long for you guys to review my contract?" (Second only to, "Why are our contracts so damn long?") The answer, as you suspect, is complicated. Legal is a limited resource, typically a small team that reviews hundreds, possibly thousands, of contracts in a given year. While a lot of contracts are fairly routine, many involve complicated provisions or transactions with millions of dollars on the line. Sometimes you have to create a contract from scratch, meaning you do not have a form or something to easily model from. Frequently, things like litigation or large M&A deals take up substantial amounts of lawyer time—time that cannot be spent on contracts. Finally, legal generally will prioritize contracts based on the strategic objectives of the business. Deals that better support the strategy/objectives get more attention more quickly. From an administrative viewpoint, you have to make considerations when people are out on vacation or ill. Unfortunately, giving it to somebody else is difficult. A new attorney will not have the history or understanding of the business deal necessary to finish the contract quickly Also, they would need to reprioritize their workload to handle the deal, meaning someone else's project will get less or no attention.

As the perceived lack of speed with contract turnover can diminish the legal department's value proposition, it is important that in-house lawyers educate the

---

47 *See, e.g.*, a recent *The Wall Street Journal* story on the start of the opioid trial on Long Island involving pharmaceutical companies. The plaintiffs opened by showing the jury emails from pharma employees mocking customers as "pillbillies" and with a "funny" picture of Kellogg's Honey Smacks cereral photoshopped as "Killogg's Smack" with the cartoon character holding a syringe. *See* online story *New York Opioid Trial Opens Wwth Emails Joking About Epidemic*, THE WALL STREET JOURNAL, June 29, 2021, *https://www.wsj.com/articles/new-york-opioid-trial-opens-with-emails-joking-about-epidemic-11625001834?mod=djemRiskCompliance*. None of these documents were needed to advance the business interests of the respective companies.

business on all of these issues. Moreover, if you can teach the business certain key steps regarding contracts, you can help them help you, i.e., hasten the contracting process by allowing them to take some ownership in ensuring things are done with speed in mind.

To start, if one is available, teach the business to always use the company's form agreement and to be willing to insist that the other side do so. Nothing saves contracting time like sticking with a well-vetted form agreement. Nothing adds time like drafting a custom contract or using the other side's standard procurement agreement, which will require hours of redlining and negotiating to cover the services or products the company is providing (something the company's form agreements do nicely.) As discussed earlier, this is the perfect time to consider hosting contract boot camps, where in-house lawyers meet with a large group of clients and walk through one of the company's applicable form contracts section-by-section. This includes providing the business with an annotated version of the contract spelling out the what and the why of section provision. This is great for developing relationships and helping the business understand why the contract is like it is. It also provides quality feedback to the legal team, helping them to shorten the contract, change terms, rewrite provisions to be more market and easier to understand. In other words, you'll create a form agreement customers will more easily accept.

To truly partner with the legal team, the business must read and understand the business and deal terms of the proposed contract. Any business person negotiating contracts should understand the terms of their deal and what the other side is proposing. Do not let them get away with asking the legal team if the contract looks okay and then run off and hide. Require that they read the term sheet and contract drafts and understand their deal. Most importantly, they must know how the deal can make money or lose money. To pull this off, in-house lawyers must invest an hour or two with some of their clients to help them to understand the contract, teach the negotiating process, and their role in helping get deals done. They will likely appreciate the attention. (In fact, this may be the first time anyone has ever sat down with them and walked them through the process.) Additionally, as the client becomes savvier in their business dealings and negotiating prowess, their use of the legal function will be much more efficient (saving time and dollars).

Emphasize that the company's many different business units/staff groups may need to sign off on a contract, e.g., finance, tax, human resources, insurance, product development, operations, etc. The business must drive this process, not the lawyers. It does not require a law degree to ask finance if they are okay with the relevant terms of the proposed contract. Consequently, the business person/team assigned to the deal should ensure all key groups are signed off on the agreement, especially when work is required by that group to fulfill the agreement. They should not assume that the legal department is taking care of this basic contract legwork. That said, the legal team definitely adds value when it helps the business navigate this process and spots situations where the ball got dropped and moves to help fix it before it is too late. In other words, while it is not the legal department's job, do not let the contract fall apart or not get signed because the business failed to do its job. When in-house lawyers spot issues, legal or otherwise, raise them and use this situation as a teaching moment for the business. Put the counsel back into legal counsel.

In most companies, there is a lot of demand for legal services, but there are only so many lawyers. Rarely, does a legal department have all of the resources it needs to do all the work on its plate. As a result, your business clients must understand that the department has to balance the needs of many competing contracts and other projects. The math is simple, working on contract A, necessarily means less resource and time to work on contract B. To do its job, the legal team must constantly make judgment calls on what gets its attention and when. That said, be willing (in fact, invite your clients) to discuss how contracts are prioritized in the department. Have and keep open communication with the various business leaders about what is important to the business. Be open to changing priorities based on these conversations. Align with the business, get agreement, and focus the department's efforts on what the business sees as priorities. One way to do this is to start each week by asking each business leader in the company to identify their top two"[48] priorities for the week. Tell them that the legal department will take steps to prioritize these projects over other projects. It does not mean the department will ignore other legal work, but it will show that the in-house team is listening to the business and prioritizing the things the business believes are important. Nothing demonstrates value more than the business believing that its in-house legal team is focused on the right priorities and is listening to the business.

If the business will be discussing or exchanging confidential information, teach them to always put a non-disclosure agreement (NDA) in place that covers the discussions. To make this as easy as possible, the legal department should have a short, standard-form NDA available to the business that can be used with little, if any, involvement of the legal team. Create an NDA that is fair and balanced, make it easy for the other side to agree to it. Otherwise you will find yourself redlining and negotiating an NDA, which is not a productive way to spend valuable attorney time. As mentioned earlier, make the form NDA available on the department intranet site with a link or button that is prominently displayed so the business can spot it easily. Tell the business that if used unaltered, they do not need to involve the in-house legal team other than to provide it with a copy of the signed NDA. This is a great transition to a related point, when to involve the legal team. The message to the business should be to get in-house lawyers involved early in the contracting process to avoid fire drills. Even though the business

48 There is nothing magical about two. It could be one, three, or whatever makes the most sense. You do need to keep the number small or else everything becomes a priority, which does little to help the department prioritize deals.

seems to love emailing you at 5:00 p.m., asking you to give the sixty-page contract they want to sign in the morning a quick look to see if there are any issues. There is rarely a quick legal review. There are simply too many minefields in most contracts, regardless of value or length, for in-house lawyers to give anything a quick look and a thumbs up. Planning ahead minimizes pain for all involved. Teach the business to build in time upfront to go over legal and business comments, recognizing additional changes may be needed before the next draft goes out to the other side. Additionally, if the other side sat on the contract for two weeks and just returned an intensely marked-up document, set expectations that it is not reasonable to expect the legal team to turn it around in a few hours or overnight. I know from experience this is nice in theory, but all in-house lawyers know that sometimes regardless of how much time the other side took, the business will demand that you turn the agreement quickly. However, if you speak with the business about this issue in advance they tend to advocate for reasonable turnaround times with the other side instead of advocating for a time frame the other side set.

Another key teaching point is deciding in advance how much the deal is worth in terms of time and concessions. For example, if a party to a $25,000 contract sends back redlines to the entire agreement, the business must align with the legal team to tell the other side to either sign it or not, or to pick their top three or four issues and that is it. It comes down to this: how much time and legal resource can the company spend on a $25,000 deal? This is often easier to say than enforce in practice. To a front-line salesperson, a $25,000 deal might be huge in terms of meeting their sales goals for the year. And if the customer wants to redline every page in the draft, generally they do not see why this is a problem and expect the in-house lawyers to engage fully. Obviously, for the company, this is not a smart use of legal resources. To prevent these awkward discussions, have the talk about the number of changes before the contract goes out the door. And do so not only with the salesperson, but also with their supervisor. Get alignment upfront about the problem of sucking up a disproportionate amount of legal resources to get a small contract across the finish line. If you cannot get alignment, my trick was to go to the head of the sales team and ask him or her which agreements did they want us to stop working on so we could spend hours and hours on the $25,000 deal. That usually cleared things up for everyone involved pretty quickly. Another idea is to have a small law firm or solo lawyer available for overflow deals where the money spent with them can be justified in terms of the volume of deals they can get through, while leaving the more complicated and strategic contracts for the in-house team (contracts where the value of the in-house lawyer can really shine through). Sometimes you can even get the business to pay for the overflow lawyer.

One consistent hurdle to getting contracts done faster is the failure of the business to provide the in-house legal team with the right information at the beginning of the project. Invest time in teaching the business what core materials they need to provide to get the contract process off on the right foot.

- term sheet;
- any presentations discussing the parameters of the deal;
- the history of the deal (including key emails);
- concerns the business has about the deal; and
- any important issues (good or bad) that may have arisen in the past with the other side or that have arisen over the course of the negotiations to date.

The legal department can move contracts along much faster, and draft a better agreement, if it knows about any issues upfront instead of several drafts down the line. That said, whether in-house lawyers consistently get all of the materials will be hit or miss. If materials are missing, use your best judgment to determine if you can get what you need simply from the materials you do have in hand, or if you need a call or meeting with the business. If possible, stop by the business person's office, and get what you need. That will inevitably lead to a helpful conversation about the deal, and the personal touch will pay off in terms of how the business views you and your approach to getting things done.

While in-house lawyers know that the business wants to be helpful when it comes to the contracting process, one thing that usually is highly counterproductive is when the business drafts the contract themselves, using something they found on the internet or, worse, using a highly negotiated existing contract as a template.[49] While they, and sometimes their counterpart at the other company, may think they have helped to speed things up by drafting the contract themselves, they have likely missed a lot of issues and their draft will need to be substantially amended, such as limits of liability, warranties, indemnities, and so forth. The contracting process actually will go faster if you teach the business to stick to getting to a preliminary agreement on the high-level terms (i.e., a non-binding term sheet), but let the lawyers draft the actual contract using the term sheet as the starting point.

Everybody is excited when a deal is signed and the parties are getting their business relationship underway. What is often forgotten is the process by which the contract comes to an end, such as expiration of the term, material breach, a

49 Using an existing, heavily negotiated contract can cause plenty of problems. Typically, the company may have given in on certain issues due to the negotiating leverage of the other party or if circumstances demanded that the deal get done regardless of what the company needed to give up to get it across the finish line. Using such an agreement as a starting point means that the company has likely lost those issues as it will be hard to negotiate backwards off language already offered to the other party. In a worst-case scenario, it can even mean starting over with the right version or form which will probably make the other side mad. And it is not like they will not forget what clauses and language they saw in the other contract—they will still expect the company to deal on those terms.

wind-down provision, or other triggers. Ensure that the business is spending time upfront thinking about how they want to see the relationship end as, inevitably, it will. Then, the in-house lawyer's job is to make sure things are clearly spelled out in the contract and that the business will not be unexpectedly impacted in a negative way when the agreement ends. Work with the business on the endgame at the beginning, and figure out how to structure the deal to mitigate negative impacts. The one thing you do not want to hear is someone ask,"How in the hell did we end up with a contract that ends like this?"

To sum up, it is important to discuss the contracting process with the business and set expectations with them as to their role and what you need from them to make the process work for everyone. It takes teamwork from both the legal department and the business to make the process work properly. Do not underestimate the power of a short meeting or a quick phone call to solve problems quickly (Instead of long email threads). You will find people much more reasonable when you have them on the phone or in a room and you are discussing how you can help them and how they can help you. If the business understands why there is a delay, or why certain provisions of the contract are needed or do not work, you will find they are far more willing to wait and to help you than if you kept them in the dark.

Teach the Business How to Read a Contract

If you think about it, when it comes to contracts, the input of the business is critical. Yet, in many circumstances, business people stay away from reviewing and marking up contracts under the mistaken belief that this is legal's job and not something the business should be doing. When faced with this reluctance, I usually said something to the effect of, "Hey, it's in English and it is discussing your deal, you should be able to read it, understand it, and help draft it. Your helping me can only make it better and get it done faster." That last part usually got the attention of the sales team member I was working with because they knew that getting a contract done faster meant signatures and that meant commissions. Regardless of the motivation, I was happy to have the help. Well, I mostly was.[50] When I first started as an in-house lawyer, one thing I quickly realized is that most business people have no idea how to read a contract. Actually, many in-

---

50 I also remember distinctly a contract negotiation where my co-negotiator on the sales team had not read the contract and knew nothing of the terms of the deal. In the room, he started advocating the positions of the other side. I asked for a break, pulled him outside the room, and told him to pack up his [expletive] and go get on a plane back home because he was done for the deal. He did exactly that. I got the deal done, and we later became pretty good friends. He acknowledged he should have prepared for the deal and that I did him a favor sending him home so he would learn that lesson. My finest teacher moment? Probably not, as this will not work in most situations but it sure worked for me this one time.

house lawyers do not know how to read a contract, but that is for another book. One way you can be a teacher in a way that has a meaningful impact, both on the ability to get more done as well as on how favorably the business thinks of the legal department, is to spend time teaching the business about contracts. In particular, how to read one.

Start with teaching them that contracts are a different type of animal and are unlike any other type of writing you have ever seen before. Those other formats are structured with the intent that you read them front to back, sequentially, with introductions, transitions, summaries, and more. Contracts, on the other hand, are structured to collect certain related provisions together, with all sorts of cross-references and other tricky stuff in there (including the use of defined terms and documents incorporated by reference.) This structure is not intuitive, which means that your head will explode like that guy in the movie *Scanners* if you try to read a complex contract carefully, from front to back, and expect to understand it on just the first read-through. That is wishful thinking (and potentially very messy). Instead, think of contracts like a nice big, juicy algebra problem. And, like algebra, it takes practice to get it down.

The best advice anyone ever gave me about reading contracts was to print them out and not try to read them on a computer screen. Seriously. Time to fire up the printer. If you try to read a complex contract online only, your head may once again explode. Most contracts require you to flip around a lot, especially when you are dealing with many defined terms. So, step one is to print out a hard copy of the contract. Then make a separate copy of the defined terms and use it as a glossary. This is much easier than trying to read the contract on a computer screen or continually flipping back to the definitions page. Fortunately, all commercial contracts have the same basic categories of stuff, typically:

- ☐ Preamble: Gives the name of the contract (e.g., Master Services Agreement), the names of the parties, and the date entered into.
- ☐ Recitals: These background sections are supposed to provide context for the contract (though rarely do so in any useful manner—but where else will you ever see the word "whereas" unless you are a member of Congress or Parliament?). I prefer to get rid of recitals, but most lawyers want them because they feel they are supposed to be there. If so, spend some time making sure the recitals set out the background correctly and, if you think they are important to your deal, add a provision stating they are part of the operative terms of the agreement. Otherwise, courts tend to view recitals as subordinate to the operative provisions of the agreement, or worse, not part of the contract at all.
- ☐ Defined terms: Think of these terms like formulas you will need for your algebra equation. The written meaning of a defined term (usually capitalized words in a contract) tells you what that term means for the purposes of the contract. For example, "cost of production" may have a customary

meaning in the industry your company operates, but what is written as the definition in the contract controls what that term actually means in your deal. Consequently, the guts of any complex deal usually turn on the defined terms and you need to understand them and make sure they are correct for your purposes. Moreover, defined terms, like those Russian nesting dolls, often rest within lots of other defined terms, and have carve outs for other defined terms. When this happens, you move from algebra to calculus.

- ☐ Term and termination: How long does the contract last? Under what circumstances can it be extended or terminated early? Often the stated term will be in one section and the early termination provisions will be in another section. As to the latter, one thing that is typically important to most companies is how to get out of the deal if it stinks. This is a place you're going to want to wallow in the details. Also, watch out for ambiguity around dates/times (termination, notice, etc.). Make things simple, and state something like "This agreement terminates at 11:59 pm central standard time (CST) on October 21, 2022." This way, the time and date of the action are clear.
- ☐ Representations and warranties: These are promises that certain statements of fact in the contract are true. Make sure what you promise as true in a contract is a promise you can keep. Regarding warranties, parties typically set out expressly what they will warrant about the product or service and then expressly disclaim any other warranties (including implied warranties) to the extent permitted by law.
- ☐ Covenants: These are promises made by each party about what they will do under the contract. For example, a vendor typically agrees to provide services or goods. Their customer generally agrees to pay. You should generally look to the business folks to know they can deliver what is promised, but if you ever have doubts, take steps to confirm that the company can indeed deliver.
- ☐ Conditions: These are not promises about facts or about what the parties will do. Instead, they are qualifiers. For example, a contract may have conditions that, if not satisfied by a given date, result in termination of the contract.
- ☐ Payment: Typically, there is a section for the payment provisions. Look closely at what happens if payment is late or is missed. And if your company is the one getting paid, be sure the contract addresses what happens if payment is late or missed (especially around termination rights and the ability to recoup the cost to collect what is owed).
- ☐ Risk allocation: This is one of the most important sections in a contract. Indemnification, for example, is an allocation between contract parties about which one of them bears the risk of specified third-party claims.

Other ways risk is allocated between the parties include waivers of certain types of damages (e.g., punitive, lost profits, consequential, etc.), limits on liability (e.g., the value of the contract or some multiple thereof), mandated insurance coverages, and hold harmless clauses (clauses that release and hold harmless one of the parties from liability to the other). As a lawyer, you need to carefully read and understand the risk allocation provisions, because if something goes wrong these provisions will limit recovery to some extent.

- ☐ Boilerplate: These are the standard legal provisions, such as governing law, choice of forum, dispute resolution processes, notice, assignment, confidentiality, force majeure, etc. Many lawyers make the mistake of thinking they can gloss over the boilerplate. Wrong. There are actually a lot of traps for the unwary here.
- ☐ Exhibits and schedules: Crucial information, such as the description of services, service level agreements, or pricing, often is tucked away in exhibits and schedules to the contract. These require the full attention of the business and the lawyers.

Teach the business the three passes approach to reading a contract. When reading a commercial contract for the first time, try approaching it in three passes, where you dive deeper into the material with each pass:

- First Pass: This is a high-level scan of the document. Do not read it too carefully, just get a good sense of how the contract is structured and where all the stuff outlined above is located.
- Second Pass: Now, go through the contract more carefully. Start with the defined terms and read them carefully once through. Then make a careful second pass through the contract. When a defined term uses another defined term, stop at that place in the sentence and flip to the other defined term. If necessary, use some scratch paper to diagram relationships among defined terms and take notes. Understanding defined terms is often crucial to understanding the contract. Keep your glossary of defined terms handy. As you read the rest of the contract, if the use of a defined term in a sentence doesn't seem to make sense, check your glossary. Keep making notes on observations and questions as you read.
- Third Pass: Skim back through the defined terms now that you have read the contract more carefully, and see if your understanding of any of them has changed. Find the term and termination provisions and make sure they make sense and fit your deal. Next, focus on the payment provisions (same process). Then make a pass through the balance of the provisions in whatever order makes sense to you.

Now you are ready to discuss the contract with others. You will come to the discussion with questions as contracts *always* have ambiguity, early drafts *always* have mistaken, and *all* contracts ultimately require interpretation. But you will come to the discussion prepared and with a view of where to go next.

A really challenging task when reading a contract is figuring out what is missing. This can be tricky, like trying to prove a negative, but it is important to watch out for what is *missing* as you read through the contract. One thing that can help a lot is a checklist, either one you create on your own or one in use generally by the legal department. This list should contain key deal terms your company needs to see (or *not* see) in every contract. Another idea is simply to stop and think about all the things that can go wrong, no matter how improbable, and whether there are provisions that deal with your list of horrors. Alternatively, there may be a section that purports to deal with an issue but the discussion is incomplete. You may need to fix it. Part of your goal when reading a contract is to think through any such provisions and ensure they get edited to get the job done the way you/the company want it done.

As you read through a contract, watch out for some big potential high-risk clauses:

- Most favored nation (MFN) clause: An MFN requires a party to offer the same services, products, prices, or whatever on the same terms and conditions they offer it to any other party or category of parties. Watch out for anyone trying to impose such a requirement on your company or, if you're offering one, that the company is truly prepared to give it and understands the repercussions.
- Exclusivity: Does the contract require exclusivity on the part of one party/both parties? Is the company truly prepared to do that? Is there any whiff of competition law problems with your exclusivity provision (same for MFNs)?
- Liquidated damages: You should always pause whenever you see a liquidated damages provision in a contract. These clauses provided for a fixed amount of damages for breach of the agreement or some specific term.
- Subcontractors: Does the contract permit or prohibit subcontractors? Depending on how your company operates, this can be an issue. If subcontracting is permitted, be sure the company is protected in the event the subcontractor fails to perform properly.
- Service levels: Does the contract require or lack service levels, i.e., metrics of performance where failure to meet them results in a penalty of some nature? Again, it depends on whether you are giving or getting them but, regardless of which side you are on, ensure that any contract containing an SLA provides for service levels you can live with along with acceptable remedies in the event the levels are not met.

Many contracts start as form agreements. This means there are likely blanks to fill in. As you read, watch for those, and make sure you note them and that they are properly completed when the time comes. On the other hand, you must also watch out for documents and other agreements incorporated by reference into the contract. Many short contracts include hyperlinks to web pages. Unfortunately, you will need to gather up and read through the relevant web pages to ensure you understand how they embellish and impact the contract you are reading. Skipping this step is not an option. And watch out for language that gives the other side the right to unilaterally change the incorporated documents (e.g., terms and conditions incorporated via a hyperlink). At a minimum, ensure there is a termination right if any such changes would materially impact the company's benefits or obligations under the core contract.

A step that many gloss over is ensuring that the right parties are entering into the contract, i.e., teach the business to be sure the parties signing the contract are the parties who will provide or accept/pay for the services, goods, or whatever (or, if not, that the contract spells out the relationships). This includes not only the preamble but, more importantly, the signature block. This can be very important when one party ends up in a potential bankruptcy situation or there is trouble and litigation is brewingwhen having the right parties on the hook matters. Here are some other things to teach the business to watch out for as you read through a contract:

- ☐ Whenever you see the phrase "provided, however" or "provided" this flags that you are about to read an exception to the contract rule you just finished reading.
- ☐ If you see a phrase "notwithstanding the foregoing" or "notwithstanding any provision to the contrary," this flags that you are about to read a rule that trumps all other contract rules on that topic.
- ☐ The phrase "for the avoidance of doubt," means the contract author really, really, really wants to make sure there is absolutely and emphatically no confusion on whatever comes next.
- ☐ Watch out for double negatives. Sometimes it helps to diagram these to make sure you understand exactly what the contract says. Ultimately, you may need to rewrite the sentence with the double negative so the meaning is clear.
- ☐ If you think a sentence is ambiguous, ask yourself whether that ambiguity helps the company or hurts the company. If it hurts the company, ask yourself whether you have the leverage to clarify it in negotiations. If not, do not raise the issue in negotiations because, if you do, it will only get clarified against you.
- ☐ Contract sentences can be long. Dreadfully long. So, mark the logical breaks in long sentences, and work section-by-section. Then put the sentence back together as you read back through it.

Teaching the business how to read contracts may be one of the single most valuable things a legal department can do to help the business, enhance value, and minimize value destruction. Make it part of your legal department's value checklist.

Give Them a Contract Playbook

Above, I make mention numerous times about the value of a contract playbook. Especially one tailored for use by the business. It is one thing to teach the business how to read a contract and how contracts work, but it is a completely different matter to teach them how to negotiate a contract. That is where a contract playbook comes in. The value of a negotiation playbook is that it allows everyone in the legal department, executive team, and the sales organization to understand which contracts are acceptable to the company and which contracts the company will walk away from. Despite this value, only twenty-five percent of in-house legal departments use playbooks. Consequently, one quick and effective way to add value is to create playbooks and teach the business how to use them to negotiate contracts. Not only will you get better contracts, the legal department can be less engaged in the process as the recipe for a good contract is set out in the playbook.

A contract playbook is a document that, in some fashion, breaks down the company's standard contract terms, sets out an explanation of each clause along with fallback clauses (i.e., variations of the standard clauses that the company would accept if the customer wants to negotiate a standard clause), and notes when the company will walk away from a contract. The last part means the customer/other party is insisting on changes to the standard contract that the company cannot accept based on risk-management, economic reasons, or some other criteria. While companies want to sell their products or services to as many customers as possible, they will only do so to the extent the contract makes financial and other sense to the company (e.g., acceptable limitations of liability). A properly prepared contract playbook allows the legal and business teams to stay aligned and close contracts faster (or know when it is time to walk).

The benefits of a contract playbook are numerous:

- A playbook aligns key groups such as legal, sales, and finance up front and makes it more likely they will stick together and not snipe at each other throughout the contracting process. If you have worked on enough contract negotiations, you know there is little more frustrating than when the sales team becomes an advocate for the customer's contract positions versus the company's position. A playbook can help solve this.
- A playbook is a lifesaver to new attorneys joining the department because they can get quickly up to speed on the parameters of the company's contract negotiation positions. It also captures years of legal department tribal knowledge about the contracting process. Similarly, a playbook helps reduce renegades, i.e., those lawyers or business people who want to do things "their way" which may not be the best way.
- A playbook helps your business colleagues understand the contract and the issues at play. This makes them better negotiators and partners on deals. Moreover, it takes away, to a large extent, the easy path of blaming

the legal department for contracts being delayed or for not being able to reach agreement at all. A playbook that tracks what the company finds acceptable, means that contracts fail or are delayed because of the company's positions and not because the legal team is killing deals.

- Many in-house teams have been asked to do more with less. A well-prepared contract playbook allows you to do that as you and the legal team will spend less time in contract negotiation and drafting when the company's negotiation positions are already set out in writing. Just follow the playbook.

A contract playbook can take many forms. One version is simply a document setting out general contract negotiating principles that the company follows, e.g., no unlimited liability, company employees will negotiate in good faith, signature/approval process, and so forth. It may also contain checklists and link to form agreements or a contract clause library. Likewise, it may link to different company policies and procedures related to contract negotiation and approval, including a deal review process and/or some type of grading criteria (discussed earlier). The more common type of contract playbook may include some or all of the above, but typically takes the company's standard contract template and for each clause explains why the clause is important, any acceptable changes to that clause, and when the company will walk away. The contract playbook may be different based on geography and you can have different playbooks for different lines of business/contracts. Here is the first page of a sample contract playbook I created based on past experience with SaaS contracts. The columns across the top are: "Section and Issue," "Standard Agreement Language," "Purpose/Meaning of Language," "Potential Customer Objections and Response," and "Alternatives."

Sample Agreement Playbook
(hypothetical software provider based in USA)

Section and Issue	Standard Agreement Language	Purpose/Meaning of Language	Potential Customer Objections and Responses	Alternatives
	This Master Agreement (the "**Agreement**") is made and entered into effective as of ________, 20 ("**Effective Date**") by and between ________, a ________ corporation with its principal offices located at ________ ("**Customer**") and Company X, a Delaware corporation located at [X] ("**Company X**").	The introductory clause identifies the parties to the Agreement. Be certain to include the complete legal name of the Customer and their registered or primary address. As a general rule, Company X is the correct Company X contracting party but consult with Tax Department for all foreign contracts. "Company X [DBA1]" and "Company X [DBA2]" are not legal entities and should never be used as a Company X contracting company.		None
	The terms of this Agreement shall apply to each Work Order and to all System(s) and Services provided to Customer by Company X hereunder. The terms and conditions set forth in this Agreement and in any Work Order shall control if there are different or additional terms in any Customer purchase order form or Company X's acceptance form or invoice. In the event of a conflict between the terms and conditions of the Agreement and any Work Order, the Work Order shall supersede the Agreement only for the engagement covered under the specific Work Order.	The Master Agreement serves as the governing document for all transactions with the Customer. Specific solutions and services will be added via Work Orders. This paragraph rejects conflicting terms that may be set out in the Customer's purchase order form. For internal control, some Customers require Purchase Orders be issued before payments can be initiated through their internal systems. To avoid a "battle of the forms" conflict, this provision clarifies the Master and Work Orders control. NOTE: if a Customer requires a Purchase Order, ensure the copy of the Purchase Order includes a provision clarifying that the terms and conditions of Purchase Order will not apply.	**No Master Agreement.** Some customers do not prefer master agreements, but would rather negotiate terms and conditions separately for each solution/services. Since the Master Agreement only contains base legal terms and conditions, we have found it helps expedite the contracting process. Any necessary revisions to the Master Agreement for a specific Work Order can be documented in the "Special Terms and Conditions" section of the applicable Work Order. **Master Agreement controls.** Some customers prefer the Master Agreement to control since it may be subject to more scrutiny/legal review that Work Orders. Since very different types of solutions	**Alternative 1:** The terms of this Agreement shall apply to each Work Order and to all System(s) and Services provided to Customer by Company X hereunder. The terms and conditions set forth in this Agreement and in any Work Order shall control if there are different or additional terms in any Customer purchase order form or Company X's acceptance form or invoice. In the event of a conflict between the terms and conditions of the Agreement and any Work Order, the Agreement ~~Work Order~~ shall supersede the Work Order unless the Work Order expressly refers to the conflicting provision in this Agreement ~~Agreement only for the~~

Confidential – For Internal Use Only/Subject to Non-Disclosure Agreement Page 1

It takes some effort to create a contract playbook, depending on the sophistication of your business and the number of standard contracts utilized. If your department has not created a playbook before, you should start with something relatively easy, like your standard NDA agreement which is typically just a couple of pages long with roughly twelve or so sections. Cut and paste each section of the NDA into a spreadsheet and for each section prepare a summary of the purpose of the language. Then discuss common objections from customers. Finally, propose alternative language for the clause that is otherwise acceptable to the company. For example, your standard choice of governing law may be New York, and you may have customers object to that choice, especially those located outside the United States. So, for fallback you can note that you will accept Delaware, Florida, and Colorado law in the United States, and the laws of England or Singapore outside the United States. And any situation where the customer objects to these options must go the General Counsel or a deal review committee to accept something different. Once you have created a playbook for one of your simpler contracts, you can start to tackle your more complicated ones. For any contract playbook, you must do the following:

- Review your existing contracts to determine what positions the company has agreed to in the past. Note material differences between geographies and line of business, you may need multiple versions.
- Understand where the company has deviated from the template and how. But do not rely solely on the fact that the company may have accepted a different clause once or twice. It may have been in a position where it had no choice, but otherwise would not want to accept the clause again.
- Find your company's bottom line, i.e., where the company has walked away.
- For each clause, create the acceptable fallbacks (if there are any).
- Do not create a contract playbook in a legal department vacuum. Loop in the other key players in the contract process to get their input, such as finance, sales, IT security, etc. This way you can reach a consensus on business priorities and tolerance for risk. A collaborative approach means everyone is invested in the playbook and the agreed-upon limits.
- Determine the escalation process. What happens when the customer will not agree to the standard terms or agreed on fallbacks? This is where the company, not the legal department, decides what it will or will not accept, balancing the risk and reward with all affected parties having the opportunity to weigh in.

If your sales team understands the contract and the company's positions on various material clauses, you can save yourself a lot of headaches because you can start to turn them into advocates for the contract versus advocates for what the customer wants. When the latter occurs, it drives bad behavior on the part of the sales team and forces the in-house legal team to have two negotiations, one with the customer and the other internally with sales. A well-written contract playbook can bring sales over to the right side. However, to do this means you must keep the playbook relatively short and written in a way non-lawyers can understand. If you give the sales team a hyper-detailed, 100-page playbook to use, it will sit on the shelf gathering dust. That said, you do not want to dumb it down so much that it is not helpful to your lawyers. One solution—though extra work—is to create two playbooks, one for the lawyers and one for sales. You cannot dump a playbook on someone's desk and run away. For a contract playbook to be effective, you need to spend time training people annually on how to use it and the different provisions, fallbacks, and other items contained in the book. The level of training you conduct for lawyers will be different than what you provide to the business. For the former, you can set aside several hours and drill into the details of the wording and the law. You cannot do that with the business. Consider setting up several one-hour (or less) sessions on the playbook. These can be live, by webinar, or a mix. Record them so others can view them when they have the time or when joining the company. The purpose of the business training is to get them familiar with basic legal concepts and the what and the why of the company's positions on different clauses in the contract. If the business understands the difference between a limitation of liability clause and an indemnity clause, they are much more likely to be helpful during a negotiation. That said, do not expect miracles. Most of the sales team will not care, and it will show. That is normal. A solid minority will care, though, and they will be your champions within the organization for the value of the playbook and how it can lead to faster (and better) deals. If you can convince the head of sales of the value of the playbook, that can drive converts within their organization as well. Usually, the one phrase that gets their attention and buy-in is "faster deals," which always appeals to a head of sales who is running behind on revenue targets.

While most contract playbooks deal with the entire contract, that is not always feasible, especially if you are pressed for time or you are preparing something for the business versus for your lawyers. If so, focus on the most important clauses for your business in your playbook. For example, while commonly called boilerplate, these are some clauses that can substantially reduce the risk your company faces in entering into any contract.

- Legal parties. Getting the legal parties down correctly can be important for multiple reasons, the least of which is tax treatment and the ability to hold the correct party responsible.
- Indemnities. Indemnity provisions place the risk of something going wrong on one party or other. For example, if you are providing software, typically you will indemnify the other side against third-party claims alleging IP infringement.

- Limitation of liability. These clauses typically put a cap on the overall liability of one or both parties in the event something goes wrong. They can also exclude recovery of certain types of damages, e.g., punitive.
- Warranties. Usually, the party providing the good or service will give a warranty that the product will work versus some set of specifications. Many contracts specifically exclude any implied warranties.
- Dispute resolution/arbitration. While everyone is happy when the contract gets signed, the smart lawyers are already planning for the divorce.

Plan on reviewing the playbook annually so you can keep it current and fresh. Add it to your department's official goals each year. While you will focus on updating the playbook for changes to your contract, updated contracting processes, customer feedback about clauses, or changes in the law, the annual review is also an opportunity to make your playbook more user-friendly. For example, consider adding flowcharts and graphs. Visuals are always helpful for creating understanding. Checklists are helpful, too. Include a discussion about the contracting process generally, including signature authority and the approval process. Set out how company contracts are stored and managed after signing.

A contract playbook is the crown jewel in your program to teach the business about the company's contracts. It also is the epitome of value creation. The key things to keep in mind are, 1) make it as simple to read as possible, 2) get a wide variety of inputs—not just lawyers, 3) the importance of training users, and 4) annual updating of the playbook. Once you launch your contracts playbook, contracting becomes a faster and less stressful process.

Legal as a Profit Center

One hurdle in-house lawyers face when trying to show value is that the money flow typically goes one way, from the business to the legal department. Unlike many other parts of the business, legal does not generate revenue which makes it a cost center. While other parts of the business also generate costs, the fact that they bring in revenue means that company leaders are generally looking to funnel money to those groups and away from pure cost centers—to the extent feasible (and sometimes even beyond what is feasible). However, if the legal department can find ways to generate revenue, or at least return revenue, you can turn the value discussion on its head in a positive way for the in-house lawyers as they become highly visible value creators. Moreover, the value created is easy to show, i.e., dollars coming in the door. As a result, all legal departments should spend time trying to find ways to generate or bring in revenue. Fortunately, there are a number of ways to do this, and I discuss them below.

Create a Formal Recoveries Program

One thing I always enjoyed announcing to senior management was when the legal department brought money *into* the company. There is perhaps no clearer way to show value than pulling in some cold, hard cash for the business, cash that typically drops right to the bottom line. While this was usually an ad hoc development, over time I tried to develop a more systematic way to capture the potential value through a formal recoveries program. The notion of a formal recoveries program the legal department runs is not new. DuPont pioneered such efforts back in the 1980s and 1990s. Regardless, it is a relatively foreign concept to the business side of the house. They simply are not used to thinking of the legal department as something other than a cost center. This means floating the idea of the department becoming a cash-generation machine is bound to increase the positive perception of the legal department as adding value to the company. That alone is helpful. Remember, a big portion of the value equation is simply marketing the department. A little P.T. Barnum showmanship does not hurt in this regard. That said, actually pulling off generating revenue is even better than just talking about it.

Here are some ways the legal department can go about systematically looking to generate revenue for the company. While some of these ideas can and do occur randomly, i.e., when the opportunity arises, the real value comes from instituting a plan to constantly and consistently scour the company's operations for opportunities. In other words, you have to get your hands dirty every day if you want to make money:

1. Litigation. While it may seem counterintuitive, in-house counsel should embrace the fact that going on the offensive with litigation can be a tremendous way to generate value.[51] This generally requires a mind shift away from taking defensive postures and looking to minimize disputes, to one of not waiting on the business to bring you a dispute and actively looking for instances where a third party may have breached the company's contracts or damaged its business rights. This includes claims:
   - ☐ For simple breach of contract, the other party is not living up to the terms of the agreement and, by doing so, has caused damage to the company.
   - ☐ Involving defective products (breaches of representations and warranties) seeking damages, refunds, replacement products, etc.
   - ☐ For competition law violations, i.e., antitrust, where single firm conduct or agreements involving multiple parties have damaged the company. There is little scarier to a defendant than a well-founded antitrust claim.
   - ☐ Other business torts, including tortious interference, violations of restrictive covenants, trade secret theft, unfair competition, business libel/

51 *See* my discussion infra at page 163.

slander, fraudulent or negligent misrepresentation, civil conspiracy, breach of fiduciary duty, and so forth. Not only is there money to be had, including statutory and/or punitive damages, there is also the added benefit of getting the tortious behavior to stop.

- ☐ To enforce settlement agreements, i.e., where the other side is not living up to the terms of the settlement of a prior dispute.
- ☐ Involving real estate disputes, including whether the lessor is living up to the terms of the lease or, for example, failure on the part of the contractor when engaged in construction.

2. Class Actions. If your company has received notice that it may be a member of a class action do not throw it away! The fact that your company received such a notice means there is good reason to believe that it is, in fact, part of the class. In many cases, there is some work to do to prove that the company purchased the products or services in question, but with some basic fact-gathering, the legal department can usually substantiate the scope of the damages set out in the notice or, even better, show additional purchases that would entitle the company to a larger share. Additionally, you may wish to opt out of the class and proceed on your own, seeking a bigger recovery than what is available via membership in the class.
3. Intellectual Property. Following, I discuss ways to generate patents, which hold value in and of themselves both in terms of limiting others from using the invention, but also seeking and obtaining payment from others for allowing them to use the technology. I am not talking about becoming a patent troll, but rather a business that rightfully seeks to enforce its patents and seeks appropriate compensation from anyone using the patented technology without paying. This applies to trademarks and copyrights as well. It can also mean simply spot-checking licensing agreements to ensure that licensees are paying the correct amounts, e.g., are they underpaying royalties or licensing fees?
4. Post-M&A. While due diligence will tell you a lot about the target, it is rare that anyone is reviewing the target's contracts and relationships for potential legal claims. Post-close is the perfect time for the legal team to do some investigating to see if there are any such opportunities, that is, claims the target simply chose not to pursue for some reason or ones it missed. Likewise, there may be new intellectual property ripe to exploit or rights to protect.
5. Accounts Receivable. This one could have gone above under litigation but it deserves its own place in the Parthenon of value generation. This involves chasing people or companies for monies owed to the company. It can be something the department does itself or that it outsources to outside counsel. One mutually beneficial idea here is to work with your outside counsel to get a special rate or cap or percentage of recovery arrangement in exchange for

allowing the law firm to let their younger litigation lawyers use the case as a way to get real litigation experience. Also, there is certainly value in bringing in monies owed, but there is more value in bringing in monies that the business has written off as uncollectable. In such a case, no revenue is recorded and therefore any recovery is pure profit. It is also a good reminder to ensure that your contracts, at a minimum, include a standard provision allowing the recovery of attorney's fees, in the event you have to file suit for relating to payment.

6. Insurance Claims. Any time there is a coverage dispute with an insurance company, there is money to be had. I would argue that any money the insurer pays out above the original number offered to the company is money (or value) the legal department generated. Further, sometimes reminding the business that insurance may cover a claim versus needing to be paid out-of-pocket can generate savings that would have been otherwise missed. (Another number you can capture for your KPIs.)
7. Unclaimed Property. While you typically hear of unclaimed property in the form of individuals failing to claim stock certificates or money left in old savings accounts, such property is not limited to individuals. Many companies appear on the rolls of unclaimed property notices. All you have to do is check unclaimed property websites for the states where your company operates.[52] It is an easy task, one that could be delegated to a paralegal or even an administrative assistant. One year, I asked a law firm to put a summer associate on the task, which worked out great for the company and for the firm.
8. Taxes. There is a whole new world out there when it comes to getting money back from a government. This is especially true in foreign countries where your operations may not rightly be subject to taxes, or the result is a double tax in violations of a tax treaty. One year, my department got back about $30 million from several European tax authorities for failing to properly refund VAT taxes. That was a good day to be general counsel! In addition to income taxes, you can fight property taxes and other assessments. When it comes to taxes, leave no stone unturned.
9. Hold onto the Money. This is a slight variation of items one through eight in this list. Instead of bringing litigation against someone, the legal department develops a strategy for the company to withhold monies otherwise payable to another party as a lever to force that party to comply with a contractual obligation due to the company. A starting point for such a strategy is working in cross-breach provisions into your standard contracts. If the other side breaches any contract between it and the company, the company can take some action under the instant contract, even if it has no direct rela-

52 *See, e.g.*, www.unclaimed.org.

tionship to the contract in breach. It is just leverage. Otherwise, in some situations, courts have found that two contract breaches (one by each party) cancel each other out if they involve the same issue.[53] For example, a company refuses to provide an indemnity owed under a contract, so the other company stops making payments otherwise due. Granted, this only works if there is an ongoing business relationship between the parties. Finally, there is an old truism in the law, it is easier to keep the money than to get the money. Holding onto money to drive behavior is a common strategy as it forces the other party to consider its options to get paid,, ranging from just complying with the demand to all-out litigation (and the expense and uncertainty that can entail). For more on this, see the next section discussing the strategic use of the law to drive value.

While the above is a fairly comprehensive list of opportunities, there are some realities that must be dealt with if you wish to start down the revenue-generation path. The first is that the business may simply not want to sue the other party. They could be a strategic customer for example. This is fine. The business runs the business. And if this is the case, simply make note of the statute of limitations around the claim, and be sure to revisit it with the business before the expiration thereof. A strategic customer or vendor today may be someone no one cares about in twelve months. There is also the issue of time and resources, especially money to pursue litigation or recovery. When it comes to the best use of the time of the legal department, only you can make the call whether the value of pursuing an effort like this is worthwhile. If you feel overly stretched trying to get something like this off the ground, you may be able to bring on a temporary lawyer from an alternative service provider to help get the program off the ground without adding head count. Another idea is to outsource the investigation of claims and the litigation to outside counsel based on some type of alternative fee arrangement, or to a low-cost solo litigator. Likewise, you can seek litigation funding[54] to pay such claims. Successfully doing so takes all of the cost of the litigation off of the P&L with little to no risk for the company. Lastly, if you have a legal operations function, spotting and analyzing potential claims could be something it runs with much less involvement of the department's lawyers.

Regardless of how you do it, the fact that the legal department would present a plan like this to the business will, as noted above, have benefits in and of itself. And, only hitting on one or two of the potential claims will likely more than fund the cost and provide actual revenue to the company above and beyond those costs. In my words, turn the "Department of No" into the "Department of Dough!"

---

53 *See, e.g.*, *Los Angeles Mem'l Coliseum Comm'n v. Nat'l Football League*, 791 F.2d 1356, 1362 (9th Cir. 1986).

54 See infra at page 171 for a discussion of litigation funding.

Strategic Use of the Law

Generally, the business thinks about the legal department as the function that keeps them out of trouble. As the discussion above touched on, smart in-house lawyers and business people understand that the proactive use of the law to impact competition is a way to create value, not only for the company, but also the legal department as well.[55] An easy example is obtaining patents that are government-issued monopolies to practice the patent and exclude all others from doing so. Aggressively obtaining and enforcing patents is a legal way to put up barriers to entry, barriers that make the company and its products and services more valuable. The same is true for trademarks and copyrights, the latter an often-undervalued competitive weapon. Similarly, you can view contracts as the rules of the road to the relationship between two companies. A failure to play by the rules is potentially a lawsuit. As a business, you must decide whether you will let the other side cheat or will you enforce the rules you agreed to? For example, a confidentiality or non-compete agreement can sideline a high-powered executive with intimate knowledge about the company from taking that knowledge and their skills to a competitor. It may not seem fair to everyone, but the bottom line is not about fair,[56] it is about creating and protecting value and enforcing contractual rights. When in-house lawyers are reviewing options and making recommendations, there should not be a knee-jerk reaction to shy away from a fight. In fact, the option to fight, and fight hard, should be on the table along with settlement, doing nothing, or any other option. The best business decisions get made when all of the information and options are available for the business to consider and the legal team is counseling the business on how everything fits together, from risk, to reputational issues, to cost, to rewards. Do not predetermine that fighting it out is the option of last resort. It may be the option of first resort. Or, as Mike Tyson famously said, "Everyone has a plan until they get punched in the nose." Meaning, being the aggressor can often change the business dynamic dramatically, and in your favor.

Taken further, every in-house lawyer needs to consider how the law can be used to advance the interests of the business at every opportunity. This does not mean that the company actually does so, but if no one is thinking about it, discussing it, weighing the pros and cons, then it is simply a lost opportunity. "[B] usiness leaders should not be closed-minded about potential benefits of legal action to protect their interests and to advance their business strategy . . ."[57] I

---

55 *See generally*, Constance Bagley, *Winning Legally: How to Use the Law to Create Value, Marshal Resources, and Manage Risk* (Boston: Harvard Business Review Press, 2005).

56 As a friend once told me, "It doesn't say 'Justice School' on the door, does it?"

57 *Power of Litigation as a Strategic Weapon in Business: The Law is Used (Abused) for Competitive Gain . . . (quoting Litigation and Business Strategy by* Gallion & Spielgel)(emphasis added), available at https://bizshifts-trends.com/litigation-weapon-business-strategy-companies-use-abuse-law-competitive-gains/.

understand this may not be appealing to everyone, but it is a valid strategy within the confines of the ethical rules. Consider the case of real-estate developer (and now former President) Donald Trump. Love him or hate him, he and his company have been masters at using litigation as a strategic weapon to advance the interests of their business, be it through bankruptcy, short-paying vendors, or attacking with a legal vengeance anyone they deem a threat to their business (including claims for defamation and breach of contract). To be clear, I am not touting baseless litigation as a way to show value, but I am saying that ignoring litigation and other legal options as tools to advance the interests of the company is a disservice by the legal department. The mere fact that most businesses recoil at the thought of litigation means that there is a potential opportunity in taking advantage of that dread.

Another legal option is to make your case to regulators that your competitor or vendor or customer is doing something that violates some statute or regulation. If you are successful, getting the regulators to take your fight to your opponent versus the company spending its own resources to do so. The classic example here is antitrust where competitors and others often spend significant amounts of money on white papers and economic analysis to hand to competition regulators at the federal and state levels to get them to go after the bad actor. Once an investigation starts, the cost and reputation harm (even if the bad actor has done nothing wrong) can often cause the target to enter into stipulations or a settlement to change their behavior in ways that favor the parties who complained to the regulators in the first place. Similarly, ballot initiatives are another avenue of competitive advantage whereby laws can be changed or enacted and politicians recalled through a simple vote of the people. This is exactly how, and why, the California Consumer Privacy Act was enacted.[58]

Why does all this work? There are several reasons:

- The claim is 100 percent valid. Litigation, which includes regulatory investigations, works because right is on your side, and the other side knows it and does not want to stand firm on a losing position.
- Litigation is a costly slog. Regardless of whether you are right or not, it will cost you a lot of money to find out. Litigation in America is not cheap and is getting more expensive each year. The inability to afford the fight is reason enough to compromise. On the flip side, so-called patent trolls have perfected a model where they make the cost to settle much less than the cost to fight it out in court to prove you are right. And because

58 While often sold as grassroots initiatives of the "common person," do not fool yourself. There is often big business and big money behind any ballot initiative or recall effort. This is not *Mr. Smith Goes to Washington*.

attorneys' fees are generally not recoverable in the U.S. system,[59] the hard math of patent litigation almost always forces companies to take the quick settlement instead of the expensive road to possibly vindication. We called this the "Seven Stages of Patent Troll Grief"[60] when explaining to the business why a settlement was the likely next step.

- Litigation is risky. Few people like to gamble with big numbers. Litigation is often a gamble because there are so many variables, including the judge, the jury, the quality of the lawyers on either side, the law (or uncertainty thereof), documents, and so forth.
- It is public. Unless you are in confidential arbitration, the litigation process in America is very public. In court, it is difficult to keep all but the most sensitive trade secrets confidential, and even then, it often depends on the judge's discretion. Just because something is embarrassing is not a reason to preclude its use at trial or in public filings. Many companies avoid litigation not because of the merits of the matter, but because of the exposure of embarrassing documents, which is why teaching the business to write smart is such a value-add by the legal team.
- Distraction. In addition to costing a lot of money, litigation or a regulatory investigation is not something that only the lawyers have to deal with. There will be significant time sucks on the business to locate and produce documents and draft answers in the discovery process, to prepare for and be deposed, to simply be interviewed on the background of the case. Many executives when faced with spending their time fighting such a battle versus working on the business, often choose the latter and look for ways to get out of a fight as quickly as possible.

These intertwining dynamics, along with leveraging the natural aversion to litigation of most businesses, can be used to advance the interests of the company under the right circumstances. In his book *Make the Rules or Your Rivals Will*,[61] Wharton professor G. Richard Shell discusses what he calls competitive legal strategy, which includes the use of contracts, courts, regulation, and lobbying to

59 A loser pays system, that is, the loser of litigation pays the winner's attorneys' fees would likely cause a dramatic shift to less litigation in the United States. Many countries have such a system and much less litigation than here in America.

60 That is: 1) shock, 2) disbelief, 3) anger, 4) bargaining, 5) depression, 6) resignation, and 7) payment. Feel free to use it for yourself the next time to have a conversation with the business about why settlement makes the most sense.

61 G. Richard Shell, *Make the Rules or Your Rivals Will* (New York: Crown Publishing, 2004). *See also*, Adam Kline, *The Current War: A Battle Story Between Two Electrical Titans, Thomas Edison and George Westinghouse* (Scotts Valley, CA: CreateSpace, 2017)(a masterful book on the fight between Edison and Westinghouse over direct and alternating current—not only a primer in how to use litigation, regulation, and propaganda to drive business results, but also about the formation of the modern law firm model).

secure and advance the competitive interests of business. Professor Shell discusses how many current business figures such as Bill Gates and Rupert Murdoch a) forced business rivals to the bargaining table through the leverage of litigation, b) redefined markets by obtaining favorable regulatory outcomes, and c) used politics to fight business battles (think tariffs and taxes, as in tax him and not me!). If you think a government affairs function is not important in business, think again.[62]

Finally, there is the value in being known as a tough out, that is, if the company has a reputation for fighting hard if involved in litigation or regulatory disputes, many potential adversaries will leave the company alone and many defendants will look to settle quickly because they know the company is willing to go to trial. This reputation for being a wolverine also brings value to the business.

Create an In-House Patent (and Other IP) Development Program

There are many types of intellectual property (IP), for example, trademarks, trade secrets, copyrights, or patents. These are all valuable assets of the company. One way the legal department can help generate money for the company is to find ways to monetize the company's IP. Being aggressive with enforcing patents is a good strategy, but the strategy goes nowhere if the company does not have any patents to fight with. To get over this hump, the first step is creating or enhancing a patent development program. It is a fairly straightforward process to generate patents. The licensing half, however, is not easy, but can be very lucrative if the patents are valid, have value, and you find the right targets.

A patent is a government-granted monopoly to build, sell, and use your invention (and prevent others from doing so). If you are issued a patent in the United States, it is typically good for twenty years, after which time your patent expires and anyone can copy, build, and sell your invention. In exchange for a short-term monopoly, you must disclose the details of your invention to the public so that someone practiced in the arts could recreate it. To receive a patent, your idea must meet four requirements.

1. The subject matter must be patentable,as defined by Congress and the courts.
2. Your idea must be new.
3. The idea must be useful.
4. Your idea must be non-obvious.

Additionally, there is what lawyers commonly called the *Alice*[63] decision whereby the U.S. Supreme Court established a two-part test to determine if a

---

62 *See infra* at page 232 for a discussion of the value of teaming with the government affairs group.

63 *Alice Corp. v. CLS Bank International,* 134 S. Ct. 2347 (2014).

software patent was patentable or not as pertaining to ineligible subject matter. To sum it up quickly, under *Alice*, simply reciting the use of a conventional computer in the claims to implement the known idea does not make the idea for a utility patent patentable subject matter.

There are three types of patents you can file for:

1. Utility patents may be granted to anyone who invents or discovers any new and useful process, machine, article of manufacture, or composition of matter, or any new and useful improvement thereof (good for twenty years).
2. Design patents may be granted to anyone who invents a new, original, and ornamental design (good for fourteen years).
3. Plant patents may be granted to anyone who invents or discovers and asexually reproduces any distinct and new variety of plant (good for twenty years).

There is a lot that goes into determining if your technology or idea is patentable and, if so, which type of patent is best. Unless the company has the money to have its own patent attorney on staff, you will need experienced outside counsel to help you with this process and draft the application. Simply put, getting a patent is not easy (unless you buy them from someone looking to sell or in bankruptcy, which is always an option). The overall process takes a lot of work and time. It can also be expensive—roughly \$15,000 – \$25,000 to get a patent issued. Buying already issued patents is likely far more expensive. To start, in the United States, you need to file a patent application that sets out in detail a description of your idea. These applications must be filed by a patent attorney (in-house or outside) skilled in the art of drafting a patent application. You must also review publications and other sources to make sure there is nothing already out there that overlaps with your idea or would allow someone skilled in the arts to build your invention just from reading what is already out there. (This is called prior art.) Then an examiner from the USPTO reviews your application. They might reject it in total, or they might reject part of it (for any of the reasons noted). You have a chance to appeal (called an office action) and the examination process (with the exception of design patents) generally goes back and forth for several years before either your patent is issued or finally denied. At each stage, you must determine whether it is worth the cost and the effort to continue or, depending on the objections from the examiner, whether the changes you must make to your patent leave you with anything good after it is all said and done.

You also need to decide in which jurisdictions you will seek patent protection. Patents are only valid in the country where they are issued. You cannot enforce a patent issued in the United States against a business operating within the European Union or in China. You would need patents issued in those countries. Additionally, in the United States, you must seek patent protection within one year of when you first sold or disclosed the patented material. If you wait too long (more than twelve months), you cannot get a patent. Finally, one neat trick in the U.S. system is filing for what is called a provisional patent. This is a relatively inexpensive process that allows you to get an application on file quickly (with far less detail and expense than a regular patent application). The provisional patent application is good for one year and buys you time to decide if you truly want to pursue a full patent while preserving your position as first to file.

Given the cost, the business side will ask why they should get a patent. It is a fair question, especially if you are going to be spending time and treasure trying to get inventions patented. Ultimately, the answer to the question depends on the company's strategy concerning IP generally and patents specifically. You can break the reasons down as follows.

- Protect innovations. The most straightforward reason to get a patent is to protect a valuable invention, in particular, one you believe competitors or others may reverse engineer or invent on their own.
- Offensive use. This means getting patents to use for licensing purposes (i.e., money) or to preclude others (competitors) from practicing your invention which, if done correctly, could mean they are no longer competitors.
- Defensive use. This contemplates getting patents to use to defend the company in the event a competitor or other patent owner tries to assert their patent against you. If the party asserting the patent operates a real business (versus being a patent troll) then you may own a patent that you could enforce against them. When this happens, the parties often agree to a cross-licensing program that allows each party to use the other's patents.
- Increase shareholder value. Patents have value. A portfolio of patents can increase the value of your company for its shareholders, particularly in cases of a potential sale of the business. You will always see questions around patents (and other IP) in a due diligence request. Additionally, if your company is publicly traded, a fulsome patent portfolio (or simply obtaining a single new, but important, patent) can mean an increase in share price.
- Taxes. Being able to demonstrate that you apply for and have patents can be used as a justification for research and development costs, which typically qualify as deductions for purposes of corporate income taxes.
- Prestige. Companies with large patent portfolios (or even just a handful of important patents) are viewed as innovators in their field. Employees, especially for technology companies, take pride in the innovations developed by their companies, including patents. This can lead to an improvement of morale generally, especially among the technical teams.

Another important consideration regarding any particular piece of intellectual property is whether you should protect it with a patent or treat it as a trade secret. Not all ideas are worth the cost of trying to obtain a patent. Additionally, once the patent issues, the particulars of the invention are disclosed to the world and your protection only lasts for twenty years (and it also depends on how willing you are to enforce your patents). Accordingly, there are times when a patent simply does not make sense. For example, the good folks at Coca-Cola could have patented the formula for Coke. But, for obvious reasons, it was a far better decision to treat the formula as a trade secret and keep it out of the public realm. A patent only lasts twenty years. A trade secret can last forever. So, when deciding to patent something, you need to think hard about whether this is, in fact, the right course or if you are better off keeping it as a trade secret.

There are two key documents you must have in place as you look to develop your company's IP. The first is an invention disclosure form. This is a form you require inventors to fill out so their inventions can be properly evaluated. The form should only be a few pages long to encourage inventors to complete it. The inventor should provide information such as:

- a description of the technology, how it operates, the identity of competitors in the field, and their products/technology;
- how the invention will make a difference in the marketplace for the company and allow the company's products to surpass others (i.e., why is it worth seeking a patent);
- are there easy ways to design around the technology; and
- the date the invention was created, whether the invention has been offered for sale and, if so, when?

The second document is a form whereby all employees who join the company agree to assign ownership of any inventions that employee creates on company time or using company resources to the company. This form is often combined with other agreements such as confidentiality, non-solicitation, and non-compete agreements. You do not want to be in a position where the company is defending challenges to its attempt to obtain a patent from an employee claiming she is the real owner.

Before embarking on a program to generate patents, you must be sure that you understand and have alignment among the senior management as to the company's goals and strategy around obtaining patents. For some companies, they will only want to do the minimum needed to obtain a handful of patents. Others may not want to get any patents at all. While some will be willing to create an entire group whose sole responsibility is to generate patents and seek licensing revenue. Some companies may want patents only for defensive purposes and will do anything to avoid a patent war among their competitors. The company's strategy around patents will determine how much funding there is for the program and how much cooperation you will get from different groups, especially the software engineers or research and development (R&D) teams. The easiest way to figure out where your company sits on the spectrum of patent creation is to ask.

This will be a high-level meeting with the senior management. This means you will need to be prepared to set out the pros and cons of a patent program, including the costs, the specific reasons why the patent program you are proposing makes sense for your company, and the process you recommend following to generate patents. If you have outside patent counsel, they will likely be willing to help you prepare materials for the meeting and may, if helpful, even attend. A meeting like this is a perfect showcase for the legal department to demonstrate value by bringing to the table an opportunity for the department to be a money generator and not just a cost center.

Next is the most critical part of any patent program. A patent harvesting meeting is a meeting where the right people gather to discuss all of the different types of innovation going on at the company and which ideas, if any, should the legal department seek patent protection. This is the meeting where you make determinations about what to patent, using the company's patent strategy as your guide. Here are the key points

- The right people must attend. Typically, a mix of legal, marketing (for design patents), R&D, finance, CTO, CIO, and outside counsel. Unless you have experienced patent counsel in-house, outside counsel is important for analyzing ideas and whether they are patentable or not.
- Meeting frequency/length. Meet every quarter for about ninety minutes. You can meet more frequently if your program is active. Any longer than ninety minutes, and people drift off and lose interest.
- Understand how patents work/what is patentable. Start each meeting going over the ground rules about the patent process and, most importantly, what constitutes a patentable idea. This meeting is also a place to discuss whether an idea should be treated as a trade secret or a patent.
- Encourage creativity. While not every idea will merit a patent filing, even the goofiest ideas can often spark other ideas. In other words, it is important to have fun and to encourage people to think freely, no matter how wild the idea is.
- Prior art database. One overlooked benefit of the patent harvesting meeting is the collection of all of the ideas, including inventor notebooks, patent disclosure forms, and even drawings on the back of a napkin. All of this material, even if not something you can patent, should be saved in some type of database so that if your company is ever the victim of a patent suit you can comb this database to see if there is any prior art the company created that can be used to defeat the patent asserted against it.

Some additional ways the legal department can add value to the process include (a) lobbying for incentives for inventors, e.g., cash for ideas that the company submits a patent application for or bigger amounts if a patent is granted; (b) communicating that every employee is encouraged to submit ideas on the patent disclosure form (you never know where the next brilliant idea will come from); or (c) a yearly luncheon to recognize all of the inventors who had a patent application filed or had a patent issued. All of this is designed to create a virtuous cycle where employees get excited about submitting their invention ideas. Lastly, even if no one on the in-house legal team is a patent lawyer, there are plenty of ways to show value around the patent program process, including:

- managing deadlines;
- reviewing the patent portfolio regularly to ensure valuable patents are kept alive and abandoning those that are no longer useful (why pay expensive maintenance fees for such patents?);
- helping prepare patent applications (directly or by assisting outside counsel as a liaison with the inventors).
- being a cheerleader for the patent program and ensuring that it is easy for inventors to get their ideas in front of the right people;
- educating senior management and employees on the patent process and the value of patents, including ongoing training to encourage patentable ideas and the protection of IP generally whether by patent or as a trade secret; and
- walking the halls and talking with employees and inventors about ideas they have or are working on. There is no need to wait until a patent harvesting meeting to bring forward potentially patentable ideas. In-house lawyers may spot ideas that might be patentable and they may bring the right people together within the company to flesh out ideas and encourage employees to file an invention disclosure form.

You do not need a degree in computer science or have spent your career working in patent law to be a valuable part of your company's patent strategy. All you need is a willingness to get involved and recognize that your company may be missing an opportunity regarding patents (or not fully taking advantage of the program it does have in place).

Utilize Litigation Financing

A common refrain in legal departments is how to get enough money to do the things we need to do to protect the company. There are always more matters clamoring for money than there is money available. This is especially true with litigation. If your company is being sued, you have little choice other than to spend the money needed to defend your interests (unless a quick settlement is available and a smart deal). On the other hand, if the company has meritorious claims, then it often faces the difficult choice of whether to spend the money needed to proceed. If not, valuable claims may be lost. If yes, then the money that could be spent on other parts of the business is rerouted to legal fees. Unfortunately, under accounting rules, money invested in a litigation claim is not treated the same as money invested in the business generally. Over the past five years or so, however, a potential solution has emerged. The solution is called litigation financing. It is something every in-house counsel should be aware of and be thinking about as it offers multiple ways to bring and show value to the company.

In its most basic form, litigation financing means a third party agrees to finance your litigation (usually the plaintiff side, but it works for the defense side as well) in exchange for a percentage of the recovery (settlement or post-trial) or some other agreed-upon return on investment. The financing is usually without recourse, meaning that if you do not win your case, nothing is owed to the group financing the litigation, they take all the risk. This is very different from a contingency fee arrangement with a law firm. With litigation financing, your agreement is with a third party, not the law firm. Moreover, the financing can and does cover out-of-pocket costs in addition to legal fees, i.e., depositions, travel, expert witnesses, copies, and so on. The financing can occur at the beginning of the claim, in the middle, on appeal, etc. It can cover legal fees, legal fees and costs, just costs, or half a dozen or so other ways of financing the lawsuit or paying your company for the value of the suit.

There are many litigation financing companies (LFCs) operating in the United States (and elsewhere) today. These companies tend to manage a large pool of venture capital funding with the objective of investing in litigation. Like any investment company, a litigation financing venture heavily analyzes cases it may invest in. Some common aspects of this due diligence include:

- ☐ Nature of the dispute (Contract, tort, antitrust, etc.)
- ☐ Plaintiff or defendant (The plaintiff side is generally easier to fit in the litigation financing model.)
- ☐ Where the case is pending (The court, the judge, the country, the state, and the county— it does make a difference.)
- ☐ Potential payout (Not on the face amount of the claim, but the likely amount that can be won at settlement or from a jury.)
- ☐ Merits (Including key evidence such as emails, contracts, etc.)
- ☐ Budget (Cost in terms of legal fees, experts, and other expenses.)
- ☐ Timeline for the case to get resolved and money changes hands (including appeals)
- ☐ Lawyers representing both sides (Experience, reputation, results.)
- ☐ Ability to recover the monies awarded (Is the defendant good for the money, how easy will it be to get paid or find and attach assets, if necessary.)

Many LFCs use a sophisticated statistical model to analyze the above and other factors. The companies take all of the information and match it up against their risk profile and other parameters. This is not simply an educated guess about which cases to take, it is a data-driven exercise. Funding companies are not looking for frivolous lawsuits, they want lawsuits with merit and high potential recoveries. Assuming the LFC is satisfied that the case meets its investment parameters then the parties sit down and negotiate a detailed litigation funding contract setting out the responsibilities and obligations of both sides along with the percentage of the recovery the financing company gets if there is a win. All of which means a lot of thought goes into defining winning. How much of the recovery will go to the LFC versus your company, ultimately comes down to how much risk there is in the merits of the case. How solid is the chance of winning? The less favorable the odds, the higher the percentage of the recovery going to the LFC. The percentage return on investment is directly related to the risk of the investment.

While funding the plaintiff side of the equation is more common, litigation funding can work for a defendant as well. Bringing money into the company's coffers as a plaintiff has obvious value, but litigation funding may have the most value to in-house counsel if they can obtain it to defend a case because defending expensive litigation is likely a bigger problem for companies than bringing litigation. One key to litigation financing of defense claims is the willingness of the company to pay a premium for success, but still generally paying less than the cost of defense otherwise. Much like a law firm's success fee, this means that if certain parameters are met, the LFC gets a larger return on its investment. If there is no success, then the risk, in terms of the cost of defending the lawsuit, is borne by the LFC. In exchange, the company gets relief from funding the cost of the litigation while it is pending and, hopefully, a win at trial if it goes that far. Here are some ways where litigation financing can work in the defense context.

- Funding an entire claim—The LFC funds the entire defense cost in exchange for a multiplier or bonus in the event of a successfu" outcome (or hitting a certain level of success). Typically, this type of funding hinges on the analysis of how weak is the claim against the company? For example, if the LFC believes the case is worth $15 million to the plaintiff, but believes it can participate in a defense that limits damages to $5 million, then the difference in those values becomes the area where the LFC can make money. The success fee concept is usually tied to a substantial discount upfront on legal fees, e.g., 25–30 percent off standard rates. If the case is resolved at $X, then the company pays the firm the amount held back. If the case is resolved at the lower amount $Y, then the company pays the firm the hold back plus a bonus/multiplier. This solves a problem with contingency fees whereby most law firms will not go below 70 to 80 percent off of their regular rates, which may not be enough of a discount for the company to proceed. The LFC can step in and fund the entire cost of defense, covering the law firm's risk (though the firm must agree to a discount off its rates to make it work), as well as that of the company.
- Portfolio funding—The claim is part of a larger portfolio of claims that include claims as plaintiff so that the LFC's risk is diversified across good

cases and bad cases. This means companies must think about litigation financing across multiple claims versus a one-off claim.

- Reverse contingency fees—The financing company collects a fee that is a percentage of the difference between the amount a third party originally demands from a lawyer's client and the amount that client must ultimately pay the third party, whether by settlement or judgment.

Like anything, there are good points and bad points that go with litigation funding. Here are several positive points for litigation funding.

- The cost of the litigation becomes secondary. Litigation funding can reduce or eliminate the problem of budget-breaking litigation. Rather than having to pay out of current cash flows and impacting current budgets, the LFC pays the costs of the litigation and the company only pays when the litigation is over, either in terms of a share of the win or some type of success fee tied to the defense of the claim. Any payments advanced by the LFC are typically without recourse. This means a relatively risk-free reduction or elimination of what is usually the largest and most unpredictable cost in a legal department budget—litigation.
- The CFO will love it. The added benefit of taking the cost of litigation off the company's books is that the company's earnings, cash flow, and other measures of financial success (think of the basic financial measure discussed earlier in this book) are not burdened or diminished by big, hard-to-predict legal fee payments. While a litigation claim is an asset of the company, just like any other receivable, it is not treated as a receivable under the accounting rules. This means costs related to litigation are usually not capitalized, they are expensed, so they hit the bottom line as incurred. Moreover, the unpredictable nature of legal fees, especially in big litigation, can drive problems with earnings for publicly traded companies as even a penny or two difference off expectations due to unexpectedly high legal fees can negatively and materially impact stock price. Litigation financing can remove a lot of these problems.
- Lawyers of choice. With litigation financing in place, your legal department has more flexibility concerning the choice of counsel as the cost/legal fees become a secondary issue. Your choice becomes more about which law firm you think is best for the case not which law firm can do the job within a certain budget. It also removes the battle over how low the law firm can go on fees and still be incentivized to work for you or do its best work on your matter. Litigation financing can better align the interests of the company, the law firm, and the LFC.
- Getting paid. Any win is useless if you cannot collect the money owed from the defendant. It can be even more complicated if the other side is a foreign company located outside the United States or if you are in arbitration and

need to locate assets in countries that accept arbitration awards. An LFC specializes in locating assets and collecting damages.

Here are some of the negative issues associated with litigation financing.

- Champerty. Champerty is an old common law doctrine from Medieval England barring third parties from stirring up litigation and financing another party's claims. The goal was/is to discourage frivolous litigation and to protect against harassment by wealthy backers of litigation. The doctrine still exists and, as you can imagine, litigation financing appears to fall squarely within the doctrine. Yet, many states have relaxed prohibitions on third-party litigation financing. The key attributes necessary to avoid champerty are:
  - o The financing agreement does not assign ownership of the claims to the financier;
  - o The financier does not have any rights to direct or control the litigation; and
  - o The plaintiff retains an unfettered right to settle the litigation at any time for any amount.
- Attorney-client/work product privilege. Any time privileged information is shared with a third party, i.e., anyone other than the law firm and the client, there is a risk of waiver of the privilege. That risk certainly exists in the context of litigation funding where the LFC will want to get as much information as possible to evaluate your claim and set the price of the funding. The law in this is area is still very unsettled and it is wise to take precautions concerning any information you seek to share with the LFC, such as:
  - o provide documents that are not privileged (for example, pleadings);
  - o provide what you expect to turn over to the other side through the discovery process; and
  - o weigh the risk of disclosure against the need for funding and provide privileged documents understanding the risks.
- Ethical rules. Under the rules of legal ethics in the United States and the United Kingdom, for example, your outside counsel owes a duty of loyalty and independence to you, the client. The funding relationship cannot interfere with that duty and this must be crystal clear upfront with your LFC. The level of independence is necessary to prevent a successful claim of champerty. Three key points here:
  - o you must retain the right to hire and fire counsel;
  - o you retain sole right to decide if to settle and for what amount; and
  - o you and your counsel direct litigation strategy and decisions, the LFC is completely passive.

In-house counsel facing material litigation spend (plaintiff or defense) or who might otherwise pass on (or not see through to completion) valuable claims because they are too expensive to prosecute, owe it to their company to make an informed decision as to whether litigation financing makes sense or not. At a minimum, they should involve the CFO/finance team in the review as some of the most positive impacts come on the accounting/budget side of the equation, including preservation of/other uses for the company's capital. Likewise, in-house counsel should be up to speed on this issue and be able to guide the company and the senior management about whether it is something the company should explore further. A legal department that considers all options and brings those options to the business, along with its recommendation, is demonstrating value. If the option can bring money into the company and/or save significant legal spending, it can be a game changer for how the business sees the legal department.

Spot and Manage Risk

It is difficult to be part of any business and not hear about risk. It is on the mind of every CEO, CFO, and board member, as it should be. And, anything that is important to the board and the C-Suite, should be important to the legal department. As the use of in-house lawyers has evolved, one of the key responsibilities businesses are placing on in-house lawyers is spotting and managing risk. While looking backward at what risks arose and how the company responded is pretty easy, the harder task—but far more valuable skill—is being able to look forward and see new or different types of risk.

When we think of risk we tend to think only of bad things. Yet, not all risk is negative. Avoiding all risk is not the way to run a successful business, sports team, legal department, research facility, military, or pretty much any organization you can name. Taking risks is important to the success of any endeavor. There is risk in any merger for example, but companies still take that risk every day because there may be a big financial payoff. One simple way to look at risk is as a continuum where risk is plotted as varying degrees of consequences, that is, good or bad outcomes. The ability of an in-house lawyer to understand the different consequences of what the company wants to do, where those consequences fall on the above continuum, and how everything balances out when the good and the bad are added up. Value creation versus value destruction is key. The C-Suite finds tremendous value in the ability of its in-house lawyers to help spot and manage such risks.

Risk can be broken down into legal risk and strategic risk. Legal risks are things lawyers are very familiar with, including such broad categories as:

- compliance risk;

- litigation risk;
- regulatory risk;
- security risk (Asking is the physical plant a safe workplace?); and
- information risk (Data breach, theft of trade secrets).

Strategic risks are things that the business leaders tend to focus on that are critical to the survival of the business, such as:

- financial risk;
- marketplace risk (Competitors, disruptive technology/business model risk);
- succession risk (Sudden death or departure of a CEO);
- major political uncertainty risk (A political coup, currency devaluation); and
- natural disaster risk, (A pandemic, earthquake, or flood.

Of course, legal risk and strategic risk are not mutually exclusive and they often overlap. Business, political, regulatory, financial, and just about any other type of risk you can imagine have both legal and business elements. The most valuable in-house lawyers see the company's strategic and legal risks, how they interconnect, and advise the company on what to do next, both in terms of legal steps and potential business steps. The latter is a huge departure from the dark ages of in-house legal departments discussed in the introduction.

While no one person or group can spot every risk facing the company, there are steps the legal department can take to ensure that eyes are looking out at the horizon, searching for risks at the first instance and before they become unmanageable problems or lost opportunities. To start, in-house lawyers must ensure that there is a pan-company team assembled to spot and manage risk. Many companies have an enterprise risk management department. If so, the legal department must insert itself into that group in some manner; as a member, partner, subject matter expert, etc. If no such group exists, the legal team may need to take the lead in creating it, bringing together groups like internal audit, finance, legal, information security, and members of the primary lines of business to focus on the company's key strategic, operational, and legal risks.

Between meetings, and as part of the preparation for such meetings, in-house lawyers must keep their eyes and ears open at all times. Board meetings, C-Suite meetings, town hall meetings, strategy planning meetings, and staff group meetings produce an incredible amount of information that in-house lawyers can tap into. One helpful tool is a checklist to help you quickly sort through all of the information coming across your desk. I developed just such a list early in my in-house career:

Risk Evaluation Checklist

- ☐ Is this something a regulator might be interested in?
- ☐ Is this something that could make customers or vendors upset or bring on litigation?
- ☐ Is this something that if it became public or goes badly could damage the reputation of the company?
- ☐ Is this something covered by specific laws and does it comply?
- ☐ Is this something you have seen other companies (competitors, etc.) have problems with?
- ☐ Is this something that could severely injure someone (e.g., a safety or environmental mishap)?
- ☐ Is this an opportunity to create value?

Depending on the answer, this checklist will tell you if you need to do some more digging about the risks associated with the project or idea.

The business also needs the legal department to help evaluate risk and potential outcomes (good or bad). To do so, you must understand three things: (1) the company's business goals and strategy, (2) the company's level of risk tolerance, and (3) the right questions to ask about the risk. The company's business goals and strategy should be easily available to the legal department. Once the lawyers in the department know the goals and strategy, they can be on the lookout for developments that can negatively or positively impact either one.

The company's level of risk tolerance comes primarily from the board of directors and the C-Suite. Some companies are very conservative, some not so much. Company policies such as business ethics also set the bar on risk tolerance. Additionally, internal audit and the individual business units/staff groups (including members of the compliance department and the legal department) can and should weigh in on acceptable risks. The most straightforward method of getting this information is to ask the right people via interviews, surveys, workshops, offsites, etc.

When you ask about negative risk, it is important that you also ask the right questions. Go beyond discussing historical failures or problems and, instead, attempt to peer into the future and spot new or different types of risk. To do this, you need to know the following.

Questions to Ask About Risk

- ☐ *What type of risk is it?*
- ☐ *Under what scenarios would the risk arise/happen?*
- ☐ *What is the likelihood of the risk occurring?*

- ☐ *Can third parties cause the risk to the company?*
- ☐ *What type of harm can arise from the risk?*
    - ☐ *Monetary?*
    - ☐ *Operational?*
    - ☐ *Criminal?*
- ☐ *What is the best case, worst case, most likely case for the company in terms of harm?*
- ☐ *What are the ways we can deal with the risk to minimize bad outcomes and maximize good outcomes?*
    - ☐ *Policies/training?*
    - ☐ *Contractual terms?*
    - ☐ *Insurance?*
    - ☐ *Operational controls?*
    - ☐ *Take a bigger risk?*
    - ☐ *Preparation for the risk?*
- ☐ *Are there benchmarks or standards we can use to measure against?*
- ☐ *How can we best monitor the risk/what are the trigger points?*

Estimating risk can be a challenging task. You are trying to determine the cost or value of the risk, depending on whether the risk is negative or positive in nature. There is a relatively simple and standard formula for estimating risk: Risk value = Probability of event × cost/Value of event if it occurs. Basically, this involves multiplication and probability. Sometimes you will need something more visual for the business. I have found that the following works nicely when trying to evaluate risk:

(-)Impact →	1	2	3	4	5
Probability ↓	Negligible	Minor	Moderate	Significant	Severe
(81-100)%	Low Risk	Moderate Risk	High Risk	Extreme Risk	Extreme Risk
(61-80)%	Minimum Risk	Low Risk	Moderate Risk	High Risk	Extreme Risk
(41-60)%	Minimum Risk	Low Risk	Moderate Risk	High Risk	High Risk
(21-40)%	Minimum Risk	Low Risk	Low Risk	Moderate Risk	High Risk
(1-20)%	Minimum Risk	Minimum Risk	Low Risk	Moderate Risk	High Risk

Or an even simpler way to visualize "risk" is a 2×2 matrix as discussed earlier.

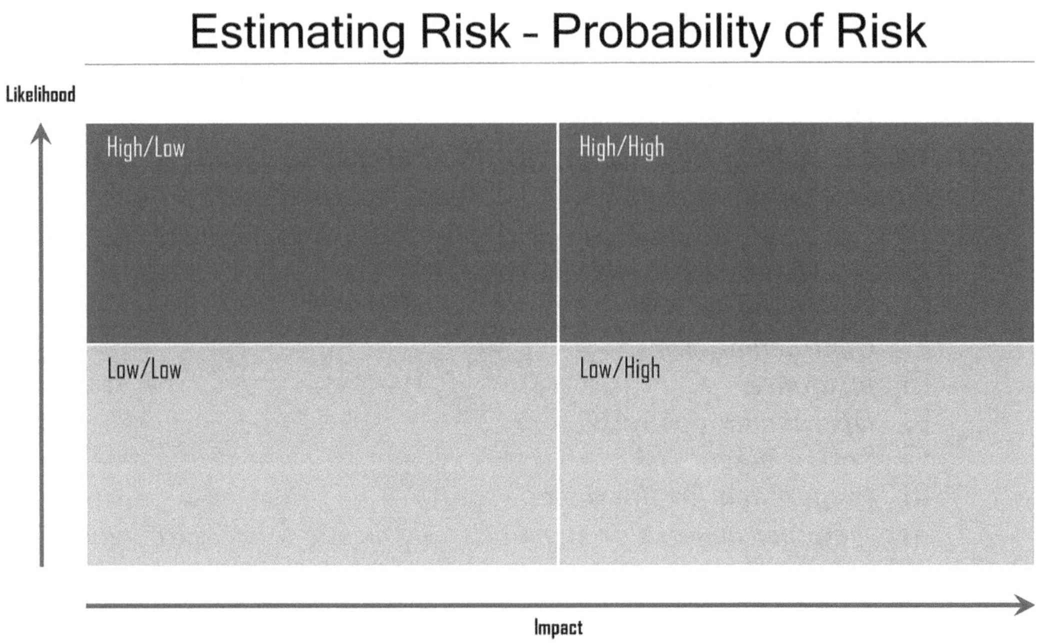

Finally, there is little value to risk analysis unless the legal department finds a way to report risk to the business, formally or informally, written or orally. Regardless of the way the risk is reported, you need to ultimately cover five things: 1) what the risk is; 2) the likelihood of the risk occurring; 3) the range of outcomes the company could face; 4) the options the company has for dealing with the range of outcomes; and 5) a recommendation about which option the company should choose and why. If you are reporting the risk in writing, take the necessary steps to preserve the attorney-client privilege. But understand that any writing (email, report, presentation, etc.) may have to be turned over to the other side in the event of a government investigation or civil litigation. Meaning, it is important to always write smart when discussing risk.

Protect the Attorney-Client Privilege

One of the company's most important assets and one of an in-house lawyer's most valuable tools is the attorney-client privilege, i.e., the ability of the client to ask pointed and raw questions for the purpose of obtaining legal advice. If not utilized properly, however, this tool can backfire in ways that hurt the company. Consequently, because of its importance and value, in-house counsel must consistently take the necessary steps to properly claim and preserve the attorney-client privilege, including teaching the business how it works.

The attorney-client privilege protects from disclosure to third parties: (a) confidential communications; (b) between an attorney and client; (c) made for the purpose of obtaining or providing legal advice. Unless all three of these prongs are met, the communication is not privileged. The purpose of the privilege is to allow clients to discuss issues openly to obtain legal advice from both in-house and outside counsel without fear that those communications will be disclosed to third parties. The parameters of the attorney-client privilege in a particular situation depend on the law of the state where the communication took place. Consequently, it is important that in-house counsel understand how the privilege applies in the state or country where their headquarters is located and/or the state (or country) where the attorney practices, if not the same as the headquarters.

If you or the business get the privilege wrong there may be numerous long-term negative consequences for your company. First, if people mistakenly think documents are privileged, they might be careless in how they write things down, thinking the document will never be seen outside the company. Not that anyone would be untruthful, just that people are more precise, thoughtful, and professional if they know that third parties may see what they write. Second, if you waive the privilege for one document, chances are high that you may have waived the privilege with respect to other documents covering the same subject matter. Third, the overly aggressive use of the privileged label can cause judges to think that the company is attempting to hide documents and find that such documents—even those legitimately privileged—should be turned over to the other side.

The attorney-client privilege applies in limited circumstances, in particular:

1. requests for legal advice from a client to an attorney;
2. requests for information from an attorney for information needed to formulate or provide legal advice; and
3. the legal advice is the attorney gave.

Many lawyers (in-house and outside counsel) mistakenly believe anything they write for any reason is protected by the attorney-client privileged. They are wrong. Unless the communication meets the test of items (a)–(c) above, it is not privileged. For example, uncommunicated handwritten notes of counsel may not be privileged. Likewise, a common area of error is the failure of the communication to contain or deal with legal advice. Legal advice covers all legal advice including litigation, transactional, and regulatory. Business advice, however, is never privileged and, for in-house counsel in particular, the line between the two can be blurry. If challenged, different judges see things differently with respect to what constitutes legal advice and what constitutes business advice and in-house counsel must be constantly vigilant regarding the scope of their communications with the business and understand when they are or are not giving legal advice and, if they are giving legal advice, that they take the extra step to clearly note in the communication that they are providing legal advice.

Additionally, it is absolutely critical that the legal department and the company keep legal advice confidential. It cannot be passed along outside that company, a frequent occurrence with business colleagues who do not understand the problems doing so can cause. Similarly, everyone needs to be extremely careful when discussing or accessing privileged communications in public areas such as restaurants, elevators, airplanes, trains, sporting events, etc. To minimize such problems, only those who need to know should receive privileged communications.

Another common misperception among the business is that all confidential information is privileged, and if they label the communication as privileged, or copy a lawyer on the email they can keep the document or communication out of the hands of third parties. Consequently, legal department training of executives and business colleagues (and fellow lawyers as necessary) on how the privilege works generates incredible value for the company. This training should include the many ways the business can waive the attorney-client privilege. Unfortunately, if you disclose a privileged communication to a third party it is very likely waived. You can also inadvertently waive the privilege, for example, by accidentally emailing a privileged communication to the wrong person.

There are several things the legal department can do to ensure the best possible outcomes with respect to protecting the privilege:

- Be sure to properly label communications that meet the test for attorney-client communications. The document/email should be labeled "Attorney-Client Communication–For Purpose of Legal Advice".
- Ensure that the document/email clearly states that the person is seeking legal advice or that you (as an attorney) are responding to a request for legal advice. For example, "I am providing you legal advice regarding [X], or "I am seeking your legal advice regarding [Y]." Ensure that any attachment you are being asked to review (or have reviewed and are sending back to the client) is also properly labeled, i.e., "Privileged and Confidential–Legal Advice/Review Sought". This will give you a better opportunity to claim that the privilege applies to both communications. It may sound a little silly, but using seven or eight words to clearly state in the cover note/email or on the face of the attachment that legal advice/ review is the purpose of the communication can go a long way in convincing an overworked judge with scant time to review materials that the privilege should apply.
- If legal advice is being sought in any email or a memorandum, be sure that the business puts the lawyer in the "to" line versus the "cc" line. It is difficult to argue that the privilege applies when it appears that the lawyer is not the primary recipient of the communication.

- Limit circulation of legal advice and privileged communications internally to those that need to know.
- Keep the communication confidential and do not permit the legal advice to be circulated outside the company.
- Do not claim the privilege when it is not applicable. Not every lawyer's communication is privileged. If you or your colleagues are incorrectly labeling everything as attorney-client communication you can hurt your chances of keeping truly privileged documents safe because a judge will, quite frankly, not believe you on the ten actual privileged documents when there are dozens or hundreds of incorrectly labeled documents.
- Write smart regardless of your level of confidence that the attorney-client privilege applies. You should always anticipate that anything you write may ultimately end up in the hands of your adversaries.
- Know the applicable laws in your state regarding the attorney-client privilege. Everyone on the legal team should know and understand the basics. Be zealous in your review of documents in production for litigation, and if you think the judge got it wrong, strongly consider appealing the judge's order and moving for a writ of mandamus if necessary.
- Understand that outside the United States privilege issues get tricky, and you should be very careful with respect to what you think might be a privileged communication.
- Train the business on all of the above and find teachable moments when you see something that jeopardizes the privilege or is not a proper use of the privilege.

The attorney-client privilege is a valuable asset of your company. Treat it as such. Train yourself, your team, and the company on best practices.[64] Be constantly vigilant and in teaching mode on the issue—and fight like hell to preserve and maintain the privilege when challenged.

Be the Watch Dog: The Value of Compliance

In-house lawyers constantly look for ways to avoid or lessen risks that can damage the company (i.e., minimize value destruction). A robust compliance function is an important part of risk-reduction at companies of any size. In-house lawyers should get behind the creation of a compliance group if there is not one or enhancing the existing compliance group, whether it sits in the legal department or not. A strong compliance department moves the company from reactive to proactive in detecting and preventing wrongdoing. Besides avoiding trouble, this

---

64 A great resource on issues involving the attorney-client privilege is the legal blog "Presnell on Privileges" available at www. presnellonprivileges.com.

can lead to substantially reduced fines with regulators. The compliance department also helps establish the right ethical tone at the company, a tone that makes it easier for employees to make the right choices. While some executives do not see the value of the compliance function, despite the many proven benefits, in-house lawyers do. However, they frequently do not know what to do next in terms of capturing or enhancing the value of compliance. Below, I discuss how to build out a value-adding compliance function along with several specific compliance issues that are most likely to land companies in hot water and, therefore, the value of compliance training and monitoring multiplies.

Setting Up a Compliance Function

The single most important need of any compliance department is obtaining buy-in from the C-suite, along with the board of directors. Both should be supportive of setting up/strengthening this function as regulators are focusing on enforcement against executives individually, as well as the company generally. The senior management of the company is important, primarily through their support, their actions (walking the walk), and by regularly communicating the importance of compliance to employees, via town hall meetings, staff meetings, large employee conferences, email, intranet, video, and whatever other means the company uses to communicate with employees. Support from the upper levels is what regulators expect to see. For example, under the U.S. Sentencing Guidelines, sentencing credit is given to companies that can show, among other things:

- ☐ Strong, explicit, and visible support for the company's compliance program from the executive team and the board of directors.
- ☐ The compliance program has sufficient stature and support within the company.
- ☐ The right culture is fostered at all levels, but especially at the top.
- ☐ Emphasis on the role compliance plays and the value it brings to the company.
- ☐ Regular communication of the company's standards and procedures.

Compliance programs are not one size fits all. They must be customized to the needs and challenges each company faces. This is why some companies may have a relatively simple program, while other programs are more complex. If you try to shoehorn someone else's program onto your company you are unlikely to get any benefits under the sentencing guidelines, which require that companies tailor compliance programs to their specific needs. This means a thoughtful review (audit) of the different compliance risks your company faces, so you can tailor your program accordingly. Ideally, an independent third party performs this audit, but you can start by using your own internal resources to scope out the relevant issues, e.g., cyber-risk, antitrust, or export compliance.

The list can vary widely, depending on the type of business you operate and its geographic location(s). To conduct a useful audit, interview employees from across the different lines of business and staff groups. As you begin to collect information about compliance risks, create a work plan setting out the different risks, the different objectives regarding each identified risk, along with timelines/deadlines to complete the objectives. This is a big job, so do not try to identify everything right away. Start with your company's five biggest compliance risks and address those first. You can embellish the program later after the most critical issues are dealt with. Once the compliance department is established, periodic third-party audits of the function and its effectiveness can be very helpful and valuable. They can also provide benchmarking data which is helpful when seeking budget, implementing new policies, or responding to C-Suite or board questions around how are we doing with compliance?—a question they should be asking regularly.

Someone must be responsible for the compliance function, so it is important to appoint a compliance officer. Often, it is the general counsel, but it does not need to be. Regardless of where it sits, the compliance function should have a direct line to the CEO and the board of directors, and to the audit committee. There should be nothing preventing the compliance officer from reporting issues to the highest authority in the company. It is also important that the compliance officer has the staff and resources to do the job properly. It does not need to be an empire, but it needs to be appropriate given the size of the company and the range of compliance risks presented. Nothing fails faster or looks worse to a regulator than an understaffed, underfunded compliance department.

The most important document for a compliance function is the employee code of conduct (sometimes called a business ethics policy). This document sets out the company's expectations for all employees (legal, regulatory, ethical, etc.) along with the behaviors and practices it encourages or will not tolerate. A company may already have a code of conduct/business ethics policy. But, if there is no compliance department focusing on it, the policy is probably overdue for an overhaul. Likewise, a compliance department needs policies and procedures, including its process for conducting internal investigations and how it will report out results. Preparing a core set of these documents is a key task for the legal team. Finally, the code of conduct and other policies need to be easily available to employees. A prominent place on the home page of the company's intranet and regular reminders of where to find the code and policies (with working hyperlinks).

A common misperception is that the compliance department is responsible for all compliance. This is not correct. Many different groups within the company are responsible for various aspects of compliance. For example, human resources is responsible for sexual harassment claims, the legal department handles antitrust and import/export, IT security handles data privacy and security training, internal audit deals with employee theft, and so on. The compliance function handles certain aspects of compliance directly (e.g., training), but often acts as the leader of the company's compliance efforts. In this role, job one is determining whether all areas of company compliance risk are sufficiently covered and, if not, how to incorporate any outliers into the overall compliance program and determine which group is responsible. The compliance function should establish regular meetings of the different groups responsible for compliance to ensure coordination between them, along with sharing best practices and common issues. One helpful task for the compliance officer is creating a matrix to ensure that different compliance issues are routed to the right group and that there is no duplication of effort, or worse, groups operating at cross purposes. The compliance officer must also ensure a reporting process to the C-Suite and the board of directors so they are aware of any material issues before any become public headlines. The board will likely want regular reporting of what compliance issues came in and how the team dealt with them, including the final resolution. Reporting to the board is the perfect time to utilize benchmarks so they can see how the company compares with others in terms of metrics like the number of hotline complaints, type of complaint, etc.

Another common mistake many companies make when it comes to compliance is forgetting about their foreign locations. To start, if you have foreign offices, you should translate your code of conduct, training, and other materials into the primary language of those locations (if not the same as headquarters). It is difficult to convince a regulator that you have an effective in-country compliance program if that program is available only in one language, and it is not the native language of those employees. Get input from your foreign offices about how effective the policies and training are, and if there are any local compliance issues that are not properly covered by the main policies and procedures—if at all. Do not assume the only compliance risks are those you can identify at headquarters. Next, find ways to underscore the importance of compliance at remote offices. It may require you to travel or incorporate a visit or meeting if you are headed that way. Do not miss out on any opportunity to appear live in front of employees anywhere. (There is always huge value upside in doing so as discussed early in this book.) Finally, be sensitive to cultural differences when it comes to compliance. For example, in some cultures, whistleblowers are viewed poorly so relying on them to come forward presents challenges. Likewise, in Europe, many countries do not permit the use of anonymous hotlines, and you must factor that into your program as well.

A code of conduct and other policies are great, but everyone knows they are almost useless unless all of the employees receive training about the code (including executives and, if possible, the board). A robust training program, therefore, is a must. Most training today is done online, but always look for chances to conduct live training. Online is fine as long as the training is tailored to your company's specific needs and risks, and it is refreshed regularly. The gamification of compliance training is growing and is highly effective in terms of ensuring employees take the training and that they retain the information. The key to any training is keeping it simple. Complex legal concepts are generally lost on the employee base. Go for the big issues, with easy-to-understand language and examples. Ensure that there is an emphasis on the spirit of the law as much as there is on the letter of the law. Employees should understand that the company wants them to do the right thing and that compliance makes the company better, protects the brand, and keeps it from getting entangled in expensive and messy lawsuits or regulatory actions.

One tough problem you might face is the group of employees who just will not get around to completing the training. Try the following to remedy this:

- ☐ Ensure all of the senior leadership team has completed the training. This allows you to tell the recalcitrant employees that they cannot be busier than the C-Suite, which found time to complete the training.
- ☐ Give the group a short, but reasonable amount of time to get the training completed, e.g., 10 business days. Inform them that failure to complete it by the deadline means their access to company systems will be suspended. This usually works.
- ☐ If they *still* fail to complete it by the deadline, give them one additional day along with a note that if they fail to complete it then, they will be ineligible for any discretionary bonus payment for the current year. This *always* works.

Crucial to any compliance program is ensuring that employees understand when they need to report something and how they can report it. The code of conduct should contain a section describing all the ways employees can raise issues, including a toll-free hotline, email to a monitored compliance email address, their manager, the general counsel, the head of HR, and so forth. Make it as easy as you can for employees to raise issues. It is far better to have employees raise issues than to have those problems buried until a serious issue explodes. The company must have, and enforce, a no-retaliation policy and make sure every employee knows there will be no such retaliation for raising a good-faith issue. Likewise, you need a general policy around ensuring appropriate confidentiality for both the person bringing the complaint and any employees implicated by the same.

When a complaint comes in there should be:

- ☐ a pre-set process for how it will be investigated, including assigning to the right department;
- ☐ procedures in place to guide how the investigation will proceed, the expected timeline, along with a form for interviews and other reports so there is a consistent look and feel to all of the company's investigations;

- ☐ a mechanism to report back to the person raising the issue (assuming they left you a means to get in touch) so they know the company took the complaint seriously and investigated it; and
- ☐ consistent punishment for any employee found in violation of the code of conduct, including executives. If there are different outcomes for different employees, there will be little faith in your process. Lack of faith in the compliance process is deadly.

Creating a strong compliance department is a tough job. But the alternative—no compliance department or a weak compliance function—is very risky. If you can get the support of top executives and the board, including the appropriate amount of funding and people, you can build a viable compliance team in a relatively short time. If your company is falling down in the area of compliance, now is the time to get the issue in front of the decision makers. A proactive legal department is a valuable legal department.

Foreign Corrupt Practices Act (FCPA) and Anti-bribery

If you work for a company that operates globally, you know that many countries have anti-bribery laws, the most prominent being the Foreign Corrupt Practices Act (FCPA) in the United States and the Anti-Bribery Act in the United Kingdom. Regardless, of where your company is located the in-house legal department must be well versed in the requirements of any applicable anti-bribery law. Given the level of fines and the reputational risk at stake, it is also important that the department take steps to help ensure the company's employees have the tools and training they need to stay on the right side of the line.

To start, you need a comprehensive anti-bribery policy in place. It can be separate or part of a larger business ethics policy (though the better practice is a separate policy). If you do not have one, now is the time to get one in place. Take the time needed to customize your policy so it tracks to and resonates with your business. Regulators will look to see if the policy and program are tailored or cookie cutter, the latter being frowned upon. If you operate globally, you need your policy translated into the local languages of your employees outside the home country. It is difficult to explain to a regulator why you think a policy, for example, in English would be easily understood and followed by an employee whose first language is not English. Every year, you should read through it, make sure it is up to date, clear, and easy to read. This last point is important. If you have a policy that is fifteen pages of dense legal speak, it will be hard to get people to read it, let alone understand it. Keep it simple, the key message being we don't bribe people. One easy trick: have a coffee or lunch with some business colleagues and get their feedback on the policy. You will learn a lot about how clear your policy is to understand when you ask non-lawyers for their thoughts and suggestions.

If your company operates globally, you can create a heat map of countries where your company should focus attention on bribery risks. If you do business in Russia, China, Brazil, for example, you will need to be more alert to bribery issues and focus extra training for and communications to employees working in those troublesome countries. Similarly, every year you should send an email reminder to all employees about the anti-bribery policy. This is an easy and effective step. A short email communication to all of your employees several weeks before the holidays, for example, reminding them about the key points of your anti-bribery policy can prevent a misstep. The holidays are an ideal time for a reminder because it is easy for folks to get carried away on gifts or expensive dinners during this time of year, not realizing that they could land the company (and themselves) in hot water. For some, just a reminder as to which of your company's customers are potential government officials can be helpful as they may not realize that quasi-governmental entities are covered under these laws (e. g., airports, hospitals, utility companies, etc.). In fact, every year, the legal department should take a look at all of the company's customers and sales targets to determine which may be caught under applicable anti-bribery law. A proactive step like this can not only prevent problems but it demonstrates real and tangible value delivered by the department.

It is also an excellent idea to review the materials and tools you use to train your employees about anti-bribery laws every year as well. Are they still fresh and relevant? Are they easy to follow and clear? Do you have special training tailored to the employees in sales or who operate in high-risk countries? Are all the members of the legal team sensitive to spotting FCPA/anti-bribery issues? Some companies use online training, but live teaching sessions (including webcasts) are highly effective too. Similarly, new training tools allow you to create apps and games to teach compliance and provide access over smartphones and tablets. Keeping training fresh and cutting edge will help it stick with your employees.

Consider whether you have the right processes in place to catch and deal with potential issues. What is the due diligence process for anti-bribery issues in mergers and acquisitions deals? You do not want to purchase a nest of bribery issues. Similarly, is there a process to research and vet the background of potential sales agents or joint venture partners? There are many do-it-yourself tools out there that make, at least the first step in this research, easier and more comprehensive. Do you have a simple process for employees to report concerns or questions (e.g., a hotline or dedicated email address)? Do you remind employees regularly of the risks of violating anti-bribery laws? Consider sending a regular monthly email to all employees that deals with business ethics issues. These are short emails that are focused on ethical issues arising from specific provisions of your business ethics policy, and remind employees about the rules of engagement in day-to-day business matters. Use examples from current headlines where companies have gotten into trouble or employees went to jail or faced heavy fines for engaging in a forbidden activity. Short emails containing real examples of how real people tripped up, bring the message home effectively. It is also a visible way for the legal department to show leadership and value.

Odds are good that the company's vendor contracts contain representations around bribery laws. If your company regularly engages sales agents in foreign countries, you must have agreements that require certain certifications and acknowledgments about compliance with anti-bribery laws. Now is the time to review those agreements and update them (yearly) as necessary. If your contracts are lacking these provisions, get them in place now. Be clear in your contracts about the importance of compliance with anti-bribery laws. The company's agreements should have audit rights and the ability to terminate immediately in the event your partner violates such laws. If a partner refuses to sign the agreement or include these provisions, that is a red flag to your company not to do business with that partner.

It is a bit of a broken record, but it is important to get senior executive buy-in that compliance with anti-bribery laws is paramount at your company. This "tone from the top" has many benefits, including helping the legal department obtain completion of training, reporting concerns or questions, and gaining compliance, generally, with the processes it set up to help ensure third parties are properly vetted before your company engages them. When you kick-off compliance training, ask the CEO to send a message out to all employees about the importance of the training and, if true, that the executive team has already completed the training first. (This helps you address employees who later said they are too busy to complete the training.)

It is not enough to have great policies and well-written emails about compliance. Consider teaming up with the internal audit team or an outside vendor to review your FCPA/anti-bribery program and benchmark it against industry-standard practices. This can be invaluable when reporting to the board, or if you find yourself in the crosshairs of a regulatory investigation. If you decide to do this, be sure to confirm that the review is being done at the request of the legal department for the purpose of providing legal advice, and be sure to take the necessary steps to preserve any applicable privileges. An audit like this is a big task, so do not rush into one lightly. It is smart to take advice from your outside counsel about such a project.

As for outside counsel, you should plan now on how you will deal with things when you have a real problem. Unless you are a particularly sophisticated in-house legal department, odds are you will not have the expertise or experience to handle a serious anti-bribery issue. Figure out what outside counsel you will call before there is a problem. When things blow up, you want to be ready to go as time will be of the essence most likely, and you will be glad to have experienced counsel helping guide you and your company through the process.

Minimize Antitrust Risk

Antitrust litigation is expensive and fraught with risk, especially for the defendant. The rules (other than for hardcore antitrust offenses like price-fixing) are murky and behavior that seems perfectly rational and competitive, may in fact not be (at least in the minds of jurors). Moreover, it is easy for business people to cross the line either by being hyperaggressive in competing in the marketplace or falling into an improper discussion when opportunities to meet with competitors arise (for example, at a trade association meeting or business conference). In addition to the expense of litigation (and the diversion of time), damages awarded in an antitrust matter in the United States are automatically trebled, which raises the stakes on compliance and the value to the company of an effective training program. Antitrust compliance comes in two parts. The first part deals with the types of agreements that can cause problems for your company. The second part focuses on the types of unilateral behavior that can land the company in a lawsuit.

Agreements

Section 1 of the Sherman Act covers agreements between one or more parties that may be anticompetitive. Section 1 states, in its entirety:

> "*Every contract, combination in the form of trust or otherwise, or conspiracy, in restraint of trade or commerce among the several States, or with foreign nations, is declared to be illegal.*"

If read literally, section 1 would prohibit every commercial contract because all contracts cause some restraint on trade. Fortunately, courts do not and have not read Section 1 literally. Instead, they have found that section 1 only prohibits unreasonable restraints of trade (though "reasonable" appears nowhere in the statute). Because companies run on contracts, in-house lawyers must understand what types of agreements provide for or create such unreasonable restraints. If not, it is way too easy for companies (especially young companies) to get into serious trouble. I'll start with the main reason: people can be stupid. Really stupid. The second reason is what I have dubbed the antitrust paradox, meaning what is good for your business is bad for antitrust exposure and vice versa. And because most rational business people want good things to happen for their business, the specter of antitrust issues will haunt the in-house legal team. Here's an example: *It would be great if all competitors charged the same price, so let's just them to do that.* Here's another: *Our business would be so much better if our competitors stayed out of each other's home markets, so let's agree to do that.* And finally, *if we and our competitors all agreed not to buy Product X from those folks at Big Corp, we could force them to drop the price.*

If you do not know already, all of these are terrible things to do from a competition law standpoint. Yet, because a race to the bottom competing on price or features or other areas is terrible for a business you can see the allure to business people of making such agreements. Further, many business people are either not be aware, do not care, or do not understand the rules of the road and they will do things that they think are great for the business. The job of in-house counsel, therefore, is to save them from themselves and before their actions can bring on significant value destruction in terms of lawsuits, fines, jail time, and reputational damage.

Courts have two core standards for analyzing agreements to determine if they contain unreasonable restraints on trade. The first is the *per se* standard. This type of agreement is so obviously anticompetitive that there is no further analysis needed. If you did it, you are in trouble. The second is the "rule of reason," where courts review agreements that are not *per se* violations to determine if the benefits outweigh any competitive harm. In doing so, courts look at the agreement and then (i) define the relevant market (product and geography), (ii) determine the market power of the defendant in that market, and (iii) look for the existence of anticompetitive effects. Assuming there are such effects, the burden then shifts to the defendant to show an objective, pro-competitive justification for the restriction/agreement. Courts look at several factors to weigh any justification:

- the intent and purpose in adopting the restriction;
- the competitive position of the defendant (including market conditions before and after the restraint was imposed);
- the structure and competitive conditions of the relevant market;
- any barriers to entry; and
- the defendant's "objective" justification for the restriction.

Most antitrust cases involving agreements fall under the rule of reason. As you can probably tell, it is an expensive and prolonged battle between the parties, fraught with risk to determine where your agreement may fall during this balancing act. Consequently, this situation is something most in-house lawyers work hard to avoid.

Here are some of the most problematic agreements:

- *Horizontal Agreements (agreements with competitors, generally per se violations)*
    - Price fixing. The king of per se violations is an agreement among competitors to fix prices. And it does not matter if you want to lower prices. Price fixing is simply bad.
    - Joint boycotts. Another per se violation, e.g., no joining together with other competitors to agree not to do business with another business.
    - Bid rigging. It is a per se violation to join with competitors to rig a bidding process.

- Dividing customers and/or markets between competitors—do not do this.

➤ *Vertical Agreements (agreements with non-competitors, generally rule of reason)*

- Tying. A vertical agreement that can also be a *per se* violation in some cases is tying, which is using market power for one product to require a customer to buy another one of your products or keep them from buying a competitor's product.
- Resale price maintenance. Occurs when a manufacturer sells a product to a distributor and then tries to control the price at which the distributor can sell the product to consumers.
- Exclusivity provisions. Provisions requiring one party to deal exclusively with another party can be challenged under antitrust law and are reviewed under a rule of reason analysis.
- Most favored nations (MFN) clauses. MFNs (sometimes called "parity clauses") have come under attack by the DOJ and in the EU. Under a pricing MFN, the other party agrees that it will not pay more to another party than it does to you, or will not sell for a different price than the one charged to you. Parties can agree to an MFN for other aspects of their agreement, for example on content.
- No poaching agreements. Over the past several years the DOJ, in particular, has waged war on agreements that prevent one company from hiring or trying to hire the employees of another. If the restraint is ancillary to a larger agreement (for example, a sale of a business), then it has a good chance of survival. If it is just a naked agreement between companies not to hire each other's employees you may have some problems, maybe even *per se* problems.

Other agreements fall under the rule of reason but the above are the most common. And you can see the antitrust paradox at work. It would be great if no one could hire your employees or undersell your price or deal with your competitors or customers and so forth. But agreeing to do so can quickly pull your company into an antitrust lawsuit, which is why it is important for in-house lawyers to teach the business where the risks are and the potential consequences—including treble damages and jail time.

When it comes to the rule of reason, most of the agreements in question are written out. They are normal commercial agreements. That makes proving that an agreement exists pretty easy, and the fight is over whether they are reasonable or not. When it comes to *per se* violations, sometimes business people are dumb enough to write out agreements to fix prices, or rig bids, or divide markets.

Writing it out does make it easy to prove an agreement but recordings, confessions, and eyewitnesses can substitute as evidence of the agreement. Your smartest move here as in-house counsel is to teach your business colleagues to act as if they were always being recorded when speaking with competitors and to never joke when it comes to antitrust issues. Also, they should always take care when writing anything down that can be misconstrued as an agreement with a competitor to take any action.

That said, most business people are not dumb enough to write out agreements to do bad things or get caught on a recording. Antitrust law has developed ways to deal with the prospect of unwritten agreements, that is, agreements can be proved through circumstantial evidence. For this, courts hold that you need more than evidence that can be equally consistent with lawful behavior. There must also be evidence that tends to exclude the possibility that the parties acted independently. There needs to be something more. The classic example of perfectly legal conscious parallelism is different gas stations located on four corners of an intersection. Because they all advertise their prices on large signs, the price at each station is almost always the same—even though there is no agreement between them to all charge the same price. Airlines matching fares is another good example. To get over the evidence hurdle, a plaintiff must show the more, i.e., something more than simply uniform action by competitors. These are called plus factors, factors that can allow the judge or jury to conclude that there was something more afoot than legal unilateral behavior, that is, the now famous "wink and a nod." The plus factors include the following.

- The defendants acted contrary to their individual economic interests (e.g., took prices up when supply was heavy).
- The defendants had meetings or conversations, that is, opportunities to agree, which is what trade association meetings are an area of concern for in-house counsel.
- The defendants had a motive to collude (for example, crushing a maverick competitor.)
- The defendants engaged in abrupt or unprecedented changes in behavior.
- The industry is concentrated with few competitors. (Oligopolies are more prone to agreement than a marketplace with dozens of competitors.)
- The hub-and-spoke conspiracy, which is trying to beat the system by arranging for competitors not to talk to each other because a middleman is serving as the hub making vertical agreements (rule of reason) with a bunch of competitor companies serving as spokes, who would not otherwise so obviously and directly agree with each other.

Trade association risks are discussed later, but for now, keep in mind that participating in a trade association does not remove your company from antitrust risk. In fact, it increases it, because trade associations often involve competitors joining together in a room to talk about business. The only thing missing is cigar smoke. While it does not mean anything bad happened, it never looks good to a jury when competitors meet, regardless of the reason.

In-house counsel must be wary of Section 1 during the merger and acquisition process, in particular when the target is a competitor of the acquiring company (that is, a horizontal merger). The due diligence process involves the sharing of incredibly sensitive competitive data about the target, such as customer contracts, financials, projections, strategy documents, employee contracts, tax returns, research and development, intellectual property, and a host of other commercially and competitively sensitive documents. Under normal circumstances, competitors sharing this information would land the parties in jail. Regulators understand that some due diligence is necessary, even among competitors. The solution is generally four-fold:

- A battle between the legal teams to minimize the data provided (versus what the acquirer wants to see).
- Reliance on aggregated and older data versus specific and forward-looking data, along with masking of customer names and redacting other sensitive data.
- Strict confidentiality agreements and secure data rooms.
- A clean team to review the information, meaning individuals at the acquiring company who are not involved in price setting, customer relationships, or day-to-day operations of that company. Usually, these individuals agree not to move into any of these competitive positions for several years, which allows the information they saw to grow stale.

Section 1 continues to apply after the deal is announced, but not yet approved by regulators. While the two companies can engage in integration planning, they cannot act as though the deal is done, They cannot reach out to customers together regarding contract terms, combine contract forms, and so forth. This is called gun jumping. And, while the purchase agreement usually puts some limitations on the behavior of the acquired company (i.e., the target company may not do anything out of the normal course), it should be, for the most part, business as usual between two competitors *until* the deal is approved.

Because the previous information is a lot to take in, I have broken things down to my five rules in-house counsel should commit to memory and train the business on. If you can get these five right, you will eliminate a lot of —but not all of —the risk of Section 1 problems:

Five Core Rules of Section 1 Antitrust Compliance

1. Do not discuss or exchange emails or other documents on prices, customers, markets, marketing, bidding, boycotts, future products and plans, or any other competitively sensitive area with competitors.
2. Do not agree to meet, talk with, signal, or enter into any type of agreement with competitors, written or oral, without first checking with the legal department. Don't try to use a middleman to get around the rules.
3. Don't write stupid [expletive]. When writing emails and company documents, stick to the facts (minimize the adverbs, adjectives, opinions, and speculation) and stick to what you know. Counsel must review all substantive merger/acquisition-related documents while they are still drafts.
4. If you are at a meeting or on the phone with a competitor, for a valid reason, act like it is being recorded. And if a competitor raises an improper topic, get up and leave (or hang up) and report the incident to the legal department immediately.
5. Check with legal before agreeing or insisting on any type of exclusive dealing or parity/MFN clause in a contract.

Unilateral Action

Now for the hard part, dealing with Section 2 of the Sherman Act. Section 2 is a minefield of traps for the unwary. In-house lawyers can find their company mired in complex litigation where every contract, clause, meeting or action, and every email or slide presentation is under scrutiny for alleged uncompetitive behavior. all because your company is highly competitive and successful. As a result, all in-house counsel should have a basic understanding of Section 2[65] so they can keep a sharp lookout for whether company actions or plans risk drawing anti-trust scrutiny or, far worse, an anti-trust lawsuit. Avoiding such a result is a true value-add for the company, falling squarely under minimizing value destruction.

Most in-house lawyers are aware of the risks discussed in the last section above, that is, their company cannot enter into agreements to boycott, fix prices,

65 Virtually all industrialized countries have equivalent national laws to Sections 1 and 2 of the Sherman Act. In-house counsel should be up to speed on competition law wherever the company operates.

divide markets or customers, or agree to bid-rigging. Unlike Section 1, however, Section 2 focuses on single-firm conduct, the unilateral actions of just one company. Section 2 is another exercise in legislative brevity stating:

> "Every person who shall monopolize, or attempt to monopolize, or combine or conspire with any other person or persons, to monopolize any part of the trade or commerce . . . "

Over the years, U.S. courts have interpreted Section 2 monopolization as requiring: a) the possession of monopoly power in the relevant market; and b) the willful acquisition or maintenance of that monopoly power (other than through superior products, business acumen, or historical accident, i.e., by acting unfairly.) This means in-house counsel should start worrying about Section 2 any time their company crosses over fifty percent market share because that is the point where competitors, customers, and government regulators can and will start to take a real interest in what the company is doing.

Once your company crosses the fifty percent market share barrier, things get different from an antitrust perspective. Actions your company took while it was small can turn into competition law problems once it gets big. While the Sherman Act is designed to protect competition and not competitors, that will not necessarily stop a competitor or customer from trying to gin up an antitrust claim as a way of trying to level the playing field or get through court action what they cannot get in negotiations, either by suing directly or by taking their claims to the antitrust regulators, for example, the Department of Justice or Federal Trade Commission.[66] Unfortunately, it often works. Antitrust lawsuits are wildly expensive, easily tens and tens of millions will get spent defending the company if the plaintiff gets past a motion to dismiss. Moreover, the Sherman Act provides for the trebling of damages along with attorneys' fees. Meaning, if the plaintiff can prove damages of $100 million, that automatically becomes $300 million (plus costs and attorney's fees, which can often be shockingly high for such cases.) All the more reason to be ever vigilant as an in-house lawyer.

In addition to money damages, the plaintiff can seek injunctive relief, attempting to get the court to order your company to stop doing something, be it behavior or even stopping the use of certain contractual clauses. An injunction can be worse than the monetary damages at issue because it may shut down your company's primary business model. If government regulators take an interest, you will probably have to deal with a costly Civil Investigative Demand, meetings with regulators, and potentially interviews of company witnesses. Government regulators can take their time with their investigation, leaving your company under a cloud, even if you have done nothing wrong. Government regulators can

---

66 *See discussion supra* at page 163 (using the law as a strategic weapon).

even seek to break up your company if it gets too big and engages in uncompetitive practices.

When thinking about Section 2, the first thing in-house lawyers must figure out is whether or not their company has a monopoly. For purposes of Section 2, this means a monopoly in a "relevant market." In particular, a monopoly concerning a certain product or service in a particular geography. Accordingly, defining the market is critical to any antitrust law analysis. The broader the market is in terms of available products and geographic scope, the less likely any company has a monopoly. A product market means all the products out there that compete (or potentially could compete) with and are interchangeable with your product or service. A simple way to look at it is if your product or service was not available, where would customers turn for a substitute? All of those substitutes comprise the product market. From an antitrust paradox standpoint, businesses would like there to be no substitutes for their product, as this would allow them to charge whatever the market will bear. From an antitrust standpoint, however, in-house lawyers want there to be many substitutes because, if this is the case, you cannot be a monopolist.

Once you know the product market, you must also define the geographic market, i.e., where does the company sell its products or services? In what region/area do all the competitors compete? How costly is it to transport products? It may be as small as a single city or town, or it could be a country or even globally, especially with respect to online services. Next comes determining whether any of the competitors in the market—including your company—have monopoly power. Monopoly power is the ability to exclude competition or raise prices and not have any competitive consequences, e.g., raise prices by five percent and keep it at that level without losing sales. An additional test is market share in the relevant market. If a company has over seventy percent market share, it is likely considered a monopolist. If the company has less than fifty percent market share, it probably is not a monopolist. If the company has between fifty percent and seventy percent, it falls in a grey zone (and this is where in-house lawyers need to start being vigilant.) Market share alone is not definitive, but it is indicative of monopoly power, especially when there are significant barriers to entry into the market (capital costs, regulations, and so on). For example, if a company has a ninety percent market share, but competitors can easily enter the market and duplicate the service or product and offer it at a lower price, then the ninety percent market share company is not a monopolist. It may briefly enjoy being able to charge whatever the market will bear, but competitors will see those profits and rush into the market to try to capture some of it via lower prices.

There is a common misperception that having a monopoly is bad or illegal. It is not. It is perfectly legal in the United States for a company to have a monopoly and to exploit it to charge the maximum amount the market will bear. This is, for all practical purposes, capitalism at its finest. The courts are clear that if a company achieves a monopoly because of superior products or business acumen, or by historical accident, there is no problem. Where a monopolist (or potential monopolist) gets into trouble is when it attempts to obtain or maintain a monopoly position through anticompetitive means, or exclusionary conduct. Here is where Section 2 gets interesting. If your company is a monopolist, there is a wide range of conduct that can raise antitrust risk. Remember, being a monopolist is not against the law, but, the willful acquisition or maintenance of that monopoly through the use of anti-competitive or predatory means is. Unfortunately, there are few bright lines for companies to follow in terms of knowing when behavior crosses the line from sharp competition (no problem) to exclusionary, anti-competitive conduct (big problem). And even if your company has no intent to act badly, you can still find yourself in the crosshairs of an antitrust lawsuit or investigation. The lack of clarity as to what constitutes bad conduct is as maddening for business executives as it is for in-house counsel. Here is a partial list of behaviors that can, but not always, cross the line if your company has a monopoly:

- refusals to deal (refusing to do business with a competitor or a disloyal customer, especially when there was a prior contractual relationship);
- tying (requiring that a customer by a company product as a condition of being able to purchase a product in which the company has a monopoly);
- use of most favored nations clauses;
- exclusive dealing contracts;
- loyalty discounts;
- denial of access to competitors;
- abuse of standard setting (especially if you have a patent);
- bundled pricing;
- predatory pricing (pricing below costs);
- product disparagement;
- abuse of government process (for example, filing bogus lawsuits or regulatory actions) and
- general bad behavior (also known as cumulate acts, where any one act alone would not be a violation, but taken together they create a Section 2 "monopoly stew," which gives the plaintiff the ability to toss stuff on the wall and see what sticks.)

If your market share is small, your company can engage in most, but not all, of this behavior with little fear of drawing a Section 2 antitrust complaint. Once it crosses the fifty percent market share threshold, however, in-house lawyers need to start thinking about whether the risk of problems is worth the payoff from the behavior as bad behavior can land the company in a world of problems.

Moreover, the risk can hinge on any one of these behaviors or a combination of them. Once the company gets big, the other side can try to make any of your actions, behavior, contract clauses, whatever, look like you are harming competition. This antitrust stew is a hallmark of Section 2 claims because it gives the opposing party many different ways to try to show that your company is acting anticompetitively, even if any one of the ingredients is not problematic or would be fine for a smaller company to engage in.

Regardless, anyone bringing an antitrust complaint must show that your actions harm the competitive process. The plaintiff must have suffered an antitrust injury of the type the Sherman Act protects. And, you can defend your alleged anticompetitive behavior if you have a pro-competitive or pro-business rationale. For example, a company might stop doing business with a competitor because the competitor is free riding on its brand or technology to the detriment of their business. Or, a company might offer loyalty discounts to provide lower pricing for volume. Because someone accuses your company of anti-competitive motives, does not mean you cannot defend your actions. In short, the court will look to see if your company is competing on the merits; whether you have a rational business purpose behind the challenged behavior. This test makes up part of the rule of reason analysis discussed previously (that is, does the pro-competitive good outweigh the anti-competitive harm?) Your job as in-house counsel (and where you bring the most value to the table) is to help ensure the business is entering into contracts and taking other actions pursuant to a legitimate business need such as:

- enhanced efficiency/lower costs;
- promotion of intra-brand competition;
- stopping free riding;
- higher quality customer service;
- increased output;
- better quality products and services; and
- creation of new products and services.

You can also see how important it is that your business colleagues write smart, as plaintiffs' counsel can twist every line in an email or slide presentation to seem like an affront to nature and all mankind.

Dealing with Section 2 claims is challenging for in-house lawyers. What constitutes a violation is difficult to ascertain or even describe to your business colleagues. Activity that on its face seems perfectly legitimate can, when combined with other actions (and clever plaintiffs' lawyers), be made to look like something sinister. Here is a list of things in-house counsel can consider doing to lower the risk of a Section 2 claim (once their company's market share crosses over fifty percent market share):

Five Rules to Help Avoid Section 2 Lawsuits

1. Do not define markets. Be watchful over documents and emails your business colleagues prepare that purport to define the market for your products or services. Such self-definition can be used against the company if it tries to define the market differently (more broadly) during litigation or investigation.
2. Cool the testosterone. Sure, it is fun for the business folks to thump their chests and write about how the company will destroy its competitors, or crush the competition, or jam price increases down customers' throats, and so on. All in-house lawyers have seen this. Guess what becomes Exhibit 1 at trial when your company is the subject of a Section 2 claim? Yep, all those testosterone-laden emails and documents.
3. Have a business justification. An in-house lawyer's best friend when facing a Section 2 claim is a valid business justification for the behavior in question. Listen closely when the business describes what it wants to do and why. Teach the business to focus on the business reasons and drop language that may falsely allude to other motives, especially motives that can be construed as anticompetitive.
4. Find good antitrust counsel. Like insurance, you may never need it, but you should have already identified some antitrust lawyers you can turn to for advice.
5. Keep your eyes and ears open. Constantly look for any indications that a customer, competitor, or the government may be contemplating some type of antitrust action against your company. Teach the business to forward to you immediately any email or correspondence where the other side is suggesting that the company is acting anticompetitively.

Lastly, value-driven in-house lawyers provide training to the business leaders on the scope of single-conduct Sherman Act Section 2 offenses (along with Section 1 training), on writing smart, and on ensuring that legitimate business justifications drive decisions.

Minimize Trade Association Risk

Most companies belong to a trade association, some to more than one. A trade association is generally made up of competitors. As most in-house counsel know, and as described previously, meetings between competitors can be tricky and fraught with risk, both for the company and the employee. Improper agreements (price-fixing, bid-rigging, dividing territory or customers) between competitors can lead to costly litigation, investigations, fines, damages (trebled), and even jail. The only 100 percent safe route is no communications with competitors ever. A restriction like that, however, is unnecessary as there are plenty of situations where conversations between competitors are needed and completely appropriate. The key (and the watchdog value-add) is for in-house lawyers to make sure that employees at the company, from the CEO on down, have a basic understanding of the rules of the road for interacting with competitors and know when to contact the legal department for guidance.

Trade associations serve many pro-competitive purposes, including lobbying the government on behalf of its members, educating the public about the services and value its members bring to the table, and sponsoring standards-setting exercises that encourage growth, interoperability, and innovation. However, any time competitors interact—a trade association meeting, lunch, email conversation—there is always a chance that a perfectly innocent conversation or document will be misconstrued or taken out of context and unfairly presented as some type of nefarious, conspiracy to thwart competition. Or, even worse, competitors may actually be engaging in prohibited conduct, often because they do not understand where the boundaries are. Consequently, there is value in ensuring that the business is trained on what they can and cannot do when working with or through a trade association. Start with basic antitrust training, which should include training about appropriate competitor interactions, including trade associations. Prepare a written policy that provides clear guidance and expectations for employees.

Next, you want your trade association set up to succeed, operating in a manner compliant with the law. This includes an informal association (a coalition) of competitors as well as a formal trade association. Here is what you need to consider:

- ☐ Start with a clear, written statement of the association's purpose and mission. It can pay off in the event anyone challenges why a group of competitors was meeting in the first place. It also sets boundaries for the group and provides guidance on the types of matters and issues the association can properly undertake.
- ☐ All trade association meetings should follow a written agenda sent out in advance to the participants and counsel approved. Once there is an agenda, the members need to stick to it. The agenda should be clear, concise, and leave no room for misinterpretation of what is being discussed. This matters because an agreement between competitors does not need to be in writing, it can be oral and informal, including what is commonly referred to as a wink and a nod among competitors sitting around the table. Having

a clear agenda (that no one varies from) can minimize the risk of bad behavior or misinterpretation/miscasting of what occurred at a meeting.

- ☐ Take minutes of each meeting that accurately reflect what occurred and have counsel prepare (or at a minimum review) those minutes before finalizing. Promptly distribute the approved minutes to all of the participants and keep a copy in case needed down the road. The final, approved minutes should be the only minutes of the meeting. Members should not keep their own minutes.
- ☐ In a perfect legal world, counsel would attend every trade association meeting or call. This is not always possible or practical. Assuming not, ensure the trade association staff is well trained on competition law issues and begin each meeting with a reminder of the antitrust ground rules. Any meeting where the agenda contemplates discussing competitively sensitive information should have counsel present or on the phone.

Additionally, ensure the business understands that participating in a trade association does not in any way transform inappropriate behavior into legal behavior. This point must be emphasized with your business team and with all members of the trade association. Problem areas include discussing current or future prices, costs, output levels, business and research and development plans, forecasts, etc. If, for some reason, an improper topic is raised during the meeting, your trade association staff and members need to know in advance how to shut those conversations down immediately. And if there is a question about whether the discussion is appropriate, the right course of action is to stop and only return to the topic after consulting counsel. Make it clear that these same rules apply outside of the formal trade association meetings, for example, at dinner, on the golf course, etc. Basically, every interaction between competitors is subject to scrutiny, and therefore, extra caution is required to ensure staying everyone stays on the right side of the line.

In addition to the promotion of their industry, many trade associations deal with lobbying, data exchanges, and standard setting. If done properly, all three can be valuable and pro-competitive. However, there is no blank check for any activity of a trade association. If you cannot do it outside the trade association then you cannot do it as part of a trade association. For example, lobbying activity needs to be reasonably necessary to the goal and not a sham. Any data exchanges between association members (for example, for benchmarking or trade association marketing purposes), must ensure that sensitive information is properly anonymized, aggregated, and historical. No current or future pricing/forecast information should be exchanged. Ideally, any such data is submitted by each member to, and compiled by, a third party. Any plan to share data must be cleared with counsel in advance of handing over the data to avoid any appearance that the process is part of an agreement to fix prices. Standard setting can be a pro-competitive action on the part of a trade association, especially if it spurs innovation and reduces costs.

Still, before a trade association engages in standard setting, counsel should vet the process and goals. Standards must be based on objective criteria and reasonably related to the goals the parties are trying to achieve. Generally, they should be voluntary in that there is no agreement to compel compliance with the standards.

When considering membership criteria, keep in mind that competitors who are not allowed to join a trade association can be the source of an antitrust complaint. Legitimate criteria for refusing membership is not an antitrust violation. Be sure your trade association's membership requirements are objective, transparent, and non-discriminatory. Similarly, if there is a process to expel a member, ensure counsel vets the process carefully. The operation and governance of the association are important, too. Play it straight at all times. Election to the board of directors should be simple, transparent, and straightforward.

The trade association should have its own antitrust policy and staff that is well trained on antitrust issues. A well-trained staff may be your best line of defense. Likewise, the company's business people who regularly attend trade association meetings should receive special antitrust training, in addition to training all employees receive. When the association meets, go over the basic antitrust ground rules before anything of substance is discussed. Every year the trade association should have a health check and work with counsel to ensure the right policies are in place and to determine if anything needs to be changed or updated. In-house counsel should also meet regularly with their internal clients to stay abreast of what is going on at the trade association meetings.

Trade association documents can be and will be used against you. Everyone—the association's board of directors, staff, and members—must understand that poorly drafted documents (email, memoranda, minutes, agenda, handwritten notes, reports, studies, etc.) can land the association, the company members, and even individuals, in hot water. Every document involving the trade association is a business document and must be professional in tone and language. The key is to draft documents that are truthful, accurate, and business like.

Even if you do all of the things discussed above, there is no guarantee a determined plaintiff will not sue your trade association or any of its members, regardless of the merits of the claim. All meetings with competitors can create risk. That said, there is nothing inherently bad about competitors meeting and talking, as long as the guidelines above are followed and those attending the meeting are thoughtful and well trained about the risk areas.[67] This is certainly an area where in-house counsel have plenty of opportunities to add value, both in terms of helping create/operate the trade association (value creation) and preventing antitrust problems from arising (value destruction). A successful trade

67 The DOJ and FTC have produced guidelines dealing with a wide range of competitor collaborations, and they are worth reading. They are available online at https://www.justice.gov/atr/page/file/1098461/download.

association is something the legal department can tout to senior management and even generate KPIs around.

Protect The Board of Directors

If you work for a company of any material size, there is likely a board of directors. For smaller, family-run companies, this usually means a board comprised of several family members with little risk of problems from outsiders. But, as the company gets bigger, and especially if the company is publicly traded, the risk of problems grows quickly. As in-house counsel, one of the most important and visible ways you can project value by minimizing value destruction is to protect the board of directors from going down the wrong path or setting themselves up for potential exposure from lawsuits or regulatory sanctions.

To start, be sure all of the directors understand their duties as members of the board. All directors owe their corporation: (a) a duty of loyalty, that is, they are disinterested (not on both sides of the transaction or otherwise stand to receive some personal benefit not shared with the shareholders of the corporation) and independent (acting in the best interests of the corporation and not themselves or another person or entity to which they may be beholden); (b) a duty of care, meaning they perform their duties after review and consideration of all applicable information reasonably available to them (a due diligence requirement); and (c) a duty of good faith and fair dealing, that is, acting with a good faith belief that the actions taken are in the best interests of the corporation.

If these duties are met, for the most part the actions of the directors are immune from second-guessing by the court under what is known as the business judgment rule. Ensure any new director receives a solid background on these duties and that you refresh all directors on these duties annually. Moreover, provide ways for directors to speak up about any potential conflicts as that is usually where trouble occurs. An annual conflicts survey is a useful tool. Additionally, be sure to keep your directors apprised of any specific obligations under the rules of the appropriate exchange if the company is or will be publicly traded.

Get in the habit of regularly updating the board on key developments in the area of corporate governance. This can mean new court decisions, new regulations, issues raised by proxy advisory services (such as ISS or Glass-Lewis), activist shareholders, and so forth. As in-house counsel, stay abreast of governance developments by reading *The Wall Street Journal* or *Financial Times*, by subscribing to capital markets alerts most large law firms prepare, finding a good blog dealing with governance issues, and by joining the Society for Corporate Governance.[68] Make providing a short update on governance issues part of every

68 *See* https://www.societycorpgov.org/home.

regular board meeting and part of the director materials. Proactively send the directors updates of critical developments as they arise.

Meetings of the board of directors go to the heart of the governance of the company. It is paramount to ensure that in-house counsel properly prepares records of what was discussed and decided at board meetings. There are three core documents to focus on, and each protects the directors by helping to show how they met their duties of loyalty, care, and good faith. These are (a) the meeting agenda, (b) the meeting minutes, and (c) any resolutions voted on by the board authorizing company actions. The agenda for each board meeting should, at a minimum, set out the time and place of the meeting, call to order, approval of the minutes of the last meeting, the topics that will be discussed (new and old business), the expected allotted time for each topic, and the speakers/presenters for each topic. The minutes are a written record of what occurred during a board meeting. The proper drafting of corporate meeting minutes is important. Minutes are not a verbatim transcript of what was said at each meeting. Instead, they should focus on summarizing things such as:

- the meeting date, time, and location;
- the nature of the meeting (regular, committee, special, telephonic, etc.);
- a list of all attendees (and a list of directors absent from the meeting and whether a quorum of directors is present);
- the general topics of discussion, the names of all individuals making specific presentations, and the general nature of their presentations;
- attaching the meeting agenda and reference any materials distributed before or at the meeting; and
- confirmation of all actions the board took, such as adoption of resolutions and the vote tally.

The most important goal of the minutes is they accurately reflect the directors exercising their business judgment when considering company matters at the meeting. To this end, accurately describe the tenor of the discussion, the length of time taken, etc. For example, "After the CEO's presentation on the need to purchase a new building, the board and members of management present discussed the issues presented in the materials at length."

Finally, where appropriate, all corporate actions taken by the board of directors should be reflected in a written resolution. A resolution is a formal document that sets forth an action of the board and records the vote. Most resolutions are voted on during meetings (in person or telephonic) and are part of the minutes, though sometimes resolutions are voted on outside of a regular meeting. In some instances, the corporate by-laws permit electronic voting via email. When drafting a resolution, keep the language formal, ensure that the title of the resolution spells out what the board is considering, and use language that walks the reader through all of the important considerations leading up to the vote of yes or no. Ultimately, in the event the action is ever challenged, the resolution should clearly set out what the directors considered and why they took the action they took.

Only the shareholders can amend the articles of incorporation. The bylaws, however, can be amended by the board of directors. To maximize flexibility, put the minimum operational requirements into the articles of incorporation and everything else important to running the company into the bylaws. One way to protect your directors via the bylaws is to include a provision setting out an exclusive jurisdiction for any shareholder-derivative lawsuits. The most likely jurisdiction for such an exclusive forum clause is Delaware, which is consistently the most sophisticated and company-friendly/director-friendly place to incorporate in the United States.

There will be times when things go off the tracks and your directors will get sued because of something related to their service on the board. Prepare for this by ensuring that the company properly indemnifies the directors and that the company has secured sufficient directors & officers (D&O) liability insurance. Both the articles of incorporation and the bylaws should contain language stating that the company will indemnify its directors to the full extent permitted by law. Doing so will prevent questions from arising later as to whether the company can or should indemnify its directors. Next, prepare and execute separate indemnity contracts for your directors. These agreements supplement the terms found in the bylaws and the articles of incorporation. One key issue here is whether the company will advance indemnity around costs of defense to directors (it should). Additionally, unlike the bylaws or articles of incorporation, the company cannot change the terms of the contract without the director's consent. Lastly, add carve outs for intentional misconduct and bad faith, where the company will not indemnify a director from his or her own bad acts.

The board is ultimately only as good as the information it receives from the company. This can be through the official board of director materials (e.g., board books made available before meetings), discussions and briefings during board meetings, informal discussions with officers and management as the need arises, and through their own diligence and sources. Regular board meetings should include time set aside for a briefing on legal issues, a way to bring forward any of the biggest risks the legal department has spotted out on the horizon, such as regulatory changes, litigation risks, and so on. It is important that the general counsel have access to the directors directly to raise issues that warrant their attention and, sometimes, their input. It is also important that the directors not receive all of their information about the company from one source or one person. While the relationship between the board of directors and the CEO is critical, the directors should also have access to key employees of the company at board meetings or on an as-needed basis so that they can get the information they need or check the information they received. The CEO should buy in and agree with how people can and will communicate directly with the board of directors. Such communications should not become a way to get around or undermine the CEO.

The directors must understand how the attorney-client privilege works. There should be no expectation on the part of in-house counsel that the directors do understand no matter how sophisticated they may appear. As discussed above, the most common mistake people make, even directors, is thinking *all* communications with lawyers are privileged or that simply copying a lawyer on a document or email will cloak it with the privilege. Neither is true. Given the amount of sensitive legal information shared with the board of directors, it is a valuable exercise to train them on how the privilege works, how to properly label privileged communications, how to protect it at all times, and to provide them with yearly refresher training. In the right type of litigation or investigation, the emails sent to and by the directors may be relevant and, therefore, called for under a document request. Your directors may even be subject to deposition under the right circumstances. Set up a company email account for each director (and their administrative assistants) and conduct all company business with the directors via company email. This way, if there is litigation or an investigation, the emails you need to search should be limited to company email accounts and not the director's personal or other business accounts.

Do not forget to include the board of directors in any compliance training provided by the company to management and employees. It is good policy that everyone in the company completes the training, even the board. For some board members, this may be the only compliance training they receive at all. Additionally, it gives the directors—especially those on the audit or governance committees—a first-hand view of what the company is doing concerning its compliance program and training. Further, it looks good to regulators if the company's directors take part in the training program. Lastly, requiring that they participate allows directors to provide feedback on the quality, ease of use, and other aspects of the training. This can only make the program better.

No one becomes a director knowing how to do it. Even the brightest and most capable people need to be oriented and protected. This is one of the prime responsibilities of the legal department. Being proactive in this area can be a boon to the department and your career as everyone will remember who had their back.

Protect the Company's Brand

Your company's brand and reputation are valuable assets worthy of the full attention of the legal department. In today's fast-paced 24-hours-a day news cycle and hyperfast social media, if a customer says or posts negative and untrue things about the company the legal team may need to scramble. The same is true if an employee (regardless of status) tweets something really stupid on the company's Twitter account. More traditionally, the legal team will swing into action if someone is using or violating the company's trademarks. And things can go sideways quickly when someone launches attacks on your company's reputation and brand. Consequently, one of the most important jobs in-house counsel can take on is protecting these assets. Customers will not buy from a company they do not like, investors will not invest in companies that have bad reputations or cannot protect their brands, and employees do not want to work for a company they do not feel good about. A bad hit to its brand or reputation can cost the company multiple millions of dollars, just like a well-protected brand and reputation can be worth multiple –millions, if not billions, of dollars. Like everything for in-house lawyers, it comes down to value enhancement and/or value protection (and it provides the legal department with another opportunity to show its value to the company).

Everything about reputation and brand starts at the top. How the C-Suite behaves and acts will roll through the entire organization. If your executives do not cut corners and do not play loose with the rules, odds are good that the organization generally will not do so either. This means in-house lawyers should counsel senior management to take every opportunity (town halls, staff meetings, emails) to communicate and emphasize to employees how important it is to act ethically and to be vigilant about how their behavior can negatively impact the company's reputation and brand. The legal department should lead the way here both with respect to coaching senior management and with helping employees understand the rules of the road via messaging, training, and real-life examples of how company reputations can be damaged quickly. As Warren Buffet says, "It takes twenty years to build a reputation and five minutes to ruin it."

There are many ways to protect the intellectual property of the company, such as patents, trademarks, copyrights, trade secrets, etc. However, when it comes to brands (names, marks, or content) the two most important are trademarks and copyrights. In-house lawyers should develop a solid strategy to apply for and maintain both. The same is true for licensing any of your marks. For trademarks, ensure that your employees and licensees are using the marks properly. A failure to do so can result in your company losing the mark as diluted, generic, or abandoned. Regarding domain names and company websites, watch out for cybersquatters and spoofing. In addition to taking various avenues of legal action, consider buying up the variations and common misspellings of the company's domain names so a competitor or someone looking to harm the company cannot use those. If someone is spoofing your website or email, you need to move quickly to stop it, including working with law enforcement, contacting the domain registrars and ISP providers immediately, and putting a notice on your actual website (and other channels) to warn customers about the fraud. The legal department should have a process to stop cybersquatters and website spoofing laid out in advance of any problems.

Today, every company should have a social media policy and provide mandatory training to its executives and employees on its provisions. At a minimum, it should set out rules for your employees using social media on behalf of the company or using their personal accounts to discuss issues related to the company. Over the years, many executives and employees have lost their jobs because humor does not always translate well outside the walls of the company. There are many examples out there that the legal team can use to train and remind employees about the risks of a poorly worded or poorly thought-out tweet. Having a social media policy is great, but to protect itself, the company must develop a systematic way to monitor the internet and social media for attacks. This can be done through the legal department, marketing, or corporate communications (or a combination thereof). However, someone must be responsible for checking the internet and social media every day and making sure all employees know where to go in the event they see something that is potentially damaging to the company.

If you do see the company's brand or reputation being attacked, it is important to not sit back and let things play out. Take some action immediately. Being aggressive, however, does not mean you have to go nuclear from the start. Most in-house lawyers have gotten a "nasty gram" from another company's legal department or law firm complaining about something. Often you think, if they had just called me and been nice, we could have solved this in five minutes. Instead, a nasty letter or email usually results in an equally nasty response. And then it can be off to the races before cooler heads prevail. It is also important to remember that whatever cease-and-desist letter in-house or outside counsel sends will likely find its way online for the world to see and judge. Sometimes that is not a good thing and can be as damaging to the company's brand as the action it was aimed at in the first place. But, when you cannot be polite about it, look for the best way to quickly and efficiently solve the issue. You can, of course, file a lawsuit alleging some type of business defamation, Lanham Act violation, or actions for trademark or copyright infringement. There are other options out there as well. If a competitor engages in advertising comparing their product or service directly to yours and does so in a manner you think is unfair or not truthful, consider filing a complaint with the National Advertising Division (NAD) of the Better Business Bureau rather than filing a lawsuit.[69] The NAD offers experienced-attorney reviews that apply precedent to determine whether the advertising claims are truthful and non-misleading. Compliance with any decision is optional, but advertisers generally comply and if not, the NAD may forward the case to the Federal Trade Commission for action. Another avenue is asking the site to take down the offending post or material. If it involves the improper use of one of your copyrights, you can send a takedown notice under the Digital Millennium

69 *See* https://bbbprograms.org/programs/all-programs/national-advertising-division.

Copyright Act.[70] Also, most websites and search engines have some process for you to request that material be taken down.

In-house counsel are in a unique position to see things such as programs, ideas, actions, investigations, and initiatives that could turn into something bad for your company's reputation and brand. You do not need a law degree to spot these issues, just a unique vantage point. Common sense will tell you when something needs to be explored more deeply and when you need to escalate a problem to a higher level. But, once you escalate a serious problem, follow through to make sure something has been done to solve the problem (or if not, why not). A good example is a controversy from several years ago involving General Motors (GM) and cars it manufactured with faulty ignition switches which led to numerous deaths, a billion dollars in recalls, more than $35 million in fines, civil damages from dozens of lawsuits, and a black eye on one of the most respected and revered companies in America. To keep it simple, lawyers in the GM legal department knew about the problem in 2004, but no one told the general counsel until 2013. That meant nine years of not dealing with the problem and letting the damage from the inevitable aftermath build. The lesson here (among many) is about creating an environment in the legal department where serious problems are raised with the general counsel as soon as possible. However, it cannot fall on the legal team alone. It takes a broad group of individuals and a cross section of business teams and staff groups to handle a serious problem concerning reputation and brand. The legal department adds value by being proactive and thinking ahead as to what this response team should look like, who should be on it, and what its charter should be, before there is a problem. If you try to create this team during a crisis, you will find yourself behind the curve when trouble strikes. The response team should include: senior business leaders, legal, corporate communications, investor relations (if the company is publicly traded), marketing, and human resources (in case the problem involves actions of an employee). All are identified in advance of trouble and trained before there is ever a need to use the group. From the outside, you will want to identify a reputation management expert and outside counsel to use in case of a serious problem.

Another critical step in brand protection is for the legal team to ensure that the company owns and controls all of its social media accounts and has a process in place to ensure the transition of responsibilities, passwords, list of accounts as employees come and go into roles involving the use of these accounts. Many companies' social media accounts are in the name of the individual who set them up and/or is in charge of social media marketing. This is especially true at start-ups. There are many stories regarding employees leaving a company and taking the company's dedicated social media accounts with them. Ask yourself this: Does legal know who owns all of the company's social media accounts? If the

70 17 U.S.C. §§512.

answer is "no," it is time to take action. As an added precaution, be sure your social media policy and employee onboarding documents clearly state that all such accounts are the property of the company and that the employee must turn over the account and passwords when departing the company.

You may not think of brand protection as a value-added service of the legal department, but it is. And savvy in-house legal teams not only prepare for and deal with any issues, but they also make sure the business knows they are standing guard.

Protect Company Trade Secrets

When you list the crown jewels of your company, it is almost certain that many of them involve trade secrets. Protecting the company's trade secrets is one of the most important and valuable tasks the legal department undertakes. Unfortunately, for many in-house lawyers the first time they worry about trade secret protection is the day a key employee with intimate knowledge of the company's most important trade secrets departs to work for a competitor. Sadly, the time to worry about this scenario was the day the company hired her. If the company does not have the right agreements, policies, training, and plans in place during her employment, it could mean a rough day in the office (or in court) when she walks out the door. Fortunately, there are a number of basic things in-house lawyers can do to harden the company's ability to protect its trade secrets and enhance value creation, while minimizing potential value destruction.

To start, most employees probably think everything the company considers confidential is a trade secret. Unsurprisingly, that is not the case. A trade secret is:

a) something not generally known to the public;
b) where reasonable efforts are made to keep it confidential; and
c) confers some type of economic value to the holder by the information not being known by another party.

What constitutes a trade secret can vary by state or by country, so in-house lawyers must be up to date on the law in their key jurisdictions. A good shorthand is any information you would not want your competitors to have. Examples include information about new business models, detailed customer and supplier information (for example, prices they pay/you pay), marketing strategy documents, new inventions, processes and formulae, and similar highly guarded information. Your company's financial information may feel confidential, but if you work for a publicly traded company, most of that information is available to the public with each earnings release, making it difficult to argue that the information is somehow a trade secret.

In addition to the narrow definition of a true trade secret, if the company does not take appropriate steps to keep sensitive information confidential, it can lose the ability to claim that information as a trade secret. For example, the company hands out copies of its future marketing plans to customers without a non-disclosure agreement in place or has failed to label the plans as confidential. Courts look at these factors to determine if something is truly a trade secret:

a) the extent to which the information is known outside of the company;
b) the measures taken by the company to guard the secrecy of the information;
c) the value of the information to competitors;
d) the extent to which the information is known throughout the company's employee base; and
e) he amount of money or effort the company spent to develop the information and how easy would it be for others to duplicate the information without access to it.

A key step is to start (or update) an inventory of all of the company's trade secrets. Interview key company employees and executives about what they believe are trade secrets and match what they say against each element of the discussion above. With a trade secret inventory in hand, you can identify what steps are needed to keep those specific items confidential and protected, and be clear with the business what items are not trade secrets (and properly set expectations in advance). Additionally, there are several key agreements to have in place and regularly update as necessary. Courts want to see such agreements in place as part of their analysis of whether the company took the proper steps to maintain confidentiality. The core agreements include:

- non-compete agreements;
- non-solicitation agreements;
- non-disclosure and confidentiality agreements; and
- work-from-home agreements/policies to ensure employees are aware of expectations around confidentiality when they work remotely, something far more common now than a few years ago. For example, requiring the use of a VPN when connecting to the internet outside of the company offices.

The enforceability of these types of agreements, especially non-competes, can vary widely depending on the jurisdiction. Trying to implement a one-size-fits-all approach is not recommended unless you want to save money and take a chance on whether your agreement is enforceable or not. The better plan given the expense of such a process, is to ensure in advance that the agreements put in place generally are enforceable as written in the jurisdictions you care most about.

Like many problems companies face, the weakest links are the careless employees. This means the right—and persistent—training and the right policies to educate employees and prevent leaks of your trade secrets are vital, especially given how much weight evidence that the company does both is crucial to convincing a court that the company is protecting its trade secrets properly. Some key policies to consider include:

- proper marking of confidential materials;
- social media policy;
- limiting disclosures to "need to know;
- procedures for visitors to the offices;
- policies around proper storage/disposal of confidential material;
- password and information security (especially training around phishing);
- guidelines regarding the removal of confidential information from the company offices;
- bring-your-own-device requirements; and
- procedures around providing confidential information to third parties, for example, requiring non-disclosure agreements.

While these agreements and policies are important, if your employees are not taught how to protect trade secrets, you still may not be able to convince a court that you are appropriately protecting the same. A comprehensive training program is essential. Training should include examples of things your company considers to be trade secrets (and not generic training modules that have little to do with your company's actual business and operations). All new hires should take the training, and there should be a yearly refresher course for other employees. Regular email reminders, short articles, examples from the headlines, etc. from the legal department about trade secrets and confidentiality are helpful as well (both in terms of underscoring the message with employees and convincing the court that the company does a lot to protect its trade secrets.)

When it comes to training employees, an easy way to ensure that confidential documents and materials are treated as such is to require employees to mark these materials as confidential so it is clear on the face of the materials they are trade secrets and extra care is needed. Another tip is to require that copies of any confidential materials handed out at meetings be returned and properly disposed of unless anyone needs to keep a copy to do their job or any follow-up task.

When an employee departs the company, a well-thought-out exit interview process is important. The legal department should partner with human resources to ensure the following:

- departing employees receive a copy of any agreements they signed during their employment dealing with confidentiality or other restrictive covenants, and that they sign a document acknowledging any ongoing obligations;
- reminders about the post-employment obligations of the employee;
- determining whether an employee has any company information at home or stored on any non-company cloud system;
- determining if the employee is going to work at a competitor. If so, and there is no applicable non-compete in place, consider a short, non-hostile

letter to the competitor explaining the departing employee's ongoing confidentiality obligations. If there is a non-compete agreement in place, determine whether the employee's new employment violates the agreement or, at a minimum, put the new employer on notice about the non-compete obligations;

- employee surrenders all company property and signs an acknowledgment that they have returned all such items (and that no copies exist anywhere);
- immediate termination of all passwords, access to systems/email, identification badge/access to buildings, parking cards, and so forth. There should be no company systems or property available to the employee once they walk into the exit interview; and
- if there is reason to suspect the employee of problematic behavior, a proper search of their company email, hard drive, computer files, and voice mail for any improper activity.

Lastly, one of the most valuable things an in-house legal department can do in this area (but hopefully never has to use) is a plan for what to do when the company's trade secrets are threatened. Here is my checklist:

Trade Secret Theft Preparation Checklist

- ☐ A strong relationship with HR, information security, and internal audit is important. Work in concert to ensure plenty of communication in the event anyone sees, feels, or hears of trouble. Get this group together in advance to map out in writing what to do and how everyone will work together if there is a trade secrets issue.
- ☐ Have your outside counsel advisors lined up in advance (for all key jurisdictions).
- ☐ Have a system in place to quickly locate any agreements signed by the breaching employee, the applicable policies, etc.
- ☐ Know who to call to terminate system access, revoke passwords, and building access.
- ☐ Think through in advance the potential legal claims available to you in the most important jurisdictions.
- ☐ Be ready to contact the party that received your confidential information and ask that your trade secrets be returned immediately and/or destroyed, along with an acknowledgment that they have done so. A form letter or email is a must.
- ☐ Develop contacts at local law enforcement and the nearest FBI field office in the event of a computer crime or theft of trade secrets

When it comes to trade secret protection, prevention is critical because once a trade secret is revealed, it may be too late to undo the harm. Being proactive and forward-looking will serve the legal department and the company well.

Prepare for Bad Things—The Ultimate Plan to Minimize Value Destruction

Unfortunately, the world we live in can go from good to shockingly awful in a matters of hours. As someone who lived through the "Great Freeze" in Texas in 2021, I saw this firsthand. Disasters arising from natural events (hurricane, pandemic, earthquake, etc.) and man-made events (plane crash, cyber attack, workplace violence, and so on) constantly lurk in the shadows. This is true for both individuals and businesses of all sizes: tragedy does not discriminate. Protection of your fellow employees and corporate assets/shareholder value should always be top of mind for in-house lawyers. Consequently, one of the most important tasks you have as in-house counsel is to help ensure that your company is prepared for when disaster—man-made or natural—strikes. In some companies, planning for disaster falls within the risk management department, in others, it is a mixture of different departments, including the legal department. Some companies simply have not gotten around to planning for disaster. Regardless of where your company sits on the disaster planning continuum, the legal department has an important and valuable role to play in assisting the company plan for dealing with a crisis. If not already the case, in-house lawyers must ensure they have a seat at the table for such planning.

To start, every business should have a business continuity plan (BCP). It is the gold standard in disaster planning. It is a big task and not something that can be thrown together in a week or two. A properly prepared BCP describes—in great detail—how a company will continue to carry on business in the event of some type of disaster. Ideally, it will be structured with checklists and step-by-step instructions that allow management to focus quickly on the specific things they need to do to get the business back up and running depending on what happened. Rather than go into detail on how to prepare a BCP, I will touch on a few basics and then discuss key parts of the plan so you have the ability to get something into place now versus waiting to create an entire plan. Doing something is much better than waiting around for perfection.

At its core, a business continuity plan requires the company to think through risks and vulnerabilities to the critical parts of its business, and then set out in detail how it will manage any such risk should it come to pass. The key takeaways are:

1) have a plan;

2) disseminate it to management and employees;
3) train on and practice it; and
4) review it annually and update as needed.

Your planning will start with identifying which executives/employees will make up the crisis team, that is, the people who will gather immediately once a crisis is declared and who will put the BCP into effect. They will also help create and update the plan. The team will largely be made up of senior executives from key lines of business and staff functions, with the goal of covering the entire business. Everyone's role and responsibilities should be set out, for example, crisis team chair, communications, security, IT, legal, etc. Establish succession planning with clear instructions about who takes over in the event someone is not available to act. Contact phone numbers and email addresses should be made available to everyone on the team. Get alternative phone numbers and alternative email addresses in case the primary numbers/email are not available. Everyone should know how, and be able to, contact other team members. Include contacts of key third-party vendors (name, phone, email, and description of service/products provided), as some of the company's vendors will need to be involved in dealing with the crisis. (This should include contacts at local utility companies.)

The plan should cover executive and employee travel, meaning what happens if there is a serious problem and how to avoid problems. First, it is best practice to ensure that not all of your senior management will be on the same flight. That way if there is an incident with the plane, other executives will be available to deal with the problem. Second, your company should know where its traveling employees are at all times. Your travel department/agent can help with this and likely has tools to automate the process. All traveling employees should have phone numbers and other ways to contact their travel planner in the event an emergency arises and travel plans need to change. Third, if your employees are traveling to foreign countries, they should take steps to notify their government. In the United States, you notify the U.S. State Department via the Smart Traveler Program.[71] By doing so, travelers will receive important information from the applicable embassy about safety conditions in their destination country and, among other things, help the traveler's family and friends get in touch with them in an emergency. Fourth, your company should have plans regarding medical emergencies and provide employees with information about what do to if they need medical attention while on the road. Lastly, you should have detailed plans around what to do if there is a kidnapping involving one of the company's employees.

In a crisis you should, if possible, have a dedicated room for managing the situation. This room can be on site or off site. The key is to plan for the room before it is needed. You will need phones, Wi-Fi, printers, and other key services

71 *See* https://step.state.gov/step/.

available, especially if the crisis room is off site. Moreover, it may not be possible to continue to operate your business from its existing location because of something like a fire, bio-hazard, earthquake, etc. Your plan should discuss where and how management and employees will work and communicate if this is the case. Many employees may be able to work from home or will simply be idle for some portion of the crisis. Others will need to be present at a temporary work location. Identifying a location (or a process to secure a location) in advance of a problem is an important step.

For each company location, local executives should know who to call for which type of emergency. In the United States, the most likely first responders will be police and fire. But do not forget about poison control, public health officials, FEMA, the FBI, Centers for Disease Control, Homeland Security (federal and state), and other public safety officials. Most countries have similar agencies. Your security manager should reach out to each and touch base as simply knowing who to call in an emergency is critical. Plus, having a conversation with these officials now, before there is a problem, can provide access to other resources, information, and guidance on how best to prepare for the worst. Once you identify the correct officials, their names, offices, and contact information should go into your business continuity plan.

It is important to ensure the work environment is as secure and safe as possible. There are no guarantees, but preventing a crisis is easier if your building is properly readied and secure before there is a problem. The most common ways to do this are registration desks, security guards, entry checkpoints, cameras, properly maintained secured access, well-lit facilities and parking areas, clean grounds, unobstructed exits, proper fire suppression system, fire extinguishers, and so on. There should also be well marked and properly stocked first-aid kits throughout the facility. Defibrillators are common, in fact, some U.S. states require them. Likewise, your list should include plans for and practice of building evacuations in case of fire, violence, weather, etc. Also have alternative locations for employees to gather in the event one selected location is not safe.

In addition to securing your building and premises, company employees should be on the ball as well. The legal team can add value to the company by assisting with developing a culture of security awareness that can save lives and property. For example, all employees should be on the lookout for people who do not belong on your premises. Train employees to, politely challenge or report people not wearing badges. Employees should also be on the lookout for anything out of place, including strange vehicles, packages/backpacks left unattended, or anything else that does not feel right. Train them on what to do under such circumstances, including the use of posters or signage with reminders and phone numbers of who to call if something is amiss. The Department of Homeland Security has a simple saying, "If you see something, say something." You can easily incorporate this into your program. Providing first aid training, CPR training, and defibrillator training are good ideas as well. Senior management support and participation cannot be overemphasized. If the senior management does not take this process seriously, then neither will the employees. All employees should be aware of the general parameters of your crisis plan and where to go for information if they suspect a problem or there is a problem.

All planning for business continuity must include insurance coverage. Many companies have business interruption insurance to cover interruptions. Likewise, many companies carry kidnapping insurance and other types of specialized insurance. A call to your insurance company may be among the first you make in the event of a crisis, so know who to call. Keep in mind, many insurers are generally happy to work with you on spotting issues, providing training, and assistance with planning around the risks they are insuring. You should regularly review the company's insurance coverage and make sure it matches up against potential risks, e.g., includes a pandemic clause. While it is unlikely the job of the legal department to run the company's insurance program, know that the legal team being involved in the process and having a real knowledge of the policy terms will pay off if all hell breaks loose.

Do not overlook the importance of the communications process—both internal and external. Several things matter. First, the company should speak with one voice in the event of a crisis. Determine who will be that voice in advance, and ensure everyone knows who is authorized to speak for the company concerning which issues. Typically, this will be the head of corporate communications. You can prepare templates (email, press releases, etc.) in advance so that your communications have a uniform tone and look. For internal communications, you have two audiences. The first is the crisis team itself and ensuring that the communication flows back and forth without problems. The second internal audience is the general employee base. They will be anxious for news about what is going on, what the company is doing in response, where they can go for more information or regular updates, and what they should be doing during this time of trouble. For external messaging, be prepared to deal with questions from the press, shareholders, government officials, family members of your employees, etc. Having a website page dedicated to making the most recent/current information available around the clock is a good idea, and the shell can be prepared in advance of a crisis. Similarly, a recorded message on a toll-free line is also a good way to mass communicate. If you have a call center and/or central reception area, you will need to keep them in mind as you prepare materials so they have guidance and talking points for any inquiries that come their way.

The legal department should be proactive and go to the business ready to raise and/or discuss the process to update or implement business continuation plans. The skills needed to prepare (and perform under) such plans fit nicely into the skills most lawyers bring to the table already. If a full business continuity plan is not in cards now, pick and choose among the items above where you can go ahead and get started. Getting any plans into place or at least started will make your company and its employees safer and protect your shareholders' investment in the company— and underscore the value of the legal department.

Summing Up

There are so many ways in-house legal departments can show their value that we often overlook the basics, i.e., the department's role in maximizing value creation and minimizing value destruction. When you analyze what in-house legal departments do on a day-to-day basis, you can put everything into one of these categories. By doing so, you start to see how crucial the legal department is to the success of the company day in and day out. If in-house counsel can package up this story for the business in the right way, it will have a tremendous platform to show why investing in the legal department makes sense for the business. To create the right value story, focus on the following.

- ☐ Create a to-do list of value-generating projects for the department to focus on every year. Make sure senior leadership is aware of the list and agrees with the projects.
- ☐ If you are not sure where to start or what to do, always focus the department's efforts on projects that generate revenue.
- ☐ Look for ways to speed up the contracting process, doing so will be noticeable and appreciated throughout the organization. Start with finding ways to make your contracts easier to sign and reducing risks overall so the focus is on getting high-quality contracts done quickly.
- ☐ Technology is your friend when it comes to creating value. Focus on technology that matters.
- ☐ There is much untapped value in finding ways to let the business help itself and only coming to legal when truly necessary. Find ways to enhance value through non-engagement including teaching the business how to write smart documents, how to read a contract, and how to use a contract playbook to get the right deals done faster.
- ☐ Do not ignore opportunities for the legal department to be a profit center, including establishing a recoveries program and finding ways to leverage legal issues to advance the interests of the company.
- ☐ Be on constant guard for ways to manage risk, both in terms of protecting against negative risks and taking advantage of opportunistic risk.
- ☐ Protect the attorney-client privilege at all times.
- ☐ Do not underestimate the value created through a fulsome compliance function. Focus your limited resources on compliance issues that matter to

the business such as FPCA, antitrust, protecting the board, and protecting the company's brand and reputation.

- ☐ Finally, use all of the special skills lawyers bring to the table to help the company prepare in advance for when bad things happen and the need for business continuity—probably the ultimate way a legal department can minimize value destruction. These are an in-house lawyer's superpowers and they are something to tout, not hide.

Partnering with the Business—Lawyers as Leaders

The legal department is not an island and it is not the only group within the company with something to contribute when it comes to value creation or minimizing value destruction. But, as noted in the discussion of the evolution of the in-house legal department, there are certain skills (superpowers) lawyers bring to the table that are difficult to find consistently throughout the company, such as dealing with uncertainty, communication skills (written and oral), managing unwieldy projects, organizational skills, consideration of multiple viewpoints, and calm leadership during stressful times, among other things. This means that in-house lawyers have tremendous value to add simply by acting as leaders and finding ways to partner with different groups so that complementary skills and expertise can meld together to generate or protect value for the company.

Set Annual Goals that Matter to the Business

One of the more daunting administrative tasks legal departments face is setting useful goals for the upcoming year. As we saw in the section on KPIs above, the work a legal department does not always lend itself to a set of neatly defined goals like other parts of the business. Yet, setting goals is important and provides a fresh opportunity to take stock of where the legal team should devote its efforts for the year. Goal setting is also an opportunity to market the department as in, here is all the great stuff we are doing. Done properly, the process gives the general counsel and legal team a deeper understanding of what is important to the business, along with feedback on how the department can improve in the upcoming year. As a result, in-house lawyers should see goal setting as an opportunity to embrace and not as a chore to muddle through. The more thought and effort you put into goal setting, the bigger the payoff.

To set goals that matter, it is helpful to create themes, or broad categories that capture the mission of the legal department. You know by now that the mission is simple: enhance value creation and minimize value destruction. When you think of what the department does (or should do) in light of this simple dichotomy, it is easy to place almost anything the department does into one of these categories, including the important need to develop and retain team members (an underappreciated part of the value legal departments provide.) Here is a set of five high-level themes to start with that you can customize as needed to set goals for practically any legal department.

- ☐ ***Build and retain an extraordinary team with exceptional people.***
- ☐ ***Meet budget targets.***
- ☐ ***Prioritize and complete high-value and strategic commercial agreements.***
- ☐ ***Deliver on strategic transactions and initiatives (including mergers, joint ventures, acquisitions, and other deal activity).***
- ☐ ***Defend and protect the interests of the company (litigation, IP, government affairs, compliance).***

Once you decide on your themes, you can develop precise goals underneath each.

Interestingly, it is important to look backward to look forward. How did the department do on the prior year's goals? Are there any goals worth carrying over to the new year or otherwise left unfinished? Did you find a better way to measure success, and should you try one of last year's goals with a new measurement process? Use the lessons of the prior year to develop better goals going forward. Also, talk to your business clients and find out what is important to them in the upcoming year. Do this at multiple layers. Talk with senior management, and then move down through the lawyers, and then those on the front lines. These people will give you more granular insight into what the business unit hopes to achieve. Then, match up the goals of the department (and individual lawyers supporting that business unit) to what the business thinks is important. Make sure the people you spoke with in the business know that you heard them and you are putting goals into place to match what they want to see. If you do not tell them, they will likely never know and that is a wasted marketing opportunity for the legal department. Do not forget to coordinate with other staff groups—they matter! Find out what they are seeking to accomplish in the upcoming year and think about how the legal department can help them either by partnering on a specific goal, adding goals that are complementary, or staying out of the way.

The general counsel must ensure that the goals of the legal department line up with those of the CEO and the board of directors, especially the committee chairs, e.g., audit committee. It is important to understand what the board is concerned about heading into the new year. And do not forget to canvas the entire legal team. Pick their brains about what should be on the list of goals for the coming year. Who knows better about specific legal issues facing your department and the company than your own lawyers? In other words, do not set goals in a vacuum.

In addition to matters that are ongoing, such as litigation, contracts, and strategic deals, consider things you know are coming down the pike for the company in the new year. This is where learning the company's business goals and strategy comes into play most prominently. For example, there may be an IPO or big refinancing on the way, start to plan for those. You know the new California and Virginia privacy laws are in place, but not effective until 2023. There is work to do now to position the company for compliance with these. Use your risk-spotting training to peer ahead, stay aware of what is going on in the world around you. Stay up to date on world events and developments in the marketplace and consider how those developments may impact the company and, therefore, the goals you set. The competitive and regulatory environment your company operates in is constantly changing and evolving (domestically and internationally). You must be plugged into that environment through internal resources (marketing, strategic planning office), as well as external sources (newspapers, websites and blogs, trade associations, and industry publications.).

It is a bit cliché, but your most valuable asset is the people you have working for you already. Goals should include helping your team upgrade their existing skill sets, develop different skills, and become more efficient and productive. It may be better or more CLE training, new technology and research resources, or moving people into different roles, or adding responsibilities. Is it time to put a succession plan into place (yes, it is), and are you ready to start that project?

Finding ways to measure success is one of the more challenging aspects of the goal-setting exercise. How do you measure success? Every goal you set should have some type of measurement associated with it, even if it is to complete review of data privacy policy by December 31. My advice: *Do not overthink it.* Unless you are directed otherwise, keep the measurement simple and straightforward, for example, the volume of contracts completed over the course of the year. As with KPIs generally, if no one has told you what to measure or how to measure it, use the opportunity to find the measure that lets you tell the narrative you want to tell about the legal department. Do not lie or sugar coat things, but if you cannot figure out what the business should recognize and value, why do you expect the business to do so? The answer? Tell them.

Once you have set goals, sit down with your team and go over them so everyone understands what is important and what they need to focus on individually and potentially add to their own goals for the year. Unless confidential, share all of the goals with everyone to ensure the entire department is on the same page. Then, have more focused discussions on goals during one-on-one meetings with your direct reports, so they can the same with theirs, and so on. And, start tracking success (or failure) immediately. Start January 1. If you wait until December to think back on how well the department did compared to your goals for the year, you probably won't remember everything you accomplished. Create some mechanism to continually save the department's achievements and successes for the year in real time, even if it is simply a folder in email.

It is unlikely that your goals will stay static over the course of the year. New issues, problems, or deals will arise that will become goal worthy. Be ready to update or alter your goals as needed—and let the business know if you are changing goals. Your themes should be flexible enough to capture important new goals. Finally, discuss progress toward the goals with your team at least monthly. Make sure everyone is aware of the progress—or lack thereof—and understands what they need to do to help the department meet its goals. Even better, share your progress with a broader audience, i.e., the business. The more the business sees what legal does, the more the value proposition will start to sink in. Sharing this information shows you are thinking strategically and about how the legal department can best add value to the company. That, in the end, is the point of setting goals.

In-house lawyers do not always recognize the value of goal setting (and measurement). It is a time to market the legal department proactively and to coordinate with senior management and other staff groups to not only understand what is important to the business, but to show them that the legal team wants to focus on things that are important to the success of the business.

Partner with HR

One of the most important internal relationships for an in-house legal department is with the human resources (HR) team. Much of the HR department's day-to-day work directly involves legal issues and analysis. Likewise, some of the nastiest and headline-grabbing litigation involves employees and their claims alleging company executive and manager mistreatment, discrimination, or malfeasance. Regardless of merit, these disputes tend to be public and can negatively impact the company's brand and reputation (along with severe economic consequences in the event the company must pay a settlement or loses in court). The legal and HR teams should closely cooperate and align on how to best protect the company from employment-related issues. To start, set up regular meetings to discuss a wide variety of issues and how best to work together to manage them. Each group brings different viewpoints and skills to the table, which is very valuable. Issues to discuss include everything from policy updates and training to cutting-edge employment-related legal risks.

Most companies offer some form of online, live, or combination training to employees on a variety of issues, including sexual harassment, compliance, business ethics, and data security. Legal and HR should meet once a year to go through the training program and materials to make sure they are relevant, effective, and updated to capture new issues. New hire orientation can be a great place to reach employees and discuss important policies and issues. Work with HR to get in-house lawyers a seat at orientation day or, if not, let the legal department help prepare materials for the sessions. Any training on legal issues will pay off down the road through a savvier workforce.

The process of properly classifying workers as exempt or non-exempt under the Fair Labor Standards Act is also important. This classification tells you which employees are exempt from overtime requirements. Misclassification of employees as exempt can set the company up for severe legal problems and potential big damages with respect to back wages and overtime. Work together to create easy to understand guidelines and processes about when an employee is exempt or not, and then train all supervisors on the distinctions and importance of getting it right. Additionally, legal should work with HR to regularly review job descriptions and do periodic auditing of employees earning below any statutory threshold to ensure they are properly classified. There is less risk of misclassification at the higher end of the pay scale. Similarly, another area of risk revolves around the use of interns. In particular, free interns. Basically, unless you can meet some pretty rigid standards, there is no such thing as a free intern. Despite someone's willingness to work for free to get experience or a foot in the door, the law is constantly changing on what types of work and under what circumstances an intern will qualify for free work. Given the potential for high penalties, tax exposure, and so forth, be sure the company has a process in place to vet any and all internships, along with regular audits to ensure compliance. The simple solution is to pay them the minimum wage even if they are willing to work for less or nothing at all.

In the good old days, the lawyers would draft employee agreements, such as non-compete, non-solicitation, and IP ownership and HR would administer them. Over time, and without coordination, agreements get modified in non-uniform ways or older versions of an agreement/clause are used when newer state-of-the-art versions exist. Additionally, when it comes time to enforce one of these agreements, you may find it difficult to locate a signed agreement. HR and in-house counsel should meet regularly to discuss the preparation and administration of these types of agreements, including a process to maintain version control and when to make changes needed because of new circumstances or changes in the law.

Many companies have an employee handbook containing key policies such as code of ethics and business conduct, anti-corruption, antitrust, insider trading, health and safety, etc. Set up a process with HR to go through these policies annually and update the handbook and relevant policies as needed. For example, without proper wording or disclaimers, an at-will employee handbook can become a binding employment contract. And, as control of the National Labor Relations Board (NLRB) shifts between political parties, guidance and enforcement priorities can change at each election cycle. Another area fraught with regulatory risk and traps for the unwary is the classification of employees versus independent contractors, something that has taken on more and more significance with the shift to the gig economy. Work with HR to periodically review all independent contractors each year, along with the latest developments under the laws of each jurisdiction where the company operates. Another key task is to ensure contractors are not being treated like employees. For example, a contractor is invited to employee meetings, is part of the employee review process, or there is close supervision and direction of the contractor's work, as if they were an employee. If you get it wrong, the contractor may be entitled to employee benefits and overtime, and the company can be on the hook for employee-related taxes. Supervisors and anyone with the ability to engage contractors should understand the proper process around hiring and managing them. Set up a procedure to flag and review contractors who have been working with the company for a set period of time (e.g., six months), and ensure high-level executive review of any decision to keep a contractor beyond the set period of time. This would make an excellent KPI.

Layoffs are not a fun topic. Regardless, a pro-active legal department will work with HR to be prepared for the possibility of layoffs at any time, including developing a process to reduce the legal risks that can arise when layoffs happen. Jointly create a checklist of all of the steps the company will need to take in the event there is a layoff. One key task is a disparate impact analysis of the potential layoffs to ensure there is no bias against any protected class. Put tools in place to run this analysis along with identifying outside counsel to help evaluate the results. Additionally, be familiar with the requirements of the WARN Act (or state-specific mini-WARN statutes) in the United States and TUPE throughout Europe (and similar laws in other countries). These statutory worker protections can trip the company up and delay layoffs and/or impose significant additional costs if not followed. Developing, and keeping current, form severance agreements/releases constitutes good planning and can be helpful when things start to pile up.

Legal should work with HR and internal audit to develop a written investigation policy and protocol. At most companies, internal investigations typically involve the participation of these three groups. The lines, however, can become blurred leading to duplicative efforts and lost or poorly managed information because there is no clear process to follow. Create a document that clearly sets out the roles and responsibilities of each group depending on the type of issue presented (for example, what to do in a sex discrimination complaint versus business ethics policy violation.) In addition, the policy should set out how information will be shared, what follow-ups are required, who is copied on what, and—critically—how to invoke the attorney-client privilege properly.

Given the potential legal exposure for making a bad hire, many companies now perform criminal background checks on all potential employees and/or promotion candidates. This is an area requiring up-to-date knowledge and care as various cities and states have enacted or are in the process of enacting laws that change the ground rules on such background checks, including when employers can ask job applicants questions about prior arrests. The EEOC has set out its expectations with respect to when and how an employer can consider arrest and conviction records. The legal team should ensure there is appropriate due diligence on any third parties the company engages to conduct background checks, in particular around compliance with the Fair Credit Reporting Act. Join together to ensure that the company is in compliance with all of the different laws in the United States (or elsewhere) and fully understand any limitations on the use of background checks.

Lastly, the legal department and HR should meet several times a year to simply discuss any cutting-edge issues in employment law. For example, remote work policies, personal device policies, the employee use of social media, Americans with Disability Act issues, dress codes/religious accommodation guidance, service animals, affirmative action plans, unionization efforts, firearms, pandemic response (including whether or not to require vaccinations), and many others. You do not need to have an answer to all of these types of issues, but you should have a plan to track issues and regularly communicate about what each group is seeing.

The takeaway here is the importance of setting up regular meetings between these two critical staff groups. If these meetings are not going on today, make it your goal to make the first move and set them up. Your friends in HR will appreciate the opportunity to work together. Talk with other senior company leaders outside of HR and get their views on what employment-type issues or problems they are seeing or think need to be addressed. The company will benefit from the legal department taking a proactive and strategic role in identifying areas of risk and working to minimize problems down the road.

Partner with IT—Preparing for a Data Breach

One thing that can lead to value destruction is a massive data breach. While some companies recover, for example, Target, many are still tainted by a breach for a long time, such as Equifax. There are several things in-house counsel should be doing to plan for in case of a breach. While everyone can debate whether a data breach is truly a matter of when versus if, there is no debate that being prepared will greatly increase the company's ability to minimize the harm. That said, as important as it is to know what to do if you have a breach, there are things that in-house lawyers should focus on before there is a breach and by doing so, can substantially limit the potential damage a breach causes. Like many things that add value to the company, this is not a solo project for the legal department. It is a project that requires cross-company cooperation, in particular, the legal team partnering with information technology (along with system security, corporate communications, and several other groups). The legal department can provide value not only by assisting with the legal issues a data breach can present but by using its unique organizational and drafting skills to help the company take steps proactively to minimize the pain and damage of a data breach. Below is what in-house lawyers should be doing while partnering with the IT group.

Before there is a breach, in-house counsel should identify the outside lawyers they will call within the first five minutes of notice of a data incident.[72] Unless you are an experienced privacy lawyer (or have one on your team), trying to handle a true data breach situation (or even figuring out whether you have a breach or not) is not the wisest thing to undertake without the guidance of experienced outside counsel. Likewise, outside counsel can help you assert the attorney-client privilege around the investigation and help you with the review and drafting of documents related to the data breach. Finally, outside counsel likely has a list of other experts (IT forensics, crisis communications, etc.) they can bring to bear to help you and your company with your situation.

Ensuring there is a written data breach response plan should be a priority. Surprisingly, most companies that handle personal data lack such a plan. Preparing one (or updating an existing plan) is instant value generation by the legal department. Your plan needs to outline the following.

1. who are the members of the response team (internal and external);
2. key contact information for everyone;
3. communications plan—external, internal, and to the C-Suite/Board of Directors (along with key contact information);
4. important regulators to contact and keep advised;
5. who will lead the investigation;
6. the cadence of communications;
7. a social media plan; and
8. document templates.

Plan on updating the plan annually.[73] Similarly, you need to practice it every year as well, using a tabletop exercise to update and enhance your plan. The communications aspect of the plan is critical. Do it poorly, and your company's reputation and brand can be tarnished for years. Companies with bad reputations lose customers, have a falling stock price, and have a tougher time with regulators. Get

72 Notice I did not use the phrase data breach. That is because you need to be absolutely sure that whatever happened rises to the level of a data breach before labeling it as such. A data breach (which involves the loss of personal data) drives a myriad of legal, regulatory, and contractual obligations, whereas a data incident does not.

73 I know I sound like a broken record with this point, but I am amazed at how many legal departments do not update policies and templates regularly, if at all. It does take time, but it is such a value generator for the department and the company. Set up a yearly calendar placing different policies or templates to update in different months to spread out the work. Once you lay out your calendar you are set year after year.

it right, and you can help put a data breach behind you in a much shorter time frame. In-house counsel should be key players in drafting and reviewing communications and in developing a communications strategy. In-house counsel that is sensitive to the need for the business not to sound like a bunch of lawyers can marry their legal skills, business acumen, and good old-fashioned common sense to draft communications that are truly helpful to the situation.

After a data breach occurs is not the best time to try to change the terms of your contracts. In-house counsel should already be looking at all of the company's contracts on a regular basis to ensure they contain the best possible protection against different types of exposure. For example, the company's website terms and conditions should contain the right limitations of liability, arbitration clause, class-action waivers, choice of law, exclusive venue and jurisdiction provisions. Similarly, the public-facing privacy policy should always be up-to-date and accurately describe how the company actually handles personal information.[74] On the flip side, do your vendor contracts contain the right contractual protections that will allow the company to recover against them if they are at fault in a data breach incident? Has the company fully vetted its vendors to see if they can live up to the promises they make regarding data? How do the company's customer contracts minimize its exposure and appropriately shift the risk of a data breach? All of these are things you must do now because once there is a breach you cannot wish your way into new contract terms. And, as you do these yearly updates, add that to your presentations to the C-Suite or the business about the accomplishments of the legal team. This is marketing 101!

If your company handles personal data, it should invest in cyber-risk insurance. Insurance may not technically fall under the purview of the legal department but you can provide a valuable service to the company by working closely with that group and ensuring the right policies, including cyber risk, are in place. Keep in mind that there is not a one-size-fits-all cyber-risk insurance policy. To be effective, you must understand what the policy covers. The best cyber-risk policies cover customer notification services, ransomware demands, forensic investigation costs, business interruption costs, your first-party expenses, your third-party obligations, litigation costs, credit monitoring for customers, regulatory costs, and so on. Keep asking questions until you are sure your policy covers the scenarios and damages you want to be covered.

The most inexpensive way to help prevent a data breach is to train your workforce properly. Training the business is also a known legal department value add. This includes training on creating proper passwords; how to spot phishing, what to do with suspicious emails, and how to be alert for industrial espionage (for example, spotting unauthorized visitors). Additionally, train the company's employees on keeping their antivirus software updated and how they may or may

---

74 And, the privacy notice should comply with applicable laws, such as the CCPA.

not use the data that sits on the company's servers. Finally, training can include teaching the workforce how to report an incident properly and how to draft such a report in a way that sets out just the facts, and not a lot of unnecessary—and usually inaccurate—commentary that you, as in-house counsel, will have to deal with as part of the breach. Teaching employees how to write smart is always a good investment of time by the legal department. The good news is most of this training is fairly inexpensive in the overall scheme of things and is proven effective in preventing problems down the road.

Data is tempting for all businesses as there is potential profit in data. This generally drives the mentality within the business that more is better. From a data breach risk standpoint, it probably is not. If your company limits the amount of personal data it collects, disposes of unneeded data promptly, and limits access to personal data to those with a need to know to do their jobs, it will take major strides in mitigating the damage from a potential breach. Simply put, the less data collected and stored, the less data the bad guys can access in the event of a breach. Similarly, the odds of breach go up when more employees have access to data because employee failure of some type is a frequent cause of a data breach, for example an employee losing a laptop packed with personal data. Make sure that employees have access only to the data they need to do their jobs. And ensure that you have prepared updated and well distributed/understood internal policies about access to, handling of, and use of personal data. Without clear guidance from the legal department, employees in various business units may feel that it is open season on any and all data they find in the company's systems. It is important everyone understands that—in addition to any data privacy laws—the company must respect its own data privacy notice to customers about how data will be used, along with any contractual commitments regarding the ownership and use of data. It is unlikely that personal data residing on the company's servers is fair game for anyone to use as they see fit.

The value destruction a company faces when hit with a data breach (treasure and reputation) can be devastating, not to mention that employees and executives often lose their jobs in the aftermath. The legal department demonstrates its highest value when it proactively takes steps to avoid or minimize value destruction events. There are no guarantees, but proactively taking measures like those listed above can help minimize the damage if your company suffers a data breach.

Partner with Government Affairs—Politics Matter

If you are in-house counsel and are not paying attention to government officials and regulators (state, local, federal, international) you are making a mistake. Companies miss opportunities to advance their interests and/or protect themselves from government action if they underestimate the importance of being plugged into the various government officials and regulators who have a say over their business (and there are a lot of them). Government action can come in many forms, such as taxation, new laws, rules and regulations, investigations, legal reform, merger control, data privacy/security, and dozens of other areas. Depending on your company's business, many of these actions can have a direct impact on the bottom line. It is no stretch to state that government action (or inaction) affect some part of your company's business daily either in or outside your home country. To be a truly effective in-house lawyer, you need to be on top of this important area. Being attuned to positive and negative governmental developments is another area where you and the legal function can add value to the company and show strategic vision by partnering with the government or industry affairs team(s). If your company does not have a formal government relations function, in-house must still stay up to speed on what various governmental or regulatory bodies are doing and consider leading or being part of any effort, your company may want or need to influence a specific or favored outcome.

One effective thing you can do in the area of government relations is to meet with officials before there is a problem. Meaning, make time to simply introduce yourself and your business to local, state, and national government officials with nothing on the line. For example, if the Department of Transportation or the Federal Communications Commission regulates your business,, make time to meet the regulators and explain your business to them and give them a point of contact in the event they ever have questions. Likewise, establish relationships with the offices of key Congressional members (for example, your state's delegation or the chairs of key committees that can impact your business). If you operate internationally, meet with the United States trade representative and remember almost all U.S. embassies have a commercial interest section. Generally, they are more than happy to meet with you and get a sense of how your business operates in that country (and can be helpful in the event you run into problems in that country or need to understand the lay of the land.) Finally, do not forget your local and state officials. The governor's office, the mayor, the city council, and so on typically will all be willing to meet with you to get to know a company operating in their states/cities.

If you have a government affairs department, part of their job is to keep an eye out for regulatory actions, new laws, hearings, and other matters that could impact your company. If not, develop your own resources to stay on top of new issues. Newspapers, websites, government-related publications, blogs, television, newsletters, word of mouth, and trade associations can all be valuable sources of information about what is going on in Washington, internationally, or locally. You should regularly and systematically sort through all of your information sources to spot issues. Stay close to your business partners and the CEO/CFO to help identify the issues worth the time and effort of the legal department. You will need to prioritize issues as you probably cannot devote time and resources to every issue you spot. Smart in-house lawyers focus on issues important to the business. The department should start each year with a list of potential government-related issues it would like to tackle. However, be prepared to change the list as circumstances warrant throughout the year.

Once you have identified any issues to focus on, you must decide whether it makes sense to go forward alone or as part of a larger group. As to the latter, you can build or join a coalition of similarly minded businesses/organizations. This can be as simple as working through an existing trade association, or as complicated as building a coalition of the willing from scratch. The rub of being part of a coalition, however, is that it requires a good deal of compromise because you must accommodate the different needs and risk tolerance of each coalition member. Before you launch your campaign, get agreement from the interested parties (internal or your coalition) as to the end goal. How do you measure success? Is it passing a new law or seeing a proposed law fail? Is it to get a few simple changes made to a proposed regulation or a wholesale rewrite? Is it to see a government regulator take action in some manner or keep the regulator on the sidelines? And no matter what your goal is, prepare yourself (and your business team) upfront to be frustrated. It is difficult to get a governmental body to take an action you want, be it passing a bill or writing a new regulation. You will find things rarely happen quickly. It will be inch by inch. It may take years to reach your goal (if ever).

All government affairs campaigns need some type of media or communications strategy. It can range from an opinion piece your CEO writes for the local newspaper, to a professionally built website dedicated to your issue containing expert-written materials, FAQs, blogs, and other media tools and techniques. Keep in mind that many effective media materials can be prepared in house. Your corporate communications or marketing departments can be helpful here and usually welcome the chance to get involved. In addition to a communications campaign, there are several other activities you should consider as part of your effort:

- Plan on wearing out some shoe leather. There is no substitute for meeting with officials, legislators, regulators, staff members, and so on to press your point.
- Prepare materials to hand out at your meetings. There are two main types of written materials. The first is a short leave-behind piece that highlights the issues and the ask or what you want the official to do. The second is a white paper, a lengthy and detailed discussion of the issues and the ask. Often, it will contain detailed legal analysis or economic analysis an attorney or outside expert (such as an economist) prepares.
- Draft sample legislation (the text of the law or amendment or regulation you want to see implemented or changed).

- Participate in hearings on the issue is another effective way to move the ball forward.
- Determine who outside the government is opposed to your positions and why. You may be able to convince them otherwise, you may be able to reach common ground on acceptable compromises that enable you to join forces, or you may just have to agree to disagree. At a minimum, you will want to understand the arguments in opposition to your views and figure out how to best respond to them as they will come up as you go forward.

Politicians and regulators listen to citizens. Voices count, and the more voices supporting your position the better. Consequently, getting citizens involved through meetings, testimony, phone calls, emails, letters, and petitions, can be tremendously helpful. This is called a grassroots campaign. Consider asking your employees, customers, vendors, and others to get involved. You can also work to create general public interest in your issue via social media, press releases, or other media events. Keep your message simple, and be sure you include a call to action so that people who want to get involved know how to make their voices heard.

There are times when you will need professional help with a campaign. If so, you will need to consider hiring a lobbyist, that is, a professional with the relationships and/or expertise needed for your particular issue. Lobbyists can be valuable additions to your campaign, and part of your planning should be dedicated to thinking about whether or not you need such help. A close second is a professional public relations firm to help develop and execute your communications strategy. Neither is a low-cost solution, so you need to weigh the costs and the benefits before going down this path.

As you develop your campaign, be sure you understand the legal boundaries. Companies with active government affairs efforts usually have some type of political action committee (PAC) to make contributions. Any and all donations—and the operation of the PAC—must be done well within the rules of the road. Be well versed in anti-bribery laws around the globe, especially if you have employees on the ground in foreign jurisdictions who may be involved in your campaign. And, while jointly lobbying the government generally is an appropriate reason for competitors to take join action, it is not fully excused from antitrust scrutiny. Take all of this seriously as the damage to reputation and the other harm that can come from not following the rules is significant.

A well-run government affairs group or campaign can help your company succeed in the business world. It takes hard work, patience, strategic vision, and a good deal of creativity to be successful. All skills in-house lawyers generally bring to the table. A government affairs campaign is also a terrific opportunity for the legal department to partner with other groups (internal and external to the company) to demonstrate and add value.

Partner with Finance

After the CEO, the most important friend of the legal department is the finance department. If they have bought into what the legal team is doing and the value it delivers, then you will have a much easier time when it comes to budget and headcount issues, and they will potentially advocate for the department with the rest of the senior management. For the general counsel, this means working closely with the CFO, ensuring that she understands what is going on with various material legal matters, why things cost what they cost, the trade-offs on certain matters or risks in terms of success or failure given the overall legal budget, or on specific projects where the cost is expected to be high (or higher than expected). This means you must be open about what the department is doing and why it is doing it, and be open to constructive criticism and new ideas. Most importantly, you must be accurate in your spending forecasts because if you mess up, it can screw up the CFO's day, especially if the screw-up is big enough to materially affect earnings or any other important financial benchmark the finance team is managing. Below the CFO, partner closely with the finance person responsible for the day-to-day profit and loss statement for the department. Include them in your monthly department budget and spending reviews and ensure they know what you are spending money on and why. This keeps surprises to a minimum. Finance does not like surprises.

The above means several things to bake into how the legal department operates:

- Always be responsive to the finance team's requests for information (no matter how annoying).
- Invite finance team members to attend budget meetings/spending reviews —make them feel like part of your team.
- Take the time to explain what matters the department is spending money on and why. Do not assume they have any understanding of the legal process or how legal issues evolve. They will appreciate you taking the time to teach them.
- Listen to their suggestions and ideas about legal spending.
- Talk to them frequently during the budgeting process, get their feedback and insider's viewpoint.
- Give them accurate information and forecasts about legal spending so they look good to their bosses and the CFO.

If you do these things, you will likely create an important ally who will support your budget request and fight for you. More importantly, someone to help best to position the legal budget to get the maximum amount possible, including additional resources.[75]

---

75 *See supra* at page 245 for a discussion on how to get additional resources for the legal department.

Partner with Everyone—Crisis Preparation

Earlier, we discussed planning for bad things generally. When a specific crisis occurs, the legal department must swing into action quickly, and run to the fire. A crisis situation falls under potential value destruction and can come in many forms, including a data breach, government investigation or criminal indictment, social media meltdown, product recalls, and death of the CEO, to name a few. How the company responds to a crisis will go a long way to preventing or limiting damage, including to its reputation and brand. In-house counsel must play a key role in the strategy and plans to manage these risks as they arise. Ask this question: If [X crisis] happened today, do we know the exact steps the company and I would take in the next 24 hours? If the answer is no, then there is opportunity afoot for the department to be proactive and generate value for the company.

Like many things, you start with the opportunity to plan before there is a problem! The most important thing to remember at this stage is that you cannot plan for everything, but you should be able to think through and prepare for the most likely five to ten situations that would present a significant crisis for your company, given its business. The first step is to create a cross-company team to flesh out the various likely risk scenarios. The legal department may be the leader of such a team or it may be part of such a team. It does not matter which. The job of in-house counsel is to help ensure the process of crisis planning gets underway, regardless of its specific role. In fact, a broad cross section of the company will give far better insight into the risks the company should be most concerned about than the legal team acting alone. This pan-company insight will enable the team to prioritize the most likely crisis situations and put together the right plans to deal with them.

A written crisis plan is critical. For this, you can have one overarching plan that contains sections dealing with different types of crisis situations, or separate plans for each type of crisis. Part of the effort here may simply be gathering crisis plans that already exist in various parts of the organization and bringing them into one document or one central location. Regardless, a written plan will give the leadership team basic step-by-step guidance as to what to do in the event of a specific crisis. Here is a checklist of things a written crisis plan should cover:

Written Crisis Plan Checklist

- ☐ Clear definition of roles and responsibilities.
- ☐ A process to triage the crisis, meaning, how serious and widespread the problem is, including impacts on customers and other parties,

litigation risk, what facts are known, and what needs to be determined.

- ☐ Where to meet (including an off-campus location in the event you are not able to meet at your headquarters).
- ☐ How people will be notified of a crisis situation, e-mail, phone call, etc.
- ☐ Crisis bridge-line number and instructions (including how to dial in from foreign countries).
- ☐ Who needs to participate (including primary back-ups in the event someone is not available)? Your crisis team will likely consist of the CEO, CFO, the general counsel, COO, chief compliance officer, HR, corporate communications, marketing, investor relations, and internal audit. Likewise, the heads of the various business units should be part of the team.
- ☐ Who is in charge of any particular type of crisis? Depending on the issue, it may be the general counsel, human resources, CFO, etc. It is not a good idea for the CEO to be in charge of the crisis team. While she will be part of the team and may have a key role in communications, the nitty-gritty details of operating the crisis team should rest with someone else.
- ☐ Contact information for internal people, including alternative phone numbers and alternative email addresses should the company's e-mail server go down.
- ☐ Contact information for external people including the board of directors and any outside resources you may need including outside counsel, media relations, security, police/FBI, etc. In-house counsel should know in advance who they will call in the event of a particular crisis. It may be a different lawyer for a data breach versus a litigation crisis. Make sure the plan contains multiple contact numbers for your outside counsel and have a backup person you can contact if the prime lawyer is unavailable. Let your outside counsel know they have been identified as someone to help in the event a crisis hits.
- ☐ Communications plan for dealing with external media, social media, employees, investor relations, board of directors, regulators, as well as who is in charge of developing the messaging and making contact with each group. While you cannot develop the exact messaging language in advance of the crisis, you can develop standard templates that will save time.

- ☐ A clear process and timeline to develop and distribute communications, updates to the team, and other documents. With respect to outside communications, it will be important to set out in detail how communications get approved as you can lose valuable time if it's not clear who needs to sign off on something before it goes out.
- ☐ Where the plan is stored and how it is accessed, and who is the keeper of the plan.
- ☐ A process to update the plan regularly. Do a health check on the crisis plan at least annually and, ideally, twice a year. Be sure to get a broad set of viewpoints about risks the company faces, in particular, if you have new executives joining the company or your business has expanded into new areas.

Once you have your plan in place, create "tabletop" exercises to practice different scenarios over the course of the year. You can eliminate a lot of the uncertainty and confusion that comes with a crisis by running through such a training exercise so people know what to do and what to expect. You may want to invest money in having a third party help you with developing and running the exercises. There is additional value in ensuring the senior executive team has media training. More advanced media training should be available to the people designated as spokespeople for the company. While the in-house lawyers may benefit from such training, they typically will want to stay out of the spotlight and help behind the scenes.

When a crisis hits the most important thing you can do as in-house counsel is to stay calm. Many in the business will take their cues from you. Even if your stomach is churning with worry, you will need to be a rock, and bring a lawyer's perspective to the situation. If you have done the right planning, you will already know what to do, who to call, and what to say. Set the tone, and keep people focused on the task at hand. Trust the plan you have put into place, and follow it. There may be a good reason to deviate from it, but the first meetings and responses regarding a crisis should track what you already have put down in writing. This is especially true when it comes to communications. The company must speak with one voice and stay on message. In these days of instant communication, the company will be bombarded with questions about your crisis (from both outside and inside the company). The worst thing that can happen is for someone to freelance a response or speculate without knowledge of the facts. Additionally, keep the board of directors properly updated. If the directors are learning about material issues from other sources first, there will be hell to pay.

Lastly, if your company is publicly traded you will need to be on top of any necessary 8-K filings.[76]

The crisis plan should identify outside resources that can help. It may be outside counsel, a public relations team, or other experts. It will be important to ensure that parts of your investigation are appropriately protected as privileged communications. This is an area where your outside counsel can be particularly helpful. Depending on the circumstances, the legal department or outside counsel should direct and lead the investigation to maximize the availability of various privileges. Regardless of privilege, ensure there is a process in place for the department to review all substantive communications with an eye toward possible litigation down the road. The legal team must partner with corporate communications in this area. If there are issues with proposed communications, you should calmly explain to corporate communications your concerns from a legal viewpoint and listen closely to their concerns from a business communications standpoint. Working together, with flexibility on both sides, you should be able to balance any competing needs. If not, ensure someone is already designated as the decisionmaker in the plan. A good way to build a strong working relationship with your communications colleagues is to provide them with training about legal issues and the pitfalls of poorly drafted documents before there is a crisis.

When the crisis is over, the next step is investing time to review what worked, what didn't work, and how best to revise your plans, behaviors, and other actions going forward. This is another place for the legal department to take the lead and add value.

Ironically, when it comes to demonstrating the value of the legal department, a crisis situation is near the top as managing a crisis requires most, if not all, of the unique skills lawyers bring to the office every day. As mentioned earlier, one general counsel once told me, "Let's not waste a good crisis!"

Send Out a Client Satisfaction Survey

Ultimately, the legal department partners with the employees of the company. Every one of them. Consequently, one clear way to show the value of the legal department is to simply ask the business if it values the services provided by the legal team. The best (and easiest) way to do this is through a client satisfaction survey, one of the oldest and most informative tools a business can use to gauge how well it is serving its customers. While primarily a tool to gather helpful data and comments about how the legal department is performing and how it is perceived throughout the organization, it can also serve as a vehicle to market and promote the department by reminding people that the department is here, that it

---

76 The Securities and Exchange Comission requires publicly traded companies to provide notification of material events to the public and the SEC by filing a form 8-K. For more on the 8-K process, *see* https://www.sec.gov/fast-answers/answersform8khtm.html.

provides valuable services to the company, and that you are directly seeking their input as to how you can improve the quality and value of the services it provides.

To start, spend some time thinking about what it is you want to know or capture with your survey. Typically, you want the survey to give insight into some measurable metrics showing how efficient or effective the department is, such as timeliness, quality of advice, accessibility of the lawyers, and so forth. You also want to some general feedback on the department as a whole and invite feedback about individual performers. Once you know your goal, there is a myriad of tools available on the internet to create and launch a survey, for example, Survey Monkey, SurveySparrow, or Google Forms. Your company may have its own tools to use.

After you selected your survey tool, it is time to prepare the questions. Do not make the survey too long or complicated. If you do, people will not complete it. The maximum number of questions should be twenty or less. Mix up the types of questions you ask, ranging from yes or no, rate on a scale, multiple choice, to open ended. This keeps the survey interesting. The survey should not take more than fifteen minutes to complete. In Appendix 3, a sample legal department survey is provided.

One important question to answer before launching your survey is who should receive it? It should go to people who are frequent users of the department, but you do not want the survey only to go to fans of the legal team, as the results will be skewed and will not be useful. To make it easy, send the survey to every employee in the company. Most will ignore it, but if you include everyone, you will get more and better information. And, the employee base will feel better about the department because you included them and asked for their opinion, even if they did not complete the survey. That goodwill alone is valuable and helps reinforce the value of the department in the hearts and minds of the employee base.

Sending a survey out more than once a year is too frequent and response levels will suffer. Allowing roughly twelve to fourteen months between surveys will get the best response rates. Avoid sending out the survey during the summer and around the major holidays. The best months tend to be September or October because most everyone is in the office and you can use the results to start to plan for next year's goals or to update your annual value-generation checklist.

Not all responses are created equal. For example, the opinions and thoughts of the frequent users of the department and those of senior management tend to carry more weight. The former because their frequent use means the feedback is more specific and useful. The latter because they control the purse strings and their perceptions of the legal department as an important and valuable part of the company (compared to a blackhole cost center) are crucial to whether the legal department thrives and has a seat at the table or is constantly fighting for funding and a voice. Consider weighting the responses from those who are frequent users or who are part of senior management a bit higher than other responses. For example, a 1.25 weight to the former versus a 1.00 weight to the latter.

Do not be disappointed if you do not get a 90 percent response rate. Realistically, a five to ten percent response rate is really good. Also, you will tend to get more responses from people who are unhappy with the legal department. This is just human nature. Accept the criticism as something the legal team needs to work on to fix. The fact that you asked for feedback has probably made some positive in-roads with these unhappy clients. And there will always be some people that no matter what you do, or how unreasonable their complaints, you will never satisfy.

Depending on the capabilities of your survey tool, as some of the initial questions you ask, you should be able to slice and dice the data in a number of different ways, for example, by region, by line of business, by type of legal matter, and so on. This will give you a lot of insight into where things are going smoothly or where you need to put in some work. Look for patterns involving certain types of matters or certain groups or members of your team (good or bad). All of these are areas for improvement or enhancement. Prepare yourself for the odd curve ball, for example, someone complaining on the survey about things that are not part of the legal department's purview, such as procurement or IT security. However, if you get that type of feedback, share it with those groups, do not just toss it in the trash. And, there may be something the legal department can do to help that group address the feedback. Be a partner.

After you have been through the results yourself, share them with the business (after sharing with the legal team first). Start with the CEO and senior management. When you do this, prepare a cover email listing the top three positives and the top three things to improve gleaned from the results. Be sure to note that you have plans in place or are making plans to address any particular shortcomings. The business loves to see plans to fix things that are not up to par.[77] Lastly, share some of the key results with the company at large. You solicited feedback from a large group of people, let them see how the department fared.[78]

Of course, the most important thing to do with a survey is to use the data and the comments to make changes. Develop a formal action plan to deal with the most important areas. Share your action plan with the CEO and senior management to let them know you are moving forward with fixing any problems.

77 If you can get it, an opportunity to present the results to the C-Suite is even better as you can emphasize value generation and get feedback in real time.

78 When sharing the data broadly with the business, be sure that what you share does not (or cannot) reveal who gave the feedback or focus on any one individual in the department. That is simply not fair. Instead, provide the high-level results about satisfaction level generally, ideas for improvement, and ideas for areas to focus on in the future. And, of course, end with asking for more feedback and any other questions employees may have. This all goes to hearts and minds.

Consider asking for a short meeting with some key members of senior management to individually go over the key survey results and get their feedback on the action plan and/or the department in general. Even if they do not take you up on the invitation, they will appreciate being asked for their input. The information you gather from all of this will help you improve the delivery of legal services to the company and build the brand of the legal department as a group that is constantly looking to improve, cares about what its clients think and need, is proactive and strategic, and is using cutting-edge technology to build a better department. All are smart moves when it comes to showing the value of the department.

Summing Up

For the legal department to effectively demonstrate its value to the business, it is important that the in-house lawyers demonstrate leadership during times of crisis and take advantage of opportunities to partner with different business units and staff groups. Even when there is not a crisis situation the department can demonstrate value simply by ensuring its yearly goals tie closely to things the business finds important, both in terms of specific projects but also in terms of goals that take on strategic problems. The point being to show that the legal team is looking at more than the purely legal issues it wants to handle or otherwise believe important:

- ☐ Use a survey tool to glean data about how the business views the legal team. While hearing good things is nice (and those are areas to continue to enhance), hearing bad things is probably more important. Those bad things are opportunities to show the business you are listening and striving to improve the services delivered by the department.
- ☐ The survey can also assist with developing yearly goals that actually matter to the business. Many legal departments develop goals in a vacuum Meaning, they create goals that are important to the lawyers or creating goals they think are important to the business (without ever asking). Seeking input from the business and then sharing the goals before they are finalized is an easy way to demonstrate value and get business buy-in that what the department is focused on is truly valuable.
- ☐ While there are many parts of the business that can provide opportunities to partner with, focus on those that provide the most valuable opportunities to generate value for the business, i.e., finance, human resources, government affairs, and IT security. These groups are natural allies of the legal team.

- ☐ Of the above, the finance team is your most important partner. Treat them right, bring them into the circle of trust, and win them over to your side. It will pay off . . . literally.
- ☐ The legal department should be out in front when it comes to leadership on creating and implementing a crisis plan. Not only do the department's superpowers lend themselves such a project, in the event of an actual crisis the legal team is probably the best suited of any part of the business to step up and lead. Remember: run to the fire!

Leveraging it All to Get More!

Let us circle back to the beginning of this book. First, congratulations on making your way through the slog! Second, you will recall me mentioning that it sucks to be a cost center. You can check. Cost centers are places the business looks to cut when times get tough or the numbers need improving. Historically, most legal departments have had a "cut my budget" sign taped to their backs. This is due partly to failing to market the legal department to the business, to take the steps necessary to show the value provided by the legal team, and, more importantly, not knowing how to show that the department can create even more value if properly nurtured. Guess what? If you have been following along closely, you now have a blueprint for exactly how to go about marketing the department, demonstrating value, and how to rip the "cut my budget" sign off your back and replace it with a "we deserve more budget" sign.

First, I hope you see how interrelated all of the various components of value are. Everything I wrote about above ties together in some way. There is a virtuous cycle created when the in-house legal team focuses some of its energy on marketing, on becoming the Department of Yes, on thinking and acting strategically, putting their lawyer hats away, and finding ways to partner with (and not dictate to) various parts of the business. This cycle culminates in two things: 1) over time, the legal department has built a reputation and veneer of value that becomes second nature in the minds of the business leaders and employees generally. The value of the legal department becomes a given; 2) the business is hungry for more, i.e., clearly seeing the value generated by the in-house lawyers they want to invest more in this resource because the payoff is clear—enhanced value creation and minimized value destruction. If the business is primed for more, then all you have to do is ask. But, as shown below, ask smartly.

Second, it is not easy. Sure, you may on occasion just luck into more resources, be it budget, people, or technology. However, that is rare and, to be honest, highly unlikely. So, if your plan is to sit back and wait for the controllers of the purse strings to say "Oh my gosh, legal is wonderful. Let's give them more." You may be waiting a while. All of which means you cannot succeed in increasing your budget and resources on a spur-of-the-moment pitch. It takes time, and it takes planning. You must understand that the natural inclination of the business is to say no to any increase in costs that do not have a positive return on investment.

Your job is to show the business how investing in the legal department leads to a positive ROI. It is going to take some showmanship, some math, and—most importantly—you are going to have to earn it. That is, by building up the reputation of the legal team in the hearts and minds of the company leadership by consistently showing the value of the legal team. In other words, doing all of the things outlined in the pages of this book. It is now time to use your lawyer superpowers for truth, justice, and more resources.

To start, you need to track key indicators that show the lack of resources for the legal department is costing the company money. Here are a few indicators to watch:

Key Indicators the Legal Department Needs Additional Resources

- ☐ Consistently high or increasing spend on outside counsel for work that can demonstrably be done in house, either with the members of the current team or by adding a head to the legal team. An example is the department's spend on outside lawyers to help with contract overflow has greatly surpassed the cost of hiring an additional contracts lawyer. The match is simple and the value clear.
- ☐ Key deals and projects not getting done because there is too much work for the legal team, too few hands to get to it all. The lost value of the deals not getting done or delayed is more than the cost of hiring another lawyer or implementing technology that would increase the speed of contract turn-around time.
- ☐ The legal team is consistently overworked, i.e., long nights, weekends, holidays, just to get basic legal work finished. I know and understand there will always be times with nights, weekends, and holidays are required, even in-house. However, if the team is consistently working at a breakneck pace, they will eventually burn out and quit. The cost of an in-house lawyer quitting is huge. Not only is there the cost of finding the replacement, but there is also all of the work that must be reassigned or put off in the interim. This adds stress to an already stressed-out team or means more things are not getting done or falling through the cracks. Finally, even when you find someone new, there is no magic process whereby that person suddenly is pulling their full weight. It takes time for new lawyers (even experienced ones) to ramp up, to understand the business and the company's legal issues, and for the business to get used to and trust the new person. This lost time and lost work add up. In fact, you can make a pretty good estimate of the cost of losing an attorney and

show that the cost of hiring an additional head is far less than the cost of losing and replacing one who quits because of the stressful pace.

- ☐ The company expands via acquisition and dramatically increases the workload on the current legal team. I have been part of many acquisitions and, typically, unless the target company has a legal department already, the increase in workload caused by adding the legal needs of the newly acquired company can cause slowdowns and burnout. While it may not be one-for-one in terms of scaling, there must be some consideration given to how legal work for the newly acquired asset will be handled. It is easy if they have a lawyer or team that can be added to the team of the acquirer. However, those people may not want to stick around (for various reasons) or they may not mesh well with the existing team. All meaning that without additional resources the legal team will start to fall behind, both in supporting the existing business and the newly acquired one.
- ☐ The company enters new markets or develops new products that dramatically increase the demand (or need for) legal services from the legal department. Simply put, you cannot enter new geographic or product markets without sufficient legal assistance. If that assistance is not sought or not available, big problems can arise bringing forward the old, but true, adage that an ounce of prevention is worth a pound of cure.

The legal department must be aware of the company's strategic plans and direction and be able to spot developments like the list above. Likewise, it is important to have developed reliable metrics that show the strain on the current level of legal resources and the impact the strain is having on the ability of the business to move forward profitably and with lower risk (or to move forward with a higher return on its investment because the new resources provide value above their cost). This comes down to math, a language the business understands. So, be armed with numbers, as well as rhetoric.

Once you believe you have a strong case for additional resources, there are several additional steps to take. To start, analyze the situation and determine what you truly need to deal with the bigger workload. It will likely come down to these three questions:

- ➤ More people to help with the work? Do you need to add full-time heads to the legal team? Do you need a contract resource to deal with a temporary surge in work? Do you need a lawyer and, if so, with how much experience (less experience is less expensive). Would a paralegal, legal assistant, or other non-lawyer employee suffice? Do you need a skill that is fairly common (commercial agreements or litigation) or do you need someone with more specialized (and therefore more expensive skills), for example, data privacy, executive compensation, corporate secretary?

- Can you handle the increase in work by getting additional funding and then hiring outside counsel? Is this a more cost-effective way to handle the increase in work? Can you find a solo practitioner to handle the extra work (and be on stand-by going forward once trained)? Can you find a small boutique firm with substantially lower rates than your usual counsel?[79]
- Will additional technology solve the issue? For example, a contract assembly tool that will allow the business to create their own contracts based on templates and an approved list of clauses that can be substituted into the standard template, e.g., choice of law options or alternative dispute mechanisms.

In other words, it is important that you understand and determine what you truly need to address the resources problem and not simply fall back on the standard we need more full-time lawyers pitch. That may be true, but if you bring forth an analysis that shows you looked at different options, the cost, and the efficacy of each option, then the option you do settle on and ask for will be the clear winner based on math—not a hunch.

The next step is knowing when and how to make the ask. Be cognizant of the company's budget and planning cycle. While it is possible to get additional money and resource mid-cycle it is much easier to get increased resources making the ask going into a planning cycle. For most companies, the budget planning season starts in the fall, around October. This means that if you see a need or gap you need to fill, the planning must start months before that deadline as it is unlikely that you will be able to properly make the case if you start the necessary work on the day the budget process starts. Likewise, if the company is engaged in an acquisition, the time to make the pitch for additional resources to deal with the anticipated increase in legal work is during the acquisition planning phase, that is, when the company is crunching the numbers of whether the acquisition makes sense financially. Note, one thing the finance team is likely doing is determining what costs can be cut. This process is called, ironically, developing synergies. If the legal department is not raising its hand and saying here is what we think we will need for resources post close, then it is likely the business is expecting to simply roll up the acquisition and handle any legal work with the existing legal department staffing. Get ahead of this thinking from the moment you first become aware of a potential acquisition. While you might be able to handle the work with the current team, do some digging into the target business, the markets it operates

---

79 This is the perfect analysis for a legal operations team or legal procurement group. *See supra* pages 54 and 88 respectively.

in, the legal issues disclosed during due diligence, its legal spending, and so on. It will be too late to raise your hand when the deal closes as all of the synergies and cost savings baked into the deal case are now set in stone. No one is going to want to hear post-close, "Oh sorry, we should have said something about needing additional resources to handle the new legal work."

The place to start to build your case is with the finance team. Hopefully, you have made some friends in the finance department and have been a good partner by including them in your budget discussions, reviews of outside counsel spend, and getting them accurate forecasts and accruals on time and without complaining. If you have done these things, then odds are good that you will get a fair hearing from them about your budget needs (even if you are making the request outside of the budget planning window). Start by previewing with your contact in finance that you are going to set a meeting with her to discuss some budget planning items and needs. This way they know what is coming and will not be caught off guard (remember, you are partners!) Then, show up to the meeting with your thoughts and plans fully baked, not thrown together at the last minute or worse showing up and just winging it on a whiteboard. Finally, be realistic with your ask. If the company is losing money like mad, you probably need to defer the conversation or note that you understand it is not possible at the moment given the financial circumstances, but when things turn around you would like this to be put on the list for consideration. Always put yourself in their shoes when developing your ask and realize that you are almost certainly not the only department asking for more. Have some empathy and understanding. Do not make it personal or predict doom and gloom for the company if your request is not granted, that is, no threats. Your job is to educate and persuade the decision maker (s) with facts and a good bit of charm. Use the goodwill you have built up from being a good partner.

An effective tool to get additional resources is to let others make the pitch for you. As general counsel, I never minded if business leaders would reach out to me to complain that the legal team was taking too much time to get deals done or turn projects. First, they were usually wrong in terms of the facts (which I—politely—would correct them on). Second, and more importantly, I would almost always say "Don't tell me. Tell the CFO/CEO that 'we need more lawyers. Things are not getting done and we're losing out on revenue deals!'" A statement like that from the head of sales, for example, is ten times more powerful than the general counsel saying exactly the same thing. Why? Because, of course, the general counsel is always going to ask for more heads. That is expected. What is not expected, and therefore more powerful, is someone from the business side demanding more lawyers. Similarly, if you are considering adding any type of technology for the legal department, try to determine if any other groups (staff or business) could find value using the technology. If so, they can help make the pitch and, potentially, share some of the cost. This is a win across multiple channels, including demonstrating leadership in addition to partnership.

As you work on your pitch for resources, do not forget to show your math. This goes back to one of the fundamental premises of this book: to show value you must speak the language of the business and that language is numbers. You cannot walk into the CFO's or CEO's office and say "I need some more people/ technology/recourses," without having the numbers to back up the ROI. Show how much better off the company will be financially if the legal department gets these extra resources. The two cleanest examples are 1) how much money can the company save if the legal department gets the resource (e.g., savings on outside counsel spend), or 2) how much more money can the company make if the legal department gets the resource (more deals). While it is usually one or the other, sometimes you make the case for both 1 and 2 for the same resource. That is a home run.

When you do the math, be sure to account for all of the costs. For example, for a new employee, the cost is not just salary, but also benefits, taxes, office supplies, bar licenses, and so forth. You want to calculate the fully loaded cost of the head. Likewise, for technology, it is not just the cost of the software, but also yearly subscription fees, support costs, fees for things not part of the plan, etc. Sure, it is a pain but your numbers will have more validity to the finance team if they see you are including all of the costs and not just part. On the other hand, you probably have far more freedom to develop numbers showing the savings or the increase in revenue you can attribute to the new resource. That said, stay within the confines of reality and come up with good faith estimates whenever you present such numbers. Be relatively conservative and, importantly, be able to defend the numbers should they come under scrutiny. If someone questions your assumptions, you should be able to easily walk them through the calculations and assumptions (and not feel sheepish doing so). The business understands assumptions (e.g., pro forma numbers) so long as they feel there is a solid basis for each assumption and things add up. If you have the math on your side, you are well on your way to justifying the additional resources.

Sometimes, your conversations are not just about asking for more resources, they are about defending what you have, that is, preventing cuts to the legal department budget. Hopefully, you have a strong relationship with the finance team and you have been a good steward of the funds you have managed to date, i. e., staying within budget, providing accurate accruals and forecasts, keeping finance in the loop on what legal is spending money on and why, and so forth. All of these things underscore your credibility when you first get a whiff that your legal budget may be coming under the knife. Granted, there are times when there is nothing you can do, and you have to take one for the team because of optics or because of stubbornness on the part of the decision makers. If this happens, make your case, but do not fall on your sword. If the budget cuts are coming no matter what, the thing to do is draw up a list of all the valuable things the legal departments does, and ask the decision makers to help decide what will not be done or get done post-budget cuts, i.e., you cannot do it all so choices have to be made. Sometimes, but usually not, this gets the business to reconsider the cuts because they see how foolish they are. Otherwise, get agreement on what the legal department will not do or will do less of and confirm it in writing— a document you can share with those same business leaders when they complain about things getting missed, not getting done, or significantly delayed. After all, you get what you pay for and if you do not want to pay for it you do not get it.

Lastly, understand that you will not be the first or last legal department to ask for more and get turned down. This is okay. Be patient, be a good corporate citizen (i.e., do the best you can with what you do have), and continue to work on building the case for more. You may not get what you want this year, but odds are good that you will have laid down a powerful marker for future years and at some point, the seeds you plant now will bloom. So, cast the seeds about, fertilize them when you can, and plan on someday reaping the harvest.

Summing Up

It may seem like wishful thinking, but you do not need to be satisfied with the resources you currently have at your disposal. This does not mean that just because you asked, you will be rewarded. However, you have to make the case to find out. As Warren Zevon famously sang, "Send lawyers, guns, and money!" Keep the following top of mind:

- ☐ Constantly evaluate the legal needs of the company—both current and future. When you see gaps and needs, bring them forward to the business at the appropriate time. Never be shy about making the case for more if the circumstances truly warrant such a request.
- ☐ Build a partnership with the finance team. If you win them over, you have overcome one of the biggest hurdles to increasing the department's resources. However, you have to be a good partner to have a good partner.
- ☐ Understand the planning and budget cycle timing. When the time is right, make your request. Out-of-cycle requests are almost always shot down, short of an emergency.
- ☐ Let the business complain to the C-Suite about the lack of legal resources. This is a far more effective way to show the need for more resources than if the legal department made the same pitch.
- ☐ Be realistic and thoughtful with your ask. If you do not need a full-time lawyer, do not ask for one. If technology will solve the problem instead of headcount, ask for technology. Showing you have thought through the need and have narrowed the request to what is truly needed will enhance your

credibility with the decision makers and more likely lead to getting your request approved.

- ☐ In a similar vein, show your math. In other words, come to any meeting where you will request additional resources with the numbers that justify the ROI, meaning that, if the business spends this dollar, it will get that dollar, plus $X back from the investment. It is okay to be creative with how you calculate the value of the additional resource, but be able to justify your numbers and assumptions.
- ☐ Sometimes you need to show your math to prevent a reduction in resources. Unfortunately, budget cuts and headcount reductions are a fact of life in the corporate world. If the legal department becomes a target, be zealous in defending a position of no reductions by showing how the company will lose value due to such cuts. But, once a final decision is made, fall in line, and do the best you can with what you have available. (However, be sure to document what the department cannot do or can no longer do because of the resource cut.)
- ☐ Do not be discouraged if you are told no. You should expect a lot of nos before you get a yes. Keep trying, keep making the case, and keep being positive about the company and the legal department regardless of the level of resources you have available.

Appendix 1 (KPIs)

As noted, there are literally hundreds and hundreds of different KPIs a legal department could devise and implement. In addition to the KPIs outlined earlier, I have kept a list of various KPIs I used, have seen, or were sent to me by readers of the blog.[80] You can use these as is or, more likely, adapt them into KPIs that work for your legal department and company. Some of the below overlap, but I think it is better to simply list the different KPIs and provide you with the freedom to pick the ones/categories you find most useful. All KPIs are measured over some period of time, a year, a month, year-over-year, etc. Some KPIs may become joint KPIs, that is the department teams up with a part of the business to create and track, such as the finance team, sales, marketing, and so on. You may also wish to assign different weighting factors to any particular KPI or any subparts of a specific KPI. Whatever you can do to make the measure more accurate (in terms of the measurement and/or the value generated). Also, the more technology you have in place (e-billing, matter management, contract management), the easier it is to generate the data needed to create and track KPIs.

Also, a word of caution, as discussed in the chapter on KPIs, it is difficult to put the value the department or an individual lawyer generated into a black-and-white number. Do not fall into the trap of false precision. KPIs are useful tools but one huge problem avoided because of something the legal department did is worth ten times (or more) of the value of cranking out template contracts. Moreover, KPIs are highly idiosyncratic, meaning, they depend on many factors that are true for the specific circumstances in which your legal department operates, including the industry (regulated or not), the company's appetite for risk, and budget. In other words, as you create and present KPIs giving context and background along with numbers, charts, and graphs is critical to ensuring that the business sees the same thing you see or are trying to convey. Numbers in a vacuum can be a curse. Lastly, remember that if your KPIs are not telling the story you want to tell (the news is bad) do not panic. The important thing is that you also present your plan

80 One person I wish to specifically thank is Scott Levinson, Vice President, Legal Services at ConEd in New York City for sharing some of his litigation KPIs with me.

to fix the problem and KPIs going forward can show the trend, the number, or the issue is improving.

In no particular order of importance, here is my list of potential KPIs (which you can use as-is or amend to fit your circumstances).

Litigation

- Litigation matters handled (number)
  - Number of matters settled
  - Number of matters litigated
- Litigation avoided (number of matters that are resolved before litigation is filed or a formal settlement agreement is needed)
- Litigation generated by different parts of the business (who is getting into disputes)
- The savings (money and time) avoiding litigation generated
- Average cost of a litigation matter (by type of matter, e.g., employment)
- Total cost of litigation as a percentage of the business's gross revenue
- Average litigation verdict
  - As plaintiff
  - As defendant
- Average settlement value
  - As plaintiff
  - As defendant
- Average time (in days) to resolve litigation
  - By type of matter
- Causes of litigation (root cause of matter)
- Number of litigation related training sessions for the business
- Subpoena response prepared/average cost to respond
- E-discovery costs by matter
  - Collection
  - Processing
  - Storage
  - Review
- Recoveries from insurance policies
  - Overall
  - Missed by the business

Attorney Efficiency

- Number of litigation matters assigned/opened over a defined period
- Number of litigation matters closed over a defined period
- Number of litigation matters currently open over a defined period
- Number of contracts assigned/opened over a defined period

- Number of contracts closed over a defined period
- Number of contracts currently open over a defined period
- Number of [*insert type of matter*] assigned/opened over a defined period
- Number of [*insert type of matter*] closed over a defined period
- Number of [*insert type of matter*] currently open over a defined period
- Total number of matters (all types) handed over a defined period
- Average time to close matters (by matter type, including a weight for complexity of the matter)
- Amount of money spent on outside legal fees/vendors per matter
- Number of matters handled without assistance of outside counsel
- Variance from assigned budget

<u>Legal Department Efficiency</u>

- Spend to budget
  - By matter type
  - By law firm
  - By business unit
- Internal spend on legal matters as a percentage of the company's gross revenue
  - By type of matter over a defined period
- External spend on legal matters as a percentage of the company's gross revenue
  - By type of matter over a defined period
- Combined spend on legal matters as a percentage of the company's gross revenue
  - By type of matter over a defined period
- Number of attorneys per 1,000 (or other number) of company employees
- Number of attorneys per $1B in company revenue
- Number of matters completed internally versus number of matters completed by outside counsel
- Percentage of time spent on substantive legal work versus non-legal work
  - By attorney
  - By the department overall
- Average legal spend by type of matter
- Dollar amount spent on alternative service providers (ASPs)
  - Versus outside counsel
- Savings generated by using ASPs
- Benchmark the last three above to similar companies, i.e., companies in the same industry, same size by revenue, or similar headcount and structure (or all three)
- Savings generated by enforcing outside counsel guidelines and/or challenging outside counsel billing

- Turnover rate
  - Voluntary
  - Involuntary
  - Regrettable
  - Non-Regrettable
- Process mapping[81]
  - Percentage of time spent on upper right quadrant versus other three quadrants

<u>Contracts</u>

- Contract cycle time from signature to renewal
  - Average days to approval
  - Days a contract is with legal versus days a contract is with the business
- Clauses in contracts most frequently negotiated (by type of contract)
  - Issues most frequently negotiated/outcomes
- Number of contracts signed
  - Without legal intervention (used form)
  - By region
  - By type
  - By line of business
  - By value
- Renewal rate (expectation versus actual)
  - Value of recurring contracts
  - Ratio of new contracts versus recurring contracts
  - Revenue lost from contracts not renewed
- Number of SOWs per MSA contract
  - Value of SOWs
- Number of missed contract completion deadlines
- Contracts signed outside of the approved signature/contracting process
- Quality of contracts signed (requires establishing a grading system for your contracts),
- Total number of matters handled by the legal department
  - By matter type
  - Compared to a year ago
  - Month-over-month
  - Quarter-over-quarter
- Number of customer complaints/disputes about contracts
  - Number resolved
  - Number unresolved
  - Number moving to formal dispute resolution

---

81 *See supra* at page 66.

Outside Counsel Efficiency

- Number of law firms used by type of matter
- Type and number of matters handled by each law firm
- Number of law firms charging
  - By the hour
    - ☐ With reduced rates
  - Via alternative fee arrangement
    - ☐ Contingency fee
    - ☐ Flat fee
    - ☐ Success fee
    - ☐ Other
- Number of law firms engaged via RFP process
- Timeliness to deliver work product (days from assignment to delivery by type of matter)
- Times deadlines missed
- Actual spend vs. budget
- Matters successfully concluded (requires a definition of success agreed upfront with law firm)
- Number of CLEs and other training sessions
  - For legal department
  - For the business generally
- Amount of free hours/services provided
- Change in composite evaluation score(s) year-over-year (requires the legal department develop a former evaluation process for outside counsel and create a composite or average number comprised of multiple weighted items, e.g., availability, value, responsiveness, practical, matter management, compliance with outside counsel guidelines, etc.)

Compliance

- Training provided to business (by type, e.g., ethics, litigation, contracts)
- Amount of fines, sanctions, outside counsel expense tied to employee violations of company business ethics policy
- Estimated savings from avoiding compliance issues due to:
  - Training
  - Legal department early intervention
- Number of government investigations by type
- Number of employee complaints filed:
  - In court
  - With outside regulator
  - With human resources
  - With internal audit

- Number of independent contracts segregated by months of engagement (the longer the engagement the less like an independent contractor)

Technology/Self-Service

- New technology implemented and cost (with description of workflow or pain point the technology enhances or solves), e.g., electronic signatures, contract management
- Number of active users of the technology compared to number of potential users
  - User outside of the legal department
- Percentage of legal matters technology allows business to avoid direct contact with legal (that is, self-service goals)
- Savings attributed to new technology (money and/or time savings—including increased turnaround times) vs. cost (return on investment)
- Number of forms and templates created or enhanced
- Number of contracts properly signed without need for legal assistance
- Number of contracts signed with e-signatures
- Playbooks created or updated for each company form agreement or template
- Percentage of contracts managed by contract lifecycle tool

Intellectual Property

- Number of trademarks filed
- Number of trademarks granted
- Average time to file trademark (from when first disclosed to the legal department)
- Average time to win trademark (from date filed)
- Cost per trademark
- Number of patent applications filed
- Average time to file a patent (from when first disclosed to the legal department)
- Average time for the regulator to grant patent
- Number of patents granted within three years of filing
- Cost per patent filed
- Cost per patent granted
- Percentage of submitted patent filings that are awarded
- Number of copyrights filed
- Number of copyrights granted
- Average time to file copyright (from when first disclosed to the legal department)
- Average time to win copyright (from date filed)
- Cost per trademark

- Number of IP-rights disputes
  - By type of IP (patent, copyright, trademark)
  - Wins/losses as plaintiff
  - Wins/losses as defendant
  - Average cost to resolve IP-rights dispute
    - By type
  - Average settlement cost
    - By type
    - As plaintiff
    - As defendant

Perceived Value

- Number of complaints about legal department
  - By type
  - By business unit
  - By geography
  - Resolutions
- Ranking of the legal department on 1 –10 scale on following attributes (via survey)
  - Adds value to my project
  - Easy to work with
  - Good communicator
    - Oral
    - Writing
  - Keeps me informed
  - Is available
  - Represents company well
  - Takes time to explain legal issues
  - Is a good business partner
  - Understands the company's goals and strategy
  - Is accountable
  - Keeps word/promises
  - My overall satisfaction with the legal department is . . .

Appendix 2 (Sample Low-Value Contract Checklist)

The following is an example of a low-value contract checklist. The idea is that if the legal department can properly train the business to understand and follow the checklist, then many low-value contracts need never go through the legal department, meaning, the business can safely sign without review or approval from legal. Value through disengagement! The trick is, of course, to provide the right training, and record the training so future users can watch it without the need to continuously provide live training sessions.

AnyCo Inc. Low-Value Contract Checklist

Background

This checklist is designed to provide certain AnyCo employees (senior manager and above) with a tool to review small vendor contracts without the involvement of the legal department. Vendors are third-party companies providing services to AnyCo. For purposes of this checklist, "small" means less than $25,000 in total contract value with the vendor. Vendor contracts valued at $25,000 or more in total contract value automatically require legal department review.

You must confirm that all the tick boxes are checked. If the appropriate boxes are checked, you may proceed to signature. If not, the agreement must go to Legal for review/sign-off. Once you sign an agreement, ensure that a fully executed copy and a copy of the completed, signed, checklist is sent to legalcontracts@AnyCo.com for storage in the company's contract management system.

Basic Information (Please complete the following before proceeding to the checklist):

- ☐ Who are the parties to the agreement: ______________________________
- ☐ What is the nature of services vendor will provide: ____________________

- ☐ Verify that Finance has approved the agreement **and** you have obtained a PO: Yes ☐ No ☐ (if no, you must have Finance approval to proceed).
- ☐ List any previous agreements with the vendor (and provide links to or attach those agreements):
- ☐ Has the vendor passed through the compliance diligence process found here: Yes ☐ No ☐ (if no, you must complete this step before proceeding)
- ☐ Does the contract provide for the right signatories, i.e., the right companies and the right individuals to sign for each company:
  - ☐ Are you following the AnyCo authorized signature policy: Yes ☐ No ☐ (if no, you may not proceed)
  - ☐ Select the right legal entity for AnyCo and ensure the contract matches:
    - ☐ AnyCo Limited (Singapore)
    - ☐ AnyCo Nordics (Denmark)
    - ☐ AnyCo US Inc. (USA)

Checklist

Scope of services provided

- The products/services the vendor will provide are clearly and correctly set out and a description/specification is provided: Yes ☐ No ☐
- If this Agreement needs to be an enterprise-wide agreement, i.e. can the services be used by the whole AnyCo group and, does the agreement provide for such use: Yes ☐ No ☐ N/A ☐
- All understandings about what is being provided are in writing in the contract: Yes ☐ No ☐
- The rights and responsibilities of both parties are accurately and fully set out: Yes ☐ No ☐
- The timeframes around when services or goods will be provided to AnyCo by the vendor are clear and accurate: Yes ☐ No ☐
- If AnyCo needs to test the services before acceptance does the agreement permit AnyCo to test the services before accepting: Yes ☐ No ☐ N/A ☐
- If AnyCo needs the right to modify the products/services does the agreement permit AnyCo to do so: Yes ☐ No ☐ N/A ☐

If you checked no for any of the above, do not proceed to signature. Please contact the legal department for further instructions.

Term and Termination

- Is this contract for a fixed term of 12-months or less: Yes ☐ No ☐

- **If for a fixed term of more than 12 months, you must obtain approval from the legal department to sign.**

- If there is an automatic renewal of the agreement after the initial term expires do we have at least 90 days to terminate prior to renewal? Yes ☐ No ☐
- Does AnyCo have the ability to terminate the agreement at any time for any reason on 90-days or less notice to the vendor: Yes ☐ No ☐
    - AnyCo must have the ability to terminate at any time on no more than 90-days' notice to vendor.
    - There cannot be a penalty/ fee for AnyCo for exercising the termination for convenience.
- Does the contract provide for termination in the event either party "materially breaches" the agreement: Yes ☐ No ☐

If you checked no for any of the above, do not proceed to signature. Please contact the legal department for further instructions.

Price and Payment

- Is the price for the product/services correct: Yes ☐ No ☐
- Has finance provided sign off on the cost and have you raised a PO: Yes ☐ No ☐
- Is the currency for payment in USD: Yes ☐ No ☐
- If not USD you must check with the Controller before signing.
- Is the total contract value less than $25,000: Yes ☐ No ☐
- Does AnyCo have at least 30 days to pay any invoice: Yes ☐ No ☐
- Any lesser period requires Finance to sign off.
- If there are late fees, are they 3% or less: Yes ☐ No ☐
- Is the price fixed for the term of the agreement: Yes ☐ No ☐

If you checked no for any of the above, do not proceed to signature. Please contact the legal department for further instructions.

Confidentiality/Data Security

- Is there a confidentiality provision that covers data AnyCo provides to vendor: Yes ☐ No ☐ N/A ☐
- Is there a data security provision whereby the vendor agrees to secure any data provided by AnyCo: Yes ☐ No ☐ N/A ☐
- Is vendor required to notify AnyCo in the event of a data breach: Yes ☐ No ☐ N/A ☐
- Does the agreement provide that AnyCo owns any data it provides to the vendor: Yes ☐ No ☐ N/A ☐

- Is the vendor limited to using data provided by AnyCo only for the purposes of vendor performing the contract and not for its own purposes: Yes ☐ No ☐ N/A ☐
- Has AnyCo Information Security reviewed and signed-off on the information security standards and infrastructure: Yes ☐ No ☐ N/A ☐

If you checked "no" for any of the above, do not proceed to signature. Please contact the legal department for further instructions.

Data Processing

- If the vendor is processing personal data of our customers or our employees on our behalf and on our instructions, has vendor signed our data processing agreement: Yes ☐ No ☐ N/A ☐
- If vendor is not processing personal data on our behalf but personal data is shared, are the approved uses by the vendor specifically set out in the agreement: Yes ☐ No ☐ N/A ☐ This should be specifically set out in the agreement using the wording found here and completed as appropriate: [*insert required wording here*]
- Are all personal data-related obligations of the vendor subject to a liability cap for vendor of no less than $2,000,000.00: Yes ☐ No ☐ N/A.
- Is any personal data we provide transferred out of the EU: Yes ☐ No ☐ N/A ☐
    - If personal data will be transferred outside the EU, the legal department must review.
        - Note: there will always be a tiny amount of personal data exchanged with any contract, e.g., personnel emails–but this is not the sort of thing Legal needs to review.

If you ticked "no" for any of the above, do not proceed to signature. Please contact the legal department for further instructions.

Subcontracting

- If the contract allows vendor to subcontract to third parties is this acceptable to the business: Yes ☐ No ☐
- Is vendor required to give AnyCo notice if it will use subcontractors: Yes ☐ No ☐ N/A ☐
- Are all subcontractors based inside the EU: Yes ☐ No ☐ N/A ☐
    - If "No," the vendor must sign the AnyCo Data Processing Agreement, found here: DPA
- Is vendor required to vet any subcontractors: Yes ☐ No ☐ N/A ☐

- Are subcontractors required to follow the same contractual obligations as the vendor: Yes ☐ No ☐ N/A ☐
- If subcontracting is permitted, does the contract specifically state that the vendor is fully responsible for each subcontractor's acts, omissions and compliance with, and/or breach of, the contract: Yes ☐ No ☐ N/A ☐

If you checked no for any of the above, do not proceed to signature. Please contact the legal department for further instructions.

Indemnification/Limitation of Liability

- Does the contract provide that the vendor will indemnify AnyCo in the event a third-party sues AnyCo regarding the contract: Yes ☐ No ☐
  If not please provide the following wording to the vendor:

  "*Vendor agrees to defend, indemnify in full, and hold harmless AnyCo, its affiliates, directors, officers and employees from and against any and all liabilities, losses, third party claims and actions, damages, costs, audits, investigations, penalties or charges (including but not limited to damage to personal and real property, personal injury and death), including legal fees and all other reasonable professional costs and expenses as a result of; (a) any failure by Vendor to comply fully with any laws and regulations, including, without limitation, any data protection legislation and any claim resulting therefrom; (b) any claim by a third party that the products or services under this Agreement, in whole or in part, infringe a copyright, patent or other intellectual property right; or (c) any misuse of AnyCo intellectual property or a breach of the intellectual property obligations contained in this Agreement.*"

If this wording is incorporated, then the legal department does not need to review.

- Are vendor's indemnity obligations to AnyCo excluded from any liability cap: Yes ☐ No ☐
  - **Note:** While not offered immediately, AnyCo will, ultimately, agree to a mutual indemnification obligation up to $2,500,000 for these three areas. AnyCo cannot accept liability of any more than $2,500,000 (our insurance coverage amount)
- Is AnyCo' liability capped at no more than $150,000 other than for breaches of confidentiality, data protection and misuse of intellectual property (IP): Yes ☐ No ☐
- Is vendor's liability capped at no less than $150,000 (Not the lower of the fees paid and $150,000): Yes ☐ No ☐

- Are vendor breaches of data protection, confidentiality, and intellectual property liability capped at the amount of at least $3,000,000: Yes ☐ No ☐

If you checked "no" for any of the above, do not proceed to signature. Please contact the legal department for further instructions.

Warranties & Insurance

- Does the vendor warrant that the products and services will adhere to the specifications and/or documentation/ accurate description of the services: Yes ☐ No ☐
- Does the vendor warrant/ commit that the services do not infringe any third party intellectual property: Yes ☐ No ☐
- Does the Vendor warrant that they provide the services in compliance with all applicable laws and regulations: Yes ☐ No ☐
- Is there a satisfactory remedy if the product/service does not conform with the specification and/or documentation: Yes ☐ No ☐
- Does the contract require the vendor to have insurance in place at a level which is industry best practice: Yes ☐ No ☐

If you checked "no" for any of the above, do not proceed to signature. Please contact the legal department for further instructions.

Vendor Performance

- Does the contract specify the key deliverables anticipated from the vendor: Yes ☐ No ☐
- Is it important to AnyCo that vendor provide reasonable support when the contract has ended (for whatever reason) to transition the services to a new vendor of AnyCo's choosing and if yes then is this provided for in the contract: Yes ☐ No ☐ N/A ☐

If you checked "no" for any of the above, do not proceed to signature. Please contact the legal department for further instructions.

Intellectual Property

- Is the vendor creating any work, deliverable, software or other material AnyCo would want to own and if yes does the Agreement expressly state that AnyCo owns this work product: Yes ☐ No ☐
- If the answer to the above is "no" please request the following language: *All Deliverables and work product developed, delivered or generated under this Agreement and any applicable SOWs, as well as any unfinished ver-*

sions of such Deliverables and work products (collectively "Work Product"), will be considered "work for hire" by Vendor for AnyCo to the extent allowed by law. As such, the Work Product and any derivative works will be the sole intellectual property of AnyCo in perpetuity, throughout the world in any and all media. If any Work Product is not deemed to be work for hire, Vendor assigns to AnyCo in perpetuity and without reservation, condition or limitation, all rights, title, and interest in and to such Work Product and all derivative works; and Vendor reserves no rights of any nature.

If Vendor refuses to include this type of language, please escalate to the legal department.

If you checked “no” for any of the above, do not proceed to signature. Please contact the legal department for further instructions.

Dispute Resolution

- Does the contract require arbitration of disputes and if yes has vendor agreed to change to one of the below options: Yes ☐ No ☐
- If “yes,” is the arbitration is before the International Chamber of Commerce: Yes ☐ No ☐
- Is the choice of law one of the following: Singapore ☐ New York ☐ Delaware ☐ Denmark ☐ Ireland ☐ No ☐
- Is the venue (where case would be heard) one of the following: Singapore ☐ Copenhagen ☐ New York City ☐ Wilmington, Delaware ☐ No ☐

If you checked “no” for any of the above, do not proceed to signature. Please contact the legal department for further instructions.

Other

- Does the contract require exclusivity by AnyCo (i.e., AnyCo will use no other vendor for the same service or product). If “yes,” insist on deleting this—has vendor accepted deletion: Yes ☐ No ☐
- Does the contract require AnyCo provide the vendor with a right of first refusal (i.e., AnyCo will give vendor first chance to win business or match bids): If “yes,” ask for this to be deleted: has vendor accepted deletion? Yes ☐ No ☐
- Does the contract provide any type of preferential treatment of the vendor by AnyCo? If “yes,” ask for this to be deleted: has vendor accepted deletion: Yes ☐ No ☐

- Does the contract require the individuals signing for AnyCo to accept any personal liability under the contract. If "yes," ask for this to be deleted: has vendor accepted deletion: Yes ☐ No ☐
- Does the contract set forth who and how each side should be contacted in the event notice is required: Yes ☐ No ☐
- Does the contract provide for notice by email with emails for notice set out in the contract: Yes ☐ No ☐

If you checked "no" for any of the above, do not proceed to signature. Please contact the legal department for further instructions.

*****

You must sign below, and verify you have complied with the terms of the checklist process. Note that completed checklists are subject to the company's random auditing.

I have carefully reviewed the contract referred to on the Contract Summary and completed the attached checklist. I have ticked all boxes and the information I provided is true and accurate.

By: ___________________________

Name: ___________________________

Date: ___________________________

Title: ___________________________

Please send all signed contracts and this signed Summary Page and Review Checklist to Legal at contracts@AnyCo.com so they can upload the contact on the contract management system which will trigger renewal reminder emails to you directly.

Appendix 3 (Sample Legal Department Client Satisfaction Survey Questions)

Below is a sample legal department client satisfaction survey. This is based on surveys I used as general counsel.

In-House Legal Dept. Customer Satisfaction

Welcome to the Legal Department Customer Satisfaction Survey

Thank you for participating in our short survey. It should only take you 15 minutes or so to complete. Your feedback is important to us and we are interested in learning what you think we do well, and those areas where you think we can improve. Your participation and responses are confidential and anonymous and will not be tied to any of the results. Again, thank you for your input.

In-House Legal Dept. Customer Satisfaction

1. Please let us know the geographical area where you work for the company.

2. Please let us know your level in the company.

In-House Legal Dept. Customer Satisfaction

3. Please identify the line of business through which you have had the most interaction with the Legal Department over the past 12 months.

4. How often do you have contact with the Legal Department?

5. Please select the type of matters you feel are the most important for the Legal Department to focus its energies on (choose up to three)

6. Please rate the following attributes about the Legal Department (N/A means "Not Applicable")

	Excellent	Very Good	Satisfactory	Fair (needs some work)	Poor (unsatisfactory)	N/A
Is responsive	○	○	○	○	○	○
Adds value to my project	○	○	○	○	○	○
Solves problems (i.e., provides me solutions)	○	○	○	○	○	○
Helps me think through business issues	○	○	○	○	○	○
Gives me practical advice	○	○	○	○	○	○
Is easy to work with/is flexible	○	○	○	○	○	○
Gives my matter the attention it deserves	○	○	○	○	○	○
Communicates clearly	○	○	○	○	○	○
"Hangs tough" when it needs to	○	○	○	○	○	○

7. How important to you are the follow attributes of the Legal Department?

	Extremely	Very	Average	Somewhat	Not at all	N/A
Is responsive	○	○	○	○	○	○
Adds value to my project	○	○	○	○	○	○
Solves problems (i.e., provides me with solutions)	○	○	○	○	○	○
Helps me think through business issues	○	○	○	○	○	○
Provides me with useful information	○	○	○	○	○	○
Gives me practical advice	○	○	○	○	○	○
Is easy to work with/is flexible	○	○	○	○	○	○
Gives my matter the attention it deserves	○	○	○	○	○	○
Communicates clearly	○	○	○	○	○	○
"Hangs tough" when it needs to	○	○	○	○	○	○

8. Like everyone, Legal has limited resources. We spend a lot of time trying to give the right level of priority to all of the matters coming to us. Please let us know how you think we are doing.

	Excellent	Very Good	Satisfactory	Fair (could be better)	Poor
The Legal Department properly prioritizes contracts and other work	○	○	○	○	○

9. Please feel free to enter any additional comments to the previous question

10. How good is the legal department around managing and predicting costs?

	Always	Most of the Time	Sometimes	Rarely	Never
Forecasts are accurate	○	○	○	○	○
Keeps me informed about the costs	○	○	○	○	○
Explains why costs are higher or lower than expected	○	○	○	○	○

11. As compared to prior years, my level of satisfaction with the Legal Department today is

12. In your opinion, what does the Legal Department do well?

13. In your opinion, what should the Legal Department concentrate on improving over the next 12 months?

14. What is your overall evaluation of the Legal Department?

15. Please feel free to provide any additional comments about the Legal Department

16. If you would like to provide any feedback or comments about any particular individuals in the Legal Department, please do so below

17. As you look out over the next three years, what areas do you think the Legal Department should focus on in terms of skills or services it provides to the company?

18. Have you used the Legal Department intranet site?

19. What type of information or services would you find most useful to have on the Legal Department intranet site?

20. What three words would you use to describe the Legal Department?

Word 1

Word 2

Word 3

21. If you would like us to contact you about any of your responses, just complete the information below. You do not need to complete this section if you wish to remain anonymous.

Name

Email Address

Phone Number

Index

About the Author

Sterling Miller has enjoyed a wide and varied 33-year-long legal career. He is a three-time general counsel, having served in that role at Marketo, Inc., Sabre Corporation, and Travelocity.com where he managed international teams handling a myriad of complex legal issues including bet-the-company litigation, M&A, government affairs, data privacy, and commercial agreements. He led the legal team responsible for the successful IPO of Sabre Corporation in 2014, along with managing multiple acquisitions and divestitures. He also led the legal team responsible for the sale of Marketo, Inc. to Adobe, Inc. in late 2018.

After law school, and before he went in house in 1994, he was an associate lawyer at Gallop, Johnson, and Neuman in St. Louis. In January 2019, after the sale of Marketo to Adobe, he returned to the Dallas office of Hilgers Graben PLLC as Senior Counsel, focusing on commercial matters, litigation, data privacy, and special projects for clients where his in-house background has proven invaluable. In January 2021, he became the CEO of Hilgers Graben, which now has offices across the country.

He earned his J.D. degree from Washington University in St. Louis (Order of the Coif, law review) and his bachelor's degree from Nebraska Wesleyan University, where he was student body president, among other honors. He is certified in data privacy/security by the International Association of Privacy Professionals (CIPP/US). He is an active speaker on legal and industry panels including presenting at the South-by-Southwest conference in Austin, TX and keynoting several ACC events. Under his leadership, *Inside Counsel* magazine named the Travelocity Legal Department one of the "Ten Most Innovative" legal departments in the United States (with the Sabre legal department winning honorable mention under his tenure). He has been a multiyear finalist for the *Dallas Business Journal*'s "Best Corporate Counsel" award.

Sterling serves on the Board of Directors of Terrasoul Superfoods and the advisory board of Travefy.com. He publishes the widely-read, and award winning, legal blog entitled "Ten Things You Need to Know as In-House Counsel" available at www.TenThings.net and has been a regular contributor to Thomson Reuters, including series on succession planning for in-house legal departments and the uses of artificial intelligence by in-house lawyers. He prepared an adjunct course on the uses of artificial intelligence in litigation for the Baylor Law School. The American Bar Association published his second and fourth books titled *Ten Things you Need to Know as In-House Counsel: Practical Advice and Successful Strategies* and *Ten (More) Things you need to Know as In-House Counsel: More Practical Advice and Successful Strategies* in 2017 and 2019 respectively. He also coaches in-house lawyers and consultants with in-house legal departments around the globe.

His third book—a cookbook—came out in November 2018, titled *The Slow-Cooker Savant* (Mill City Press). Sterling's first book, *The Evolution of Professional Football: 1920–2015*, was published by Mill City Press in 2015. You can follow him on Twitter @10ThingsLegal and LinkedIn where he regularly shares his commentary and insights on cutting-edge legal issues.

Sterling and his wife split their time between the Dallas-Fort Worth area and Santa Fe, New Mexico. They are the proud parents of two daughters (one of whom is now in law school at the University of Texas) and wrangle three rescue cats and two dogs just to keep things interesting. In his spare time, he plays guitar in an 1980s cover-band called *Big Wheel*. Sterling can be reached at sterling.miller@sbcglobal.net.